*Social Work with Black Children*

**Child Care Policy and Practice**
Series Editor: Tony Hall
Director and Secretary
British Agencies for Adoption and Fostering

*Published:*
**Adoption and Race**
Black, Asian and mixed race children in white families
*Owen Gill and Barbara Jackson*

**Specialist Fostering**
*Martin Shaw and Tony Hipgrave*

**Helping Children Cope with Separation and Loss**
*Claudia Jewett*

**Long-term Foster Care**
*Jane Rowe, Hilary Cain, Marion Hundleby and Anne Keane*

**Children in Care Revisited**
*Pamela Mann*

**In and Out of Care**
The Experiences of Children, Parents and Social Workers
*Mike Fisher, Peter Marsh and David Phillips with Eric Sainsbury*

# Social Work with Black Children and their Families

*Edited by*
SHAMA AHMED
JULIET CHEETHAM
*and* JOHN SMALL

B. T. Batsford Ltd. *London*
in association with
British Agencies for Adoption and Fostering

To our families:
Salim; Paul, Matthew, Rebecca and Sophie;
Kathleen, Jason, John Junior and Zahra

© Shama Ahmed, Juliet Cheetham and John Small, 1986

First published 1986

Printed and bound in Great Britain by
Biddles Ltd, Guildford and King's Lynn

Published by B.T. Batsford Ltd
4 Fitzhardinge Street, London W1H 0AH

British Library Cataloguing in Publication Data

Social work with black children and their
    families.——(Childcare policy and practice)
    1. Social work with black children——
    Great Britain
    I. Ahmed, Shama    II. Cheetham, Juliet
    III. Small, John    IV. British Agencies
    for Adoption & Fostering    V. Series
    362.7'95'0941    HV751.A6

    ISBN 0–7134–4888–1
    ISBN 0–7134–4889–X Pbk

# Contents

Acknowledgements                                                vii

The contributors                                               viii

Introduction

  *Juliet Cheetham*                                    1


## PART ONE – UNDER-FIVES AND THEIR DAY CARE: WAYS OF ASSESSING AND IMPROVING PRACTICE

   Introduction by Shama Ahmed                        39

1 Afro-Caribbean children in day care

  *Asrat-Girma*                                           40

2 Black children in a day nursery: some issues of practice

  *Shama Ahmed*                                           51

3 Cultural action for the under-fives : training strategies developed by the Building Blocks project

  *Judith Koetter et al*                                  64

4 Practice in a community nursery for black children

  *Syble Morgan*                                          69

5 Training responses

  *Maureen O'Hagan*                                       75

6 Policies for day care

  *Clifford Headley*                                      79


## PART TWO – BLACK CHILDREN IN CARE

7 Transracial placements: conflicts and contradictions

  *John Small*                                            81

CONTENTS

8  Some psychological models of black self-concept
   *Jocelyn Emama Maximé*                                    100
9  Reviewing black children in care: Introductory note
   *Juliet Cheetham*                                         117
10 The experience of Bradford Social Services Department
   *Mike Mennell*                                            120


## PART THREE – WORK WITH WOMEN AND GIRLS

11 An Asian mothers' self-help group
   *Samar Sheik*                                             132
12 Cultural racism in work with Asian women and girls
   *Shama Ahmed*                                             140
13 An Asian women's refuge
   *Surinder Guru*                                           155


## PART FOUR – WORK WITH YOUNG BLACK OFFENDERS

14 Developing an anti-racist intermediate treatment
   *John Pitts, Theo Sowa, Alan Taylor and Lorna White*     167
15 Towards a training for an anti-racist intermediate
   treatment
   *John Pitts, Theo Sowa, Alan Taylor and Lorna White*     187

*Index*                                                     201

# Acknowledgements

Many people have helped and encouraged us in assembling this book. In particular, we would like to thank the parents who had adopted transracially and who contributed to John Small's study, our clients and colleagues who have helped develop our ideas and our practice, and John Crook for his ready response to requests for information.

An edited collection of contributions such as these, written largely by practitioners, always has a long gestation and often a difficult birth. Its midwives, the editors, have many frustrations and could not accomplish their tasks without the help of their assistants. We therefore give special thanks to Chris Gibson who had the difficult task of cajoling all the editors into keeping, as far as possible, the appointments for editorial meetings.

We are grateful to Mary Sugden for allowing us to use the National Institute for Social Work for our many editorial meetings.

The book could not have been produced without Rachael Lawrance's patience and extraordinary efficiency in keeping track of contributions and contributors, and her skill in transforming messy papers into elegant manuscripts.

Finally, we thank our spouses and children who bore the brunt of our preoccupation and bad temper and had the forbearance not to ask why so much of our time was being devoted to other people's families.

Juliet Cheetham

*Oxford*
*December 1985*

# The contributors

**Shama Ahmed** has an M.Soc.Sci.(Sociology) and a CQSW from Birmingham University. She has worked as a probation officer and a generic social worker, has been a training officer for Coventry Social Services and is now a lecturer at Bristol Polytechnic. She is particularly concerned about monitoring departmental policies for racial minority impact and in building an anti-racist dimension to social services training. She has served as a member of the CCETSW Social Work Curriculum Study Group on 'Teaching Social Work for a Multi-Racial Society' and is currently a member of the CCETSW Steering group on 'CSS and the Multi-Racial Perspective'. She is also a member of the Black Perspectives Advisory Committee of the British Agencies for Adoption and Fostering. She is involved in a number of black community projects, and in recent years has published several articles and papers on social work for a multi-racial society.

**Patsy Anderson**, a black Jamaican, has lived in England for 21 years and is mother of a 14 and 16 year old son and daughter. She has been concerned by the effects of the kind of value system an English education has placed on her children as well as other ethnic minority children, and is presently working with Building Blocks to influence change.

**Asrat-Girma** was born in Ethiopia, and came to London in the early 1970s. After graduating from North East London Polytechnic she worked with women's groups in Notting Hill, and in 1984 was awarded a grant from the Commission for Racial Equality to do research into black children in day care. She has also undertaken field research on family life in several regions of Ethiopia.

**Juliet Cheetham** is Director of the Social Work Research Centre at Stirling University. After working as a probation officer in Brixton she taught graduate social workers at Oxford University. She has written extensively on race relations and social work and was a member of the Commission for Racial Equality.

**Surinder Guru** graduated in sociology and has been working at the

Asian Resource Centre for four years. She is also active in the black struggle in Birmingham.

**Sandip Hazareesingh**, born in Mauritius of Bihari and Uttar Pradeshi antecedents, is the father of a five year old child, Satya. His interest in early childhood education developed naturally from his parenting role, and he has also been active in campaigns to secure greater public provision for Indian Arts.

**Judith Koetter** was born in the USA. After graduating with a B.Sc.(Education) she taught for seven years in several states within the USA. As a principal research associate at Cornell University she developed, along with colleagues, a practical manual, *School Before Six*, for use by pre-school, day care workers in the Head Start Programme. In England she has acted as adviser to under-fives, and was a project leader of a community children's centre before coming to Building Blocks.

**Jocelyn Maximé** was born in Port-of-Spain, Trinidad. She has an MSc in Clinical Psychology from Birmingham University and has recently become head of Hackney Social Service Department's Clinical Psychological Service. Her previous experience includes acting as a specialist clinical psychologist to the New Black Families Unit and Independent Adoption Service. She has a two year old daughter.

**Mike Mennell** originally trained as a teacher and worked largely with black children and their families in Leeds, London and Jamaica. He joined Leeds Social Services Department in 1974, and worked in the Chapeltown area both as social worker and intermediate treatment officer until joining Bradford Social Services in 1982 as Social Worker – Afro-Caribbean Youth Families.

**Syble Moncrieffe-Morgan** has been a long-time cultural worker in the Black community. She organised the first Black community-controlled nursery in Handsworth, Birmingham in August 1976. Currently she is head of a nursery in London. She is committed to better provision for the under-fives, and to child care practices that positively promote all the cultures in our society.

**Maureen O'Hagan** is a senior lecturer at North London College. She trained as a nursery nurse and then as an SRN and held several senior nursing posts. She then trained as a teacher and after working in infant and junior schools went into further education teaching future nursery nurses. She is closely involved with local social services departments and in identifying training needs of local community groups. She holds an M.Sc. in Health Education and has long experience of work with ethnic minority groups.

**John Pitts** is at present a Senior Lecturer in Social Work at the West London Institute of Higher Education. He has worked for several years in the education, youth work and Intermediate Treatment fields and has published various research documents related to this work, including 'Young Offenders in Lambeth' (LITA – 1978).

**Samar Sheik** was born in Pakistan and educated in England. She is married with one child and works as an interpreter in a local ante-natal clinic.

**Kelvin Simms** was born in Newcastle upon Tyne in 1955 and educated at Newport College. He worked as under-fives adviser at the Council for Community Relations in Lambeth before joining Building Blocks.

**John Small** has a degree in Applied Social Studies and a CQSW from Bradford University. He worked as a generic social worker in three London boroughs and in Jamaica as a Children's Officer. He was the leader for New Black Families, the first black adoption and fostering agency in the UK, and the founder and first president of the Association of Black Social Workers and Allied Professions. He is now Assistant Director of Social Services with the London Borough of Hackney. He has published several articles on ethnic-sensitive social work practice.

**Theo Sowa** is at present a Development Worker in the Juvenile Offenders Team at the National Association for the Care and Resettlement of Offenders. She has worked for several years in the fields of Intermediate Treatment, youth work and literacy. Publications include 'Groupwork and I.T.' (LITA – 1985).

**Alan Taylor** is a white training officer with the Apex Trust, a national charity working with unemployed ex-offenders. He has also been a youth and community worker and a teacher in a community project. He has been involved in the field of intermediate treatment for many years and is currently a member of the London Intermediate Treatment Association's Anti-racism Training Group.

**Lorna Whyte** is at present a Senior Intermediate Treatment Officer in the London Borough of Islington. She has worked in the fields of Intermediate Treatment, youth work and sex education for several years.

# *Introduction* Juliet Cheetham

Black families in Britain face many problems, the consequences of racial discrimination and migration; the latter, while it gave opportunities, also imposed strains extending well beyond the generation of people who were newcomers to Britain. Black families have displayed remarkable strengths in coping with these difficulties but individual and institutional racism, poverty, poor housing and unemployment inevitably influence the quality of children's and parents' lives.

The welfare services have largely failed to deal with these problems in appropriate ways. For example, many Asian mothers have not been properly helped by ante-natal services (Allen and Purkis, 1983). The day care available to the pre-school children of the large numbers of employed black mothers is often of poor quality (CRE, 1975; Jackson and Jackson, 1979; Mayall and Petrie, 1983). Disproportionate numbers of black children are in care with less chance than white children of reunion with their parents (Ousley, 1981; Batta and Mawby, 1981; House of Commons Social Services Committee, 1984). The care provided by local authorities is often insensitive to diverse ethnic backgrounds and cultural needs (Jones, 1977; ADSS, 1978; Cheetham, 1981, 1982; Young and Connelly, 1981). Only recently have black substitute parents been found for black children and determined efforts made to advance this recruitment (Arnold, 1982; Brunton and Welch, 1983). Schools have met confusion and difficulty in responding to the needs of black pupils and establishing the priorities of education for a multi-racial society (Swann, 1985). Large numbers of black children have been inappropriately suspended from school (CRE, 1985(a)). Welfare services for young offenders have also not operated adequately for black adolescents, and so disproportionate numbers are in youth custody establishments (CRE 1985(a); Pinder, 1984; Pitts, 1986; Taylor, 1981).

All this has been well researched and documented, and social services

1

and social work have begun slowly to recognize and accept their responsibilities in a multi-racial society (BASW, 1982; CCETSW, 1982). Within the last few years some local authorities and other statutory and voluntary bodies have made efforts to remedy this by examining the quantity and quality of their services to ethnic minorities, by the appointment of specialist staff and the adoption of policies designed to reduce racial discrimination and disadvantage. There have been some imaginative responses. To recognize this is not to be complacent about the continuing failures and insensitivities of services, of which there are many; it simply acknowledges the fact of change and the possibility of progress (Connelly, 1985).

This book is devoted to describing new developments in services for black children, young people and their parents, and to exploring other possible ways of providing services appropriate to a multi-racial population. The contributors do not dwell solely on past failures but concentrate on practical ways of meeting needs, and the implications for black families and for the practitioners and administrators who work with them. The book is written for black and white social workers and for people who are outside social work but who are concerned about the contribution of welfare services in meeting fundamental human needs and reducing inequalities.

Writing for a multi-racial readership is a stimulating and challenging task. This was reflected in the work of the editorial group, Shama Ahmed, Juliet Cheetham and John Small. While there was a large measure of agreement amongst us about what we wanted in contributions, for example a focus on the methods and resources of good practice and critical analysis of theory, myths and misunderstandings, we found we responded differently to the impact some contributions made on us. Shama Ahmed and John Small rated highly those which they thought entered the subjective experience of black people and which might alert them to what could be achieved in social work. Juliet Cheetham, conscious of those white people who accept, in general terms, the inadequacies of social services for black people but who are mystified or uncertain about, for example, the precise nature and implications of discriminatory practice, welcomed especially the contributions which clarified topics which at times have become part of the rhetoric and jargon of social work, to the disadvantage of proper understanding. Differences in perceptions and disagreements about the priorities of good practice were freely and fully argued, an exercise which usually resulted in a merging of opinions. Where different emphases remained, and it is a matter of emphasis not principle, this is included in our editorial comments.

There are three themes in social work with black people which we want to underline. First is the importance of focusing on the strengths of black families, strengths rooted in cultural traditions, in the survival of generations in spite of discrimination and the disadvantages of the stresses of migration and sometimes persecution. It has proved hard in the teaching and practice of social work for white people, in particular, to recognize strengths that would be accepted as the norm in white families whose difficulties are usually seen as transitory. This distorted perspective is the consequence of white people's usually limited acquaintance with black people outside a professional context in which they are the clients, often faced with serious difficulties. These problems then come to be seen as black people's normal experience. Added to this are the expectations of pathology regarded as the inevitable consequence of the acute disadvantages and pressures experienced by black people, to which attention is increasingly, and properly, drawn. Such conclusions are, of course, crudely deterministic, the product of education or mental processes which put pathology and conflict at the centre of the analysis of black families.

The second issue is the contentious nature of some of the questions raised by social work with black families. This reflects the politics of race relations and, in particular, the arguments about assimilation, integration and pluralism which are at the heart of debates about the social policies of a multi-racial society. The answers to such questions as 'Should transracial adoption be allowed? Should there be specialist agencies for black people?' reflect, in part, views of race relations. Answers must also take account of research and other evidence about the outcome of different kinds of service. This is not as straightforward as it sounds. Research may be biased in its design and so also in its results; it may be reported selectively and more may be claimed than the data allow. Also in research on matters connected with race relations a particularly critical eye must be cast over its context, aims, methods and conclusions. There are, of course, as elsewhere in social work, questions about work with black families that cannot be answered by research, and decisions will depend on the priorities determined by experience and beliefs about the basis of good practice. These will vary from person to person; they therefore need to be exposed to examination and argument, as were the views of the editors of this collection. This does not ensure consensus but it does distinguish differences based upon facts and upon values. It may, but need not necessarily, also reveal differences of opinion according to membership of ethnic groups. Such views are not, of course, universally held by all the group's members but ethnic divisions need serious examination. They often threaten white and antagonize black people and so their context and content need to be carefully considered. So too must the divisions of opinion within ethnic groups. While they may be accepted as normal and refreshing the differences of black people are sometimes siezed upon by whites, triumphantly, as a sign of confusion when consensus would ease decision making. This expectation of one voice speaking for groups with contrasting ethnic, educational and professional backgrounds is a common manifestation of racism. No one expects white people to agree on the contentious problems of the delivery of social work; why should there be a consensus amongst black people? In America, where there is a longer history of collaboration between black and white social workers, disagreements within ethnic groups are common. This has not prevented the development of ethnic agencies, and it has stimulated a continuing lively debate about the best methods of helping minorities (Jenkins, 1981). A difference need not be a division.

The editors hope that these contributions will help distinguish certainties from confusions; they have been chosen because we believe they represent contemporary good practice or set out the theoretical premises on which this should be based. We accept that in a different political climate, in a less racist society, the components of good practice might be different. The contributors to this volume write for British social work today.

The third and final underlying theme is the acceptance of the positive changes in the experience of black people which can flow from social work practice which tries to combat racism and to reflect Britain's multi-racial society. Social work cannot bring about major changes in the life chances of its consumers, black or white, but it can make significant impact on the experience of both minority and majority groups. Many children, for example, experience day care outside their home. A little of this is provided by local authorities, but nearly all of it, through the processes of registration and supervision, may be affected by them. There are, therefore, through recruitment policies and a determination that children's environment, in play materials, culture, food and so on should reflect their life at home and in the outside world, opportunities to make positive statements about the myriad cultures of black and white children, about their identity and their relationship with each other.

Further examples of the potentially positive influence of social work, not explored in this book, are the provision of day and residential services which reflect and value the language and culture of elderly black people, who perhaps never expected to grow old and to die in Britain. For them these services mean a comfortable and comforting environment; for society they are a statement of the recognition, acceptance and value of another culture. It is worthwhile comparing the acceptance, albeit slow, which specialist provision for elderly people has received with the resistance usually met by similar proposals for children's services. This reflects confused thinking about assimilation and integration; a grudging acceptance that elderly people cannot be expected to assimilate while children can and should. This can mean children and parents discarding long-established cultures and ethnic roots; the violence this may do to them emotionally and socially is disregarded (Cheetham, 1982). The consequences of such processes and the ways of avoiding them are discussed by Maximé and Small in the section on black children in care. Social work can work with the strengths of black families; it does not have to respond simplistically to black children's flight from their parents and their confused espousal of contrary values and lifestyles.

Social work can as well resist mechanisms which may gravely disadvantage black people. These can include decisions about young black offenders which place them at greater risk of custodial penalties. As Pitts and his colleagues show, social workers often contribute to these decisions; but given clear thinking and commitment, their departments can provide services for both black and white young offenders which create credible alternatives to custody, and resist premature criminalization and incarceration to which young black people are particularly subject.

There are several other contexts, including health care, in which social work can influence the quality of life and the life chances of black families which, for reasons of space, are not discussed in this book. In particular the contribution of residential work is missing. It is too important and too complex for brief discussion and deserves proper attention in another volume.

### Definitions

Already some readers may have been perplexed or provoked by the terms used in this introduction. First is the use of 'black' to describe ethnic groups which differ widely in appearance, culture and experience. Some contributors use this as useful shorthand or a political statement about the powerlessness or collective power of people of Afro-Caribbean and South Asian descent but others employ a wider vocabulary: Asian, West Indian, black British, British Asian, black and ethnic minority and so on. All of these labels are unsatisfactory in some ways. Asian could include people from such widely differing countries as Vietnam and Pakistan. Should the term refer more specifically to country or region of birth or the vastly different cultural experiences of minorities born and brought up in Western societies? Is it sensible to call someone born in Britain West Indian or Afro-Caribbean simply because his parents had that identity? The convenient unified label black British, while it proclaims equality of citizenship, obscures the diversity and richness of minority traditions and cultures in Britain. Objections to such labels are endless and they are shared equally by black and white people. They must be acknowledged but semantic debate must not become, as it often does, an endless diversion from attending to issues of policy and practice that do not depend on nomenclature.

The editors accept that labels are used in different ways and for different reasons to describe the same people. There are well accepted precedents for this amongst white people in Britain who understand the nuances that may be implied by the use of Scottish, Welsh, Irish and English, white and European to describe a British person. It is therefore worth asking why a label is being used, whether as convenient shorthand or to convey some specific meaning: the continuity of history and culture or the power and position of visible minorities.

### Racism

A central theme of the whole book is the racism which bears so hard on the lives of black people and which is the root of so many problems. Although they may accept, in general terms, the existence of racism many white people do not understand its various manifestations, particularly those which are indirect or a part of the ordinary functioning of the institutions of society, and which go far beyond simply denying an individual something because he or she is black. So what are the various meanings of racism in this book?

Racism is rooted in the belief that certain groups distinguished by race or ethnicity share other characteristics such as attitudes or abilities and a propensity to certain behaviour. The stereotypes which emerge are usually, but not necessarily, derogatory. Lest it should be thought that crude racial stereotypes are a thing of the past, the formal investigation into the Immigration Service carried out by the Commission for Racial Equality revealed guidance documents for immigration officers which described Morrocans as 'simple and cunning' and Nigerians as 'like lost children with unrealistic aspirations about their abilities'. Such stereotypes, often interwoven with a simplistic and rigid understanding of cultural differences, sustain the dominance of more influential groups and may become part of the justification for this domination. This mechanism can be particularly powerful when it has benign intent: groups, races, people need, because of their various weaknesses and shortcomings, the protection, guidance or control of the allegedly superior. These dominant groups are usually of European origin and their ethnocentric views are likely to characterize their dealings with those who are regarded as subordinate. Thus the most normal and natural practices are held to be those of the most powerful; and diversity of response is either unnecessary or undesirable. This is a central part of the rationale of imperialism. How may it be reflected in social work practice?

First, stereotypical beliefs about minority families persist: West Indian families are weak because of some ill-understood relationship with the ways of life enforced upon them as slaves; West Indian children are said to suffer from low self-esteem because, it is argued, they have no firm cultural roots. Asian parents are likely to experience insoluble conflict with their children. Muslim families will systematically suppress their female members. There are, of course, West Indian and Asian families and individuals, and many white people, with these characteristics; racism rests on the belief they are shared by all or the majority of the ethnic or racial group in question. Such perception will naturally influence social workers' practice, and may be taken to justify such drastic and often premature intervention as removal of children from parents regarded as unreasonably strict and damaging and unlikely to change their behaviour (Ousley, 1981). They militate too against individual assessments and, a mainspring for social work, against the belief in the capacity for growth and change.

Social workers, like other professionals, have considerable power in their reaction to different cultures, and when these are regarded as in some ways inferior, attempts may be made to challenge and change them, often as we saw, with benign intent and sometimes under the flag of the liberal virtues. Thus certain patterns of child care and certain presumptions about the role of women may be attacked, more or less directly, because they are perceived as having only weaknesses, not strengths. So, for example, in the early 1960s the wish and need of young West Indian mothers to find day care for their children so that they could work and support themselves was opposed by social workers, who saw these children as needing protection from the undesirable consequences of their mothers' belief in economic independance. There are, of course, occasions when extreme behaviour, which may be claimed as part of a cultural tradition, must be resisted; there are many hard conflicts in determining this; but such occasions are rare. Practice becomes racist when it is based on the dominant group's firm prejudice that the cultures of other ethnic groups are inferior and should be treated accordingly. Ahmed explores these issues further in Chapter 12.

It is sometimes argued that racism can best be resisted by ensuring that inequalities are rooted out by treating everyone the same, no matter what their background and culture. This is the 'colourblind' approach which has always been a strong ingredient in debate on those rare occasions when social policy has been focussed on minorities in Britain. Hard though this would be it would not eliminate the racism which occurs, again often with benign intent, in the refusal to perceive different needs and the implications of different cultural traditions. At first sight this may seem to contradict what has just been argued, but it does not. Racism is not equated simply with the recognition of different cultures but with the ascription to them, derived from inaccurate and incomplete information, of inevitable, usually derogatory characteristics, and with different treatment based upon these perceptions. Treating people differently according to their real not their imagined needs or character-istics is a recognition of the equal worth of different cultures; it may be a condition of equal treatment and a method of combatting racism. What examples are there in social work?

An obvious but common example of the inequalities which flow from treating everyone the same is the failure to provide information about social services and social work in minority languages, to have poor interpreting services and, in areas of high minority settlement, no social workers who can communicate with a substantial proportion of a department's actual or potential clientele. Residential and day centres which fail to take account of the dietary, religious and social needs of their minority users again are treating people unequally by treating everyone the same. This is a subtle but common paradox which needs to be watched.

Colourblind approaches are particularly common in work with

children because many white people find it distasteful to make racial and ethnic distinctions between children, lest that should imply that some groups are getting treated unequally on racial grounds. In day care centres, schools and residential establishments there are still people who assert with considerable passion that they do not have black or white children in their care but simply children. Some, when pressed, will claim that they cannot even tell you how many black and white children or colleagues they work with because they are totally unaware of colour. This extraordinary blindness, which does not, of course, extend to gender differences, is usually based on fear of the acknowledgement of racial differences or the existence of a multi-racial society, a fear which may be a product of an individual's own barely recognized prejudices. In fact, many black children are disadvantaged precisely because no account is taken of their culture or appearance, and it is assumed that the most natural and proper way of conducting affairs is according to the norms of the majority white culture. The impact of ignoring ethnic differences on the care of under-fives is examined in detail in Parts 1 and 2.

Until recently the dominance of white culture was not questioned and when it was practices were justified, somewhat thoughtlessly, on the grounds that they would aid integration. The assumption seemed to be that recognition of differences would perpetuate them and that this was undesirable. There was an equation too of 'being British' with 'being white'. Social work practice, if it is to combat racism, must therefore reflect the multi-racial society which pays for it and take positive account of its diversity.

The broader concept of institutional racism has many interpretations (Banton and Miles, 1984), ranging from the economic and other social systems which intentionally or unintentionally keep blacks in subordinate positions to those rules and practices of individuals and public bodies which unwittingly discriminate against black people. This latter interpretation is the basis of the concept of indirect discrimination in the 1976 Race Relations Act which makes unlawful the application of a requirement or condition which cannot be justified irrespective of racial and ethnic origins and when, although applied equally to different racial or ethnic groups, is discriminatory in its effects on one particular group. Racial discrimination occurs when the proportion in the group which can comply with the condition is considerably smaller than the proportion of persons in the population as a whole, and when this is to the detriment of the minority. So, for example, a rule that the children of single parents should have first priority for day nursery places could discriminate against Asians, amongst whom there are few single-parent families, unless it could be proved that such a criterion could be justified on non-racial grounds. Since day care is a scarce resource there must be rules for its allocation; but should the circumstances of single parents always be considered more urgent then the needs of ethnic minority and other families where poverty makes it imperative for both parents to work, or where it may be desirable for isolated Asian children to be introduced gently to the world and the language they will find at school?

Another common manifestation of racism is the resistance to recognizing or trying to change inequalities which flow from ethnicity or race. Again this may be done with benign intent. These questions are often put forward as common objections. If monitoring services reveal unequal distribution will this not cause discontent where none (allegedly) existed before? Will not paying attention to the needs of different ethnic groups arouse envy and competition? Doing nothing to tackle often glaring inequalities and disadvantages may, therefore, be justified as the safer course. The experience of 40 years of differing degrees of 'race relations paralysis' shows that racial disadvantage and discrimination do not simply disappear if they are ignored. This is well demonstrated in the reports of numerous House of Commons Select Committees on immigration and race relations, in the Scarman Report on the civil disturbances in Brixton and elsewhere in 1981, in the Rampton and Swann Reports on the education of ethnic minority children in 1981 and 1985, and in the succession of reports of the Policy Studies Institute (Smith, 1974, 1981; Brown, 1984) and the Commission for Racial Equality on discrimination in employment, housing and education (1984, 1985(a)).

Social workers cannot do much to combat, in general terms, the disadvantages and discrimination which flow from economic and political systems. They must however be clear about their impact on black people's quality of life. This includes the effects of immigration policy and practice which may make it extremely difficult for black families to reunite or for relatives from the home country to visit their families in Britain (CRE, 1985(b)). They must also be aware of, and where appropriate activate, the special measures which can reduce the inequalities of groups and individuals. These are briefly discussed later in this introduction and by Pitts and his colleagues in respect of the juvenile justice system. They must try to scrutinize the effects on ethnic minorities of practices, which may be regarded as natural and the best possible, but which have developed in a culture very different from that of some ethnic minority users of social services and social work. Defensiveness about the existence of racism breeds subterfuge, rhetoric, accusation and counter-accusation. Accepting racism's endemic nature makes open discussion and challenge possible and encourages realistic means of tackling it.

## Children

The next definition concerns children. This appears on its own in the title in the interests of brevity. The contributions in the book are addressed to the needs of children and young people as defined in the 1980 Child Care Act.

## Social Work

Finally there is social work. Our interpretation goes wider than case or group work with individuals and families, but includes intervention in the systems which impinge on their lives and the management of the personal social services.

## Demography, Disadvantage and Need

The demography of the black population of Britain highlights special needs for some educational and social services, especially those concerned with children. It also disposes of some myths and misunder-

TABLE 1
*Estimates of ethnic origin of population of new commonwealth and Pakistan origin*

Composition in 1980

|  | % |
| --- | --- |
| India | 22 |
| Pakistan/Bangladesh | 17 |
| 'African Asians' | 9 |
| Caribbean | 31 |
| Africa (other than 'African Asians') | 6 |
| Mediterranean | 8 |
| Other | 8 |
|  | 100 |

Source: Brown, 1984

standings about the characteristics of the black population which can still mislead administrators and social workers about the services needed by ethnic minorities. The first myth is that black people are a major proportion of the people of Britain. In fact, they are about 3.3 per cent of the general population. The projection for 1991 is that there will be 2.5 million people in Britain, approximately five per cent of the population, whose parents were born in the West Indies, India, Bangladesh, Africa and Pakistan. Table 1 shows the proportions of the ethnic minority population from these countries.

This tiny proportion of the whole population is not, however, evenly distributed throughout Britain as Table 2 shows.

TABLE 2
*Regional distribution of whites, Asians and West Indians in England and Wales*

Column percentages

| | | 1981 Census Population in households with heads born in: | | |
|---|---|---|---|---|
| Region | UK | Indian sub-continent, East Africa, Caribbean | Caribbean | Indian sub-continent, East Africa |
| Greater London | 11 | 41 | 56 | 33 |
| Other S. East | 21 | 12 | 9 | 14 |
| E. Midlands | 8 | 7 | 5 | 8 |
| W. Midlands | 10 | 18 | 16 | 19 |
| N. West | 14 | 8 | 5 | 10 |
| Yorks/Humberside | 10 | 8 | 5 | 9 |
| Rest of England and Wales | 26 | 6 | 5 | 6 |

A third of the Asian population and over half of West Indians live in the Greater London area. In the Midlands too there are substantial proportions. Within these relatively large geographical regions there are further concentrations. In one or two London boroughs nearly a quarter of the population is black. Because of the young age of this population, at or reaching the family building stage of life, and their concentration in areas otherwise largely inhabited by middle-aged or elderly white people there are several boroughs in which the majority of births are to black mothers. A few local authorities in Britain have, therefore, relatively large black populations but, even within these, concentrations are small. There are few adjoining streets in which black households predominate.

The study conducted by the Policy Studies Institute, which in the absence of information about ethnic origin in the 1981 census, is the most recent and comprehensive demographic study of the black population, confirmed that in the vast majority of enumeration districts white people are in the majority, and all live in local authorities where they are the overwhelming majority (Brown, 1984). Although in one or two boroughs in the Greater London area 40 per cent of the school children are black, they make up only 3.5 per cent of the total school population of the region; and in only 12 out of 400 Greater London secondary schools are black pupils in the majority. A significantly larger proportion of the primary schools, especially in the Inner London area, will have a majority of black children who make up 46 per cent of the primary population; but such schools are still in a tiny minority.

This brief demographic account disposes of another myth; that is that black people are nearly all immigrants. Estimates suggest that in 1982 over 40 per cent of the black population were born here and that proportion will rise to about one-half by 1991 (Brown, 1984). This leaves, nevertheless, substantial proportions who are immigrants. The timing of their arrival varies between ethnic groups and between men and women. Well over a half of West Indian men and women have lived in Britain over 20 years. Nearly two-thirds of Asian men settled by 1968 but substantial proportions of Asian women came to Britain much later. For example, nearly one-fifth of Pakistani women and well over one-third of Bangladeshi women have been in Britain for less than six years. The reunion of Asian families continues, with many wives and children having waited several years, struggling with the bureaucracy and

TABLE 3
*Fluency in English amongst Asian adults*

Column percentages

|  | All Asians | Men | Women |
|---|---|---|---|
| Immigrant speaks English . . . | | | |
| fluently | 41 | 48 | 32 |
| fairly well | 23 | 27 | 18 |
| slightly | 21 | 19 | 27 |
| not at all | 11 | 4 | 20 |
| not recorded | 4 | 4 | 4 |

Source: Brown, 1984

obstacles of British immigration law and procedures before being given leave to settle (CRE, 1985(b)).

This pattern of settlement means that for people whose first language is not English their fluency in it will vary, as Table 3 demonstrates. It can be seen that women are particularly likely to have poor or no English.

Although Brown (1984) found some improvement in the living circumstances of black people over the last 20 years, the prevailing picture is still one of persistent and serious inequality and continuing racial discrimination in employment and education.

TABLE 4
*Percentages of indigenous, West Indian, Indian and Pakistani families living in various social circumstances*

| | National Child Development Study | | Child Health and Education Study | | | |
|---|---|---|---|---|---|---|
| | Indigenous | West Indian | Indigenous | West Indian | Indian | Pakistani |
| Father in manual occupation | 56.8 | 70.6 | 54.5 | 71.5 | 72.4 | 71.0 |
| Father unemployed for part of recording year | 7.0 | 11.8 | | | | |
| No male head of household | 4.1 | 9.8 | 4.4 | 16.2 | 2.8 | 4.3 |
| 4 or more children in household or family | 29.0 | 57.5 | 14.8 | 43.5 | 43.4 | 77.5 |
| Overcrowded (1.5 or more people per room) | 10.0 | 32.1 | | | | |
| Child sharing bed | 16.3 | 43.7 | | | | |
| Family sharing bathroom, hot water and lavatory | 2.5 | 16.1 | | | | |
| Family income less than £100 per week | | | 36.6 | 51.8 | 47.5 | 68.0 |
| Serious financial hardship | 10.1 | 27.4 | | | | |
| Child receiving free school meals | | | 15.4 | 32.5 | 9.4 | 31.0 |
| Child attended more than 2 schools | 14.8 | 29.1 | | | | |
| Neighbourhood: inner-city or council estate | | | 34.7 | 72.9 | 48.4 | 77.1 |

Black people are concentrated in some of the poorest and most disadvantaged of cities whose local authorities are likely to be facing increasing demands for expenditure and the constraints of rate-capping and diminishing resources. They live quite disproportionately in areas with the highest rates of unemployment and overcrowding and other indices of social deprivation, including poor quality private and public housing. To these disadvantages, which are the daily experience of so many black families, is added the stress and fear of substantial racial harassment (Home Office, 1981). Table 4, adapted from the Swann Report, illustrates these bleak facts. Where there is no entry, this is either because the data are not available in that study or because there is no significant difference between West Indian and indigenous children.

### Implications for Social Work and the Personal Social Services

What are the implications of this demography for the personal social services and social work?

### Positive Action

First, administrators need to remember these group inequalities when confronted with the apparent truth that the deprivations of working-class black and white families seem remarkably similar. What is true for individuals is not true for identifiable sections of the population. In short, no amount of assertion of the irrelevance of race, colour and ethnicity in determining life chances alters the fact that racial discrimination and disadvantage daily and chronically influence the circumstances of ethnic minorities. This must clearly increase the need for social services and social work, even though demand may not increase. This may be because of lack of information about available services or distate for their style of delivery.

It is the fact of continuing and often gross inequalities which is central to Lord Scarman's call for positive action.

> If the balance of racial disadvantage is to be redressed, as it must be, positive action is required. I mean by this more than the admirable approach adopted by at least some central and local government agencies at present, which is intended chiefly to persuade the ethnic minorities to take up their share of general social provisions. Important though this is, it is not, in my view, a sufficient answer. Given the special problems of ethnic minorities, exposed in evidence, justice requires that special programmes should be adopted in areas of acute deprivation. (Scarman, 1981, para. 6.32.)

Positive action can take many forms and several are discussed in this book. It can involve simply a recognition that individual minority group members may have disproportionate problems demanding appropriate attention. More strongly, it can entail policies which give priority to a group, not just a few individuals within it, because of the nature and extent of the group's disadvantage. The first definition is not particularly contentious and, if it guided practice, would make a substantial difference to the allocation of services. It would also ensure that their style of presentation and delivery maximized their accessibility and acceptability. Sadly, these relatively straightforward 'commonsense' manifestations of positive discrimination are usually lost in anxious, albeit abstract, debates about the consequences of the second definition, priority allocations to certain groups. This prompts such questions as: would the targets of such policies feel stigmatized as a group identified as especially vulnerable, or the privileged focus of a determination to ensure their equal and secure position in society? Would such privilege, however justified by circumstances, simply exacerbate the envy and understandable sense of injustice felt by poor white people who see that as individuals, if not as a group, their circumstances are the same as their black neighbours? The answers to these questions are complex, but there is now a prevailing, if untested, assumption that all but the most subtle forms of positive action will dangerously exacerbate racial hostility.

This fear distracts attention from two equally important questions. First, what will be the consequences for ethnic minorities and society of perpetuating the association of blackness with gross disadvantage? Recent history shows that the violence that can ensue may well outweigh the disruption which it is alleged will flow from white resentment about positive discrimination. Although American experience shows that the advancement of ethnic minorities through positive action provokes fierce debate and continuous reassessment of its legitimate parameters, it is not claimed there that the costs are greater than the price of the continuing gross inequalities. Doing nothing means accepting, in perpetuity, the disadvantages which affect black ethnic minorities.

Second, and here the argument is about values, is it ethical not to tackle recognized problems with the means available? Here it can help to think ahead 20 years and envisage the judgements which will be passed on such a failure.

How can administrators respond helpfully to the often angry complaint of social workers that, when faced with black and white individuals in equally desperate need, it is absurd to discriminate positively in favour of the former simply on the grounds that, as a group, they are more disadvantaged than white working-class clients. Ethnic distinctions between otherwise identical individuals are not the best way forward; but decisions about group priorities are inescapable and can most effectively be taken at policy level. All the following commonplace choices could and should take account of the special needs of ethnic minorities. For example, the location and admissions criteria of day care for pre-school children and the advice available about other substitute care should be relevant to the large proportion of working mothers from the ethnic minorities. Since disproportionate numbers of black children are received into care, at an earlier age than their white peers, with less chance of reunion with their own parents or placement in substitute families, social workers need special preparation to combat these inequalities.

Particular efforts must be made to recruit substitute families who can respond to the cultural needs of ethnic-minority children and to their experience of discrimination. Moreover, since it seems that there are disproportionate numbers of young black offenders in custody, community measures, such as intermediate treatment, must be relevant in their geographical location and their programmes to these young people and their families. The siting and staffing of helping agencies should recognize the special needs of ethnic-minority groups relatively new to Britain, who may speak little English, and be unfamiliar with the workings of the social services. Because of the problems of communicating across cultures, and the consequent dangers of wrong assessment and decisions, special efforts must be made to recruit and train ethnic-minority social workers who will enlarge their agencies' understanding, make their approach more appropriate and their staffing more representative of a multi-racial society. Here two little-used provisions of the 1976 Race Relations Act (Sections 35 and 37) allow some measure of specific positive discrimination. All these measures, while largely avoiding invidious choices between individuals, would address group inequalities and therefore mean that 'ethnic minorities will enjoy for a time positive discrimination in their favour.' (Scarman, 1981, para. 9.4.)

### The Diversity of the Black Population

Second, administrators and social workers must be prepared for great heterogeneity among the black population. An obvious but often ignored point is the diversity of ethnic and geographical origins, languages and religions. The largest of the Caribbean groups originates from Jamaica, but migrants from the West Indies included substantial numbers from Barbados, Trinidad and Tobago, Guyana, the Windward and the Virgin Islands. Asian migrants come from Gujarat, which borders on Pakistan, from the Punjab in North India and Pakistan and from Sylhet and the maritime areas of Bangladesh; most of those from East Africa had family origins in Gujarat and the Punjab. The majority of Asian migrants come from rural areas although African Asians usually from towns and cities. The significance of people's origins and the strength of their cultural traditions will vary greatly, depending on numerous factors including their length of settlement in Britain and the place they have been allowed in British society. Amongst the black consumers or potential consumers of the social services will be newly-arrived people speaking little or no English, who are enduring all the strains of recent migration, and also people born and brought up in Britain who identify themselves as black and British, established or hoping to be established in mainstream British society.

The rhetoric of race relations rightly places great stress on this black British population who should have all the rights, duties and expectations of British citizenship. What is sometimes ignored in these assertions is the heterogeneity within this group. The continuing strength of cultural and religious traditions and rampant discrimination which continues to exclude many black people from economic opportunities and social life, and which often ignores the educational needs and aspirations of minorities (Swann, 1985), may ensure strong identification with the traditions and mores of parents, or a redefinition of these which takes account of more acceptable features of British society (Ballard, 1974). This then is a world in which stereotypical or fixed notions of culture, belief and aspiration are highly dangerous. Statements about 'what Asians eat' or 'what Muslims want', which can still be heard amongst policy makers are simply racist nonsense. Expecting diversity, social workers must learn what is important for the people with whom they work by careful observation, by listening and by asking their consumers who are, of course, the experts.

## The Needs and Demands of Black People

A third important issue is the proportion of social services consumers who are or should be black. This distinction is made because there is evidence of underuse of social services by ethnic minorities particularly, given the generally disadvantaged environments in which they are likely to live (Bhalla and Blakemore, 1981; Horn, 1982; Ousley, 1981). Clearly in some parts of a few local authorities a very substantial proportion of consumers will or should be black. In other authorities significant numbers can be expected. But despite the concentrations outlined earlier it is most important to note that there are black people in every region in Britain. It must, therefore, be every social worker's expectation that at some point in his or her career he or she will work with black people. Even in local authorities with tiny numbers of ethnic minority people black children can be found, fostered privately or through local authorities, or in residential establishments for children and young people. Many of these children were placed far from their families in areas of black settlement at a time when there was less awareness than now of the long-term implications of such isolation.

*A Youthful Population*

A fourth important demographic implication is the age structure of the black population. Forty per cent of Asians and 30 per cent of West Indians are under 16 compared with 22 per cent of the whole population. While about 12 per cent of the general population fall into the 0 to 9 age group, 27 per cent of Asian origin and 16 per cent of West Indian children are in this age band.

This proportion of infants and young children can, or should, make a significant impact on the health and personal social services. Mothers in poor families of whom disproportionate numbers are black, do not use, for many reasons, ante-natal and other health services as much as their more affluent sisters. For many black women, especially the significant numbers recently arrived in Britain, there are further obstacles in trying to negotiate a health care system which takes little or no account of their language problems, the cultural expectations or the extreme problems of coping with centralized health care which may demand long and difficult journeys with no help with the care of other small children. Cornwell and Gordon (1984) have described vividly the trials of these women and their children, and the imaginative and successful use of ancillary health workers who help young families directly as well as acting as interpreters and advocates for them with other health workers.

> A lot of women would like to be seen by a woman doctor, but for our women it is very important because it is in their religion and culture that women are not seen by any man other than their husband. This is the way they have been brought up. They feel guilty and shameful. Some of them go home and ask forgiveness of God for breaking the law; some put their hands over their face while they are being examined, and some have tears in their eyes. I feel very

annoyed. I am by their side and I can do nothing to help them. I watch them tremble with fear. I also feel guilty.

We felt that we could speak for and help women of our communities through our own experiences. What we do is offer help and support . . . visit the wards . . . run groups in hospitals and health centres and visit women at home . . . we also have to tell women when there is something wrong with their baby. It is very difficult for us because we have built a special relationship with them throughout their pregnancy, so we have to prepare ourselves to give the bad news and we continue to give help and support . . . we often feel pressurised with their social problems, like housing, financial and marital. We try to offer them other organisations, but sometimes it is not possible, so we find ourselves filling in forms for them, writing letters to various officers . . . to make sure they get their rights (Zohra Ali Subari, in Cornwell and Gordon, 1984, pp. 1–2.)

The personal social services do not have responsibility for all infants and toddlers, but substantial preventative work could be done through giving information about the services most likely to be needed, including income maintenance and day care, by early contact with young families, in liaison with community health services. If Samar Sheik and her colleagues (Chapter 11) had had the help available to some of the black women of Hackney, their inevitable grief and hurt as parents of handicapped children could have been reduced.

### Implications for Particular Services

### Day Care and the Under-Fives

There are many reasons why social services departments should review and act upon the day care needs of black under-fives and their parents, both as a contribution to children's intellectual and emotional development and because of their parents' employment. First, we have seen that they are particularly likely to be amongst the most disadvantaged of British citizens whose needs are least well served. Second, in several local authorities, especially London and the West Midlands, black under-fives make up a substantial proportion of the whole under-five population: nearly a third in Birmingham and Wolverhampton; over 40 per cent in the London boroughs of Haringey, Newham and Tower Hamlets. If such authorities neglect the needs of their black children they will be ignoring a major proportion of their citizens (VOLCUF, 1984). A Hackney Social Services Department Committee paper sums this all up in putting before councillors proposals to combat racism and improve the services for under-fives in one of London's poorest boroughs.

A black child lacks a fair chance to live, learn, thrive and develop normally in

Hackney today. They are twice as likely to be sick because they are more likely to be poor. They are twice as likely to have no regular source of health care, and are likely to be more seriously ill when they finally see a doctor. A black baby today has nearly one chance in two of being born into poverty and faces a losing struggle to escape poverty throughout childhood. A black child is twice as likely to live in dilapidated housing and is twice as likely to have parents who are on welfare. A black child's mother is more likely to go out to work sooner to work longer hours and to make less money than her white counterpart. A black pre-school child is likely to depend solely on a mother's earning. Because the black woman still faces discrimination as a black and as a woman, she is the lowest paid among workers and the family she heads is the poorest in the nation. As a result black children are far more dependent on full time day care arrangements, approximately 80 per cent of the children in our day nurseries are from the black and ethnic minority community.

Three-quarters of West Indian and nearly one-third of Asian mothers are employed outside the home at some period during their children's pre-school years, many for substantial periods, compared with 45 per cent of mothers in the general population (Osborn et al, 1984). A higher proportion of ethnic-minority mothers say they work from economic necessity; in the case of West Indian and Asian mothers over 80 and 66 per cent respectively compared with 36 per cent of all mothers. Nearly one-third of West Indian households with children under 16 compared with one-tenth of similar white households are headed by a single parent, usually a woman. Five per cent of Asian households are also in this position, a fact not usually recognized. Black mothers therefore have a disproportionate need for day care, much of which is probably met, because of the gap between demand and supply, by the poorest quality, lowest paid and often unregistered child minders (Hood, 1970; Jackson and Jackson, 1979; Gregory, 1969; Mayall and Petre, 1983, CRE, 1975).

*Child Minding*
Mayall and Petrie (1983) found that foreign-born mothers, as well as getting a poorer service from child minders than mothers born in Britain, also faced substantial discrimination from about one-third of the minders.

> Minders said that caring for a foreign speaking child was too difficult; that various ethnic minority or national groups were unwilling to pay or haggled about the price; or that the children were dirty; or that the parents made unreasonable demands, especially about food and cooking methods; or that their own family or neighbours would be hostile. It is not surprising that minders should hold such views. Very many people do, as studies of attitudes and practices (especially in housing and employment) have regularly shown. (p.70.)

These attitudes must play a part in the low standard of child minding services Mayall and Petrie found were particularly the fate of the children of foreign-born mothers. These children were more likely to have changes of minder and be placed with those with the poorest housing and amenities. They were twice as likely as the children of British-born mothers to be with overburdened minders, many of whom were caring for more than four children, and so unlikely to be able to give them much individual attention. When foreign-born mothers and the minders do not share a common language it is obviously difficult for them to communicate about the child; needs are therefore more likely to be neglected and misunderstandings arise. For reasons of cost, convenience and accessibility child minders care for the great majority of children, black and white, whose parents work. Significant numbers of Afro-Caribbean children are also cared for in day nurseries and in nursery schools and classes. This is not surprising since entry to this form of day care depends largely on meeting the priority criteria, and Afro-Caribbean children and their parents are so disadvantaged. Were it not for the heavy weighting given to single parenthood in defining priority needs large proportions of Asian children, who suffer numerous other disadvantages (Table 4) would be eligible.

Local authority day care provides well for the physical needs of children and, at its best, for their emotional and intellectual development. Sadly, most day care is not the best that could be provided, partly because of the strains on resources and staff and because of disagreements about its role and the appropriate relationship between parents and children. As Chapters 1 and 2 illustrate, it is rare to find day care establishments which reflect the multi-racial character of their environment and clientele. Misunderstandings and ill-feelings between staff and parents are common, and the various forms of racism described on pp. 6–11 flourish. The Rampton Committee commented that while existing day care and education for under-fives was generally inadequate to meet the needs of the population it was particularly ill-suited to the needs of West Indian children. The Swann Committee emphasized further the need for changes in the content and delivery of education so that it would be better equipped to meet the needs of ethnic-minority children and, equally important, to underline the multi-racial character of British society. Chapters 3 to 6 show how these grave shortcomings can be tackled. It is easier to influence the policy and practice of publicly funded establishments than the behaviour of individual child minders whose relationship with parents is usually a private one.

The troubles of the day care system for under-fives are well documented (Jackson and Jackson, 1979; Mayall and Petrie, 1983; Osborn et al, 1984). As so often in British social provision they are highlighted by the vicissitudes of the black families who have penetrated the system and those who would like to but have not yet succeeded. The near-universality of the need for some kind of day care provision and the means it provides for helping a high proportion of the most disadvantaged young citizens would seem to make it an attractive target for priority action. Notwithstanding pockets of good practice and pioneering development, the major initiatives needed have not taken place. The scale of the problems must be recognized so that reforms and new developments can be set within this general context. Change *is* possible, as Chapters 2–6 show. It is tempting but wrong to assume that nothing can improve without a major restructuring of day care provision; it is also essential to press for these major changes, using as one argument the needs of a significant proportion of children in metropolitan areas, namely Britain's black under-fives.

The major problem, easier to tackle at local authority than national level, is the divided responsibility for under-fives. This reflects the artificial distinction between the educational and physical care of young children. When pre-school children are with minders or in day nurseries or play groups social services departments have formal responsibility for their welfare; this may mean minimal supervision or substantial intervention and innovation. Children in nursery schools and classes are the responsibility of local education authorities, although those children who go to minders after school then come, at least in theory, under the oversight of social services departments.

The implications are clear: education and social services departments need to liaise closely in respect of the needs of pre-school children and develop local policies in which day care is not simply seen as an unfortunate necessity for parents who have to work, but as a valuable social and educational experience and a means by which the State could intervene to change the balance between women's economic dependance and family responsibilities. Although it has largely been public policy to provide only for under-fives who are gravely socially disadvantaged and, in many cases, at risk of being taken into care, the realities of family life and, in particular, the lives of mothers and young children, are well-known and accepted in many local authorities, especially in poorer urban areas. Day care is not therefore seen as a peculiar service for the exceptional child but as part of the experience of the majority. Because national policy for under-fives does not reflect this acceptance, local authorities have found it extremely difficult to put their own beliefs into practice. Nursery places and classes, the most expensive form of provision, have declined and child minding is now provided as the major form of day care, especially for the under-threes. Between 100,000 and 200,000 children are now daily minded, and the places per 1000 children under five have grown more than any other provision. It follows therefore that 'it should be seen as a day care service, not as a quirky system subject to the care givers' private and, in some cases, racist preferences.' (Mayall and Petrie, 1983, p.191.) Too often, as we have seen, the picture is an unhappy one '. . . of sad, passive children and hard pressed minders, insensitive to children's needs and distrustful of the mothers who in turn are resentful of the minders'. This is not a case for blame. '. . . neither mothers nor minders have an easy time. They are both victims of a system which exploits and benefits from the labour of women but assumes little responsibility for their children.' (Mayall and Petrie, 1977, p.11.)

The major form of day care is therefore the one about which there is greatest concern. This fact also should be sufficient justification for social services departments to pursue energetically those practices which it is known can improve standards of child minding, although not easily or speedily, as the Jacksons and Mayall and Petrie have demonstrated. These include treating the registration process as far more than a formal examination of whether the applicant fulfils legal criteria and rather as an exploration of motives, strengths and potential, an opportunity to discuss the hazards and problems of being a minder. In short, the processes and skills now well-developed in the selection of foster parents could be adapted to child minding legislation. Second, local authorities could take on more child minders as salaried employees with contractual obligations to care for children placed with them after the necessary exploration about mutual acceptability. These child minders therefore became a local authority resource and in return can expect a regular income, training and support from the social services department. Parents should be reasonably confident that their children will be cared for competently. The history of fostering shows that these relationships are not easy; it also shows how professionalism and experimentation can be the mark of serious attempts to provide a system of substitute care which is considered a central part of a special work service, not a quasi-commercial venture with peripheral supervision from a public authority. All the recent and mostly well-researched ventures into foster parents' selection and preparation, specialist care and co-operation with natural parents and social workers have relevance for child minding programmes. So too does the work done on the placement of black children and the recruitment of black substitute parents. Child minding and fostering have many differences but these should not obscure the common needs and experience of children and carers who live together for many hours of every day or for many weeks and years.

Approaches to child minding of the kind briefly outlined could dramatically improve care for all children, but there are further issues that need to be addressed in the daily care of black children. A first priority is to tackle racial discrimination. Many local authorities have turned a blind eye to the racial preferences of registered minders, arguing either that the law was unclear or that in this kind of service it would be wrong for minders to be obliged to care for children to whom they felt hostility or awkwardness. Some of these authorities have kept various formal and informal records of minders' racial preferences in an effort to divert black parents from those minders whom they knew would discriminate.

The legal position remains somewhat uncertain because it has not been tested in court. However, in a recent case which was eventually settled out of court it was argued that a local authority, in offering services of child minders to the public, offers a service within the meaning of Section 20 of the 1976 Race Relations Act which forbids discrimination on the grounds of race, ethnicity or nationality. A member of the social services department had, in fact, not given a mother the name of a particular child minder on the grounds that this woman was known not to take black children. It has also been argued that a loophole is not provided for the local authority by Section 23 of the Act, which has allowed foster parents to discriminate on racial grounds, by excluding from its scope people who take children into their home and treat them as members of their family. A local authority is not taking children into its home or treating them as family members; and so by knowingly colluding with racial discrimination the local authority, under Section 33 of the Act, would be acting unlawfully.

The question arises as to whether a child minder is protected under Section 23 of the Act because she takes a child into her home and treats him as a member of her family. It has been argued that this could be a question of fact in each case. If, for example, a minded child is entertained, fed, washed and disciplined as a child of the family, the protection exists. If important distinctions are made between the minder's own and her minded children, and if the arrangement is largely a commercial one and an important source of revenue, then the pertinent sections of the Race Relations Act would apply. Given the argument in favour of aligning fostering and child minding services, and the fact that foster parents may be paid high salaries but still be immune from the Act, it seems likely that child minders who themselves discriminate on racial grounds may also be immune from the Act. Nevertheless, local authorities will act unlawfully if they register minders whom they know will discriminate and advise applicants for minding services accordingly. The same situation probably exists with foster parents' selection.

The legal anomalies should not, in our view, be used as an excuse for registering minders who say they will discriminate racially, that is that they will refuse to mind a child simply on the grounds of his or her racial, ethnic or national origins. That is not to say that minders, parents and social workers should not think carefully, as they should in other substitute care placements, about meeting a child's linguistic and cultural needs and about easing the relationship between minder and parents. This may make some kinds of transracial placement undesirable. It is very far from justifying a situation in which any black child and parents can be refused a service by a white minder.

If local authorities take seriously their responsibilities under the Race Relations Act they will no longer be able to ignore the racial and cultural issues in child minding. Attending to the needs of parents and children will mean trying to provide a service which does not discriminate racially and which is culturally sensitive. There is much to be learnt from the best work that has been done in the fostering and adoption of black children. Black child minders need to be recruited, partly because this is an occupation which black women might wish to follow and from which they may feel excluded, but also because they will have a special contribution to make to some black children and their parents. The successful recruitment methods used for black substitute parents may well be appropriate for potential black minders. Local authorities will also need to examine their response to applicants and their registration criteria to determine whether there are elements which would unjustifiably deter or exclude good potential minders. Registered minders, and especially those who are the salaried employees of social services departments, also need training and support in the care of a multi-racial group of children. Programmes could be shared with foster parents and day nursery staff.

This is not an easy agenda for a department which treats child minding legislation and supervision as a largely bureaucratic process, and for one which is preoccupied with bringing within its orbit unregistered minders whose practices may be dubious and who are resistant both to support and supervision. We do not underestimate the difficulties, the anomalies or the scale of the task. We do, nevertheless, see child minding policies and practice as a major means of improving the daily life of black under-fives and a clear candidate for positive action. We would have liked to include, had we been able to discover them, accounts of successful work in this area. We hope that what we have written will encourage publication of social services departments' new ventures.

## Nursery Care

Although nursery care avoids some of the worst hazards of child minding it often takes little account of black children's needs and backgrounds. Here more than anywhere you are likely to hear staff proclaiming that 'we don't care for white or black children, just children'. While there are large numbers of black children in many nurseries, it is still rare to find black staff and environments which reflect the varied cultures of the children's parents and homes. For many children and parents nurseries are therefore an alien environment. This introduction dwells little on the common shortcomings of nursery care because they are discussed in Chapters 3–6 which explore too how group day care for under-fives can combat racism, reflect Britain's multi-racial character and become more sensitive to black children's needs. The initiatives described can be undertaken by individual or staff groups in voluntary or local authority settings. They may come about because of the discontents, passions and enthusiasms of a few people but they are likely to have greater impact if they are part of a general policy for the care of black under-fives. An example of such a policy can be found at the end of the section on day care for the under-fives.

## Training

In all accounts of improving the care of black children training is constantly but usually vaguely seen as crucial. A first important step has been the requirement that training for social work and nursery nursing should take account of Britain's multi-racial society. The Central Council for Education and Training in Social Work requires students:

> to demonstrate to the satisfaction of examiners, knowledge and understanding . . . in the processes of human development, socialisation and functioning, both normal and deviant, throughout the age cycle, within a multi-cultural setting.

27

The regulations of the National Nursery Examination Board are more extensive:

Candidates will be expected to give evidence of the ability to
1 Appreciate the wide range of ways in which families can function successfully with particular reference to
  a  ethnic and religious minorities in our society
  b  class and regional variations in our society.
2 Show awareness of
  a  the need for the individual to value his own religious, cultural and/or sub-cultural background, and to feel that it is valued by others
  b  the way in which this sense of value can be encouraged.
3 Show awareness of the possibility of real or perceived conflicts between the values, beliefs and behaviours of minority cultural and sub-cultural groups, and those generally accepted in our society, with particular reference to
  a  the reasons why such conflicts may be perceived, the consequences for members of minority groups, and possible means of overcoming mutual misconceptions.
  b  the possibility of genuine conflicts, of the need to respect mutually incompatible positions, and the ways in which such conflicts can be overcome.
4 Recognise the wide range of special problems facing families belonging to minority groups and identify appropriate sources of help.

The interpretation of these requirements varies from a fleeting acknowledgement of their existence to substantial theoretical and practical content. This may simply reflect the enthusiasm of teachers or it can be required by employers or the providers of funds. The Inner London Education Authority, for example, insists on substantial teaching on racism in nursery nurse courses. O'Hagan in Chapter 5 describes how such opportunities can be exploited.

The majority of social work and nursery nurse staff have had little training which bears directly on work in a multi-racial society. This has, therefore, to be supplemented by in-service courses. Too often these courses are far too brief and ill-planned to raise questions of racism, enlarge understanding and, most important, to improve practice. There are naive and simplistic expectations of a day programme of 4 to 5 hours. The chapters by Koetter and Ahmed describe some excellently organized training with a strong practical focus.

### Black Children in Care

There has been long-standing concern about the disproportionate number of black children in care (Barnardo's, 1966; Fitzherbert, 1967;

Rowe and Lambert, 1971; Raynor, 1970; Lawson, 1977; Batta and Mawby, 1981). In 1984 the House of Commons Social Services Committee on Children in Care commented 'one of the most disturbing trends as regards children in care is the growing proportion of such children who are of West Indian, African or mixed race parentage.' (p. cxix.) They noted that the absence of precise national information about this phenomenon was sometimes explained as a consequence of a general resistance to collecting statistics of ethnic origin or as 'a conspiracy of silence'. In fact, the Association of British Adoption and Fostering Agencies has collected national data on the ethnic origin of children in care but this has still to be analysed. Several local authorities have collected their own statistics and analysed them further in an attempt to go beyond the bare facts of disproportionate representation, and to explore the reasons for it and the care and rehabilitation services provided (Ousley, 1981).

Many reasons have been advanced for the disproportionate numbers of black children in care and possibly all have some value. It has been said that, because of the established association between poverty and reception into care, the numbers simply reflect the disproportionate degrees of poverty and deprivation to which black people are subjected. This plausible explanation must be held against the conclusions of a small but detailed study in Lambeth, which found that within a generally deprived borough the parents of black children received into care had higher incomes and were better housed than the parents of white children in care. Black parents had, however, fewer relatives to whom they could turn in family crisis. They also reported considerable misunderstandings with social workers about the reasons for reception into care; the social workers emphasized difficulties in the relationship between parent and child, while parents saw problems resting more with their children's behaviour. This would be consistent with various accounts of white social workers' bafflement and fear when faced with strong and emotional disagreements and rows between black parents and their children, during which threats of rejection and physical punishment may feature. Over 15 years ago Fitzherbert reported that social workers panicked in these circumstances. Fearing for children's safety and failing to see any room for compromise in the strongly-voiced complaints of parents and children, they frequently and prematurely received children into care and saw little chance of reunion with parents. Child care officers who were known then by the West Indian community as welfare workers earned the nickname 'farewell workers', because it was assumed that once they intervened in a family it spelt 'farewell' to the children. A decade later Cheetham (1981) found this dilemma continuing, although many social workers had become more cautious about receiving black adolescents into care. This caution, however, had its own problems, and certainly did not mean that alternative methods of help would necessarily be offered. Several respondents said they knew of substantial numbers of black young people, usually of Caribbean origin, who hovered on the periphery of the department.

> This tenuous contact was at least partly collusive. Young blacks were said to be suspicious of white dominated welfare organisations, and their suspicions were confirmed by the actual or alleged failure to help them. Social workers, in their turn, were often at a loss to know what to do. They usually had little access to accommodation, apart from local authority children's homes and hostels, and they were reluctant to receive young people into care simply on the grounds of family rows which they felt were either beyond their understanding or intervention or both. Some said that they had in the past panicked and received black adolescents into care only to find that the local authority had little appropriate provision for them. They were also aware of the criticism of black colleagues and clients that black young people could use white social workers as a stick to beat their parents by 'conning' them that reception into care was the only alternative to domestic violence or life on the streets.
>
> The consequence of these dilemmas is substantial (but uncounted) numbers of 'half clients', black young people known to social services departments, sometimes on 'unallocated' supervision orders, but, if there is any action, largely referred to other voluntary agencies or to the housing department or occasionally to the Youth Services. This is a muddled, unconsidered response, not a policy. It leaves black young people in an unco-ordinated nether world of squats, temporary hostels and crash pads, sometimes suspended or truanting from school, often unemployed and commonly with little or no regular income. (Cheetham, 1981, p.51.)

The Commission for Racial Equality in its submission to the House of Commons Committee drew attention to the way eurocentric views about ideal patterns of family life concerning discipline, material and parental responsibilities could exacerbate the risk of reception into care and reduce the chance of return to the parental home. It must also be emphasized once again that a colourblind approach does not serve black people well. Having reviewed the dilemmas of black families and their social workers, the House of Commons Committee has this to say about the assessment of problems and appropriate intervention:

> We do not for one minute propose that cruelty or neglect should be overlooked in black but not in white families; a child's right to protection is absolute but

this protection must be continuously and sensitively given. If it is not, with the best will in the world, ethnic minority families will be disproportionately and unnecessarily broken up. By the same token, the same vigorous and positive social work must be taken to rehabilitate a black child with his natural family as would be taken on behalf of any other child. (p.cxxi.)

Explanations advanced for the disproportionate numbers of black children in residential establishments have usually centred on the alleged impossibility of finding substitute families for them because it was assumed either that black children would be unacceptable to white parents, or that black people would be unwilling to offer themselves as substitute parents and, if they did, unlikely to be suitable. These suppositions were successfully challenged in the 1960s and 1970s when foster and adoptive parents were found for black children. Initially these were almost exclusively white (Raynor, 1971) but later projects established both black people's interest in substitute parenting (ABAFA, 1977) and their abilities as potential foster and adoptive parents (Arnold, 1982; Brunton and Welch, 1983). Nevertheless, despite the successful experiments in recruiting black substitute parents, large numbers of black children still remain in residential care and many are still placed in white homes because there are only a few social services departments which have energetically pursued the recruitment of black substitute parents and reviewed their policy and practice in the care of black children.

The sad conclusion of a review of services for black children and parents with special needs is that they have, albeit unintentionally, through ignorance, misunderstanding, incompetence or racism frequently exacerbated rather than solved problems. Happily this is not the end of the story.

Already, a good deal has been written on those policies and practices which could improve services for black children and their families (Cheetham, 1981, 1982; Jenkins, 1981; BASW, 1982; Coombe and Little, 1986). This book concentrates on aspects of good social work practice as yet little documented. A first priority for all social services departments must be to monitor the proportion of black children in care, the reasons they are there and the quality of care they are receiving. Chapter 10 describes Bradford Social Services Department's bold attempt to review and where necessary remedy its care for black children. It provides a rare example of special sustained attention being paid to the needs of black children in care and especially those in transracial placements. The use of this form of care is now a major and contentious issue which has been the subject of both wild and informed media coverage and various research studies (Ladner, 1978; Bagley and Young, 1979; Costin and Wattenberg, 1979; Gill and Jackson, 1983).

Small in Chapter 7 argues strongly on social grounds against the widespread use of transracial placements including the damage this care can inflict on black children's sense of identity. The vivid case studies Maximé gives in Chapter 8 should leave no one in any doubt that, while this may not be the universal experience of black children brought up by white people the identity confusion of some is real, and searing; and it can be crippling if no efforts are made to reduce the confusion and distress of children and young people brought up in environments which took little or no account of their racial and ethnic identity. Happily, help can be given to such people, and Maximé describes both straightforward and complex work of this nature.

Despite the strong professional and political arguments now being made against transracial placements, some people remain unconvinced of the case against them, for practical and theoretical reasons. They argue that the urgency of some black children's need for family care cannot wait upon the sometimes extensive delays which can occur while black substitute parents are recruited; and they point to the apparently happy outcome of many transracial placements (Bagley and Young, 1979; Gill and Jackson, 1983).

This is an area of child care practice where particularly careful and critical perusal of research is required. The long-term follow-up needed in adoption research means that the outcomes of practices which were appropriate or innovatory some 15 years earlier may no longer be so relevant to adoption policy in a world where racial issues and tensions have become much more explicit, and where adoptive parents are recruited from a much wider social background than was common some years ago. Gill and Jackson are quite clear that one factor in the successful outcome, as they describe it, of the transracial placements they studied was the high social class of the families (p.134). The adopted children had benefitted in educational and other respects, as natural children would, from their parents' social class. They had a good sense of self-esteem and confidence; they mostly felt at ease in their families; they and their parents were optimistic about their future. All these criteria are commonly used in assessing the outcome of adoption and no one could deny their importance. What the children in the British Adoption Project lacked, almost without exception, was a sense of themselves as black people. Growing up in an all-white world the majority of children said they did not mind what colour they were; only a small minority wanted to be white; an even smaller number were proud to be black. These children had been placed when very young. Gill and Jackson point out that the perceptions of black children adopted when older might be very different. If they had internalized a definition of themselves as black this definition could jeopardize the possibility of integration and emotional identification within a white family (p.138).

Practitioners have to make their own judgements about the importance of black children's perception of themselves. Gill and Jackson, while concluding happily that most of the children in their study would, in their parents' words 'make it', express some caution about the implications of their lack of awareness of their colour, particularly as they move out of their family and home environments into a world where many people will characterize them on the basis of their racial background.

It is very tempting on the basis of our findings to say that the care, attention and feelings of self-worth they have been given will see them through. And yet the question remains whether these undoubted advantages will be enough. What seems certain is that racial background will become more significant in the coming years for some of these children . . . We do not know whether the 'coping techniques' they have learnt within the context of their strong white families will be adequate when they move into adult life . . . it is apparent that (their) methods and tactics are typically related more to their successfully denying racial background than seeing it as a source of positive strength. (p.136.)

Bagley and Young (1979) conclude from their review of studies of transracial adoption that, while substantial numbers of children of mixed parentage regarded themselves as white, a fact which must surely be deplored, some racially aware parents had fostered in their adopted children positive identification with black people. They go on to argue that transracial placements are most likely to be successful in multi-racial communities where parents have good and extensive contacts with black people. White families of black children inevitably face personal and family dilemmas well described by Costin and Wattenberg (1979), and by some parents in the British Adoption Project.

There will, no doubt, continue to be divided views as to whether transracial placements should continue to be made. In America, where there is a longer history of this debate in child care and greater acceptance of recruiting black substitute parents, there is no consensus among qualified social workers, black or white, about the use of transracial placements (Jenkins, 1981). In Britain one of the most important issues now in child care practice with black children is the recruitment of more black substitute parents for the large numbers of black children in care who need a family placement. Not all these children will go to black homes and when they do not their substitute parents need the special preparation and support Small outlines.

### Young Black Offenders

We have already seen that some black adolescents in conflict with their parents may be poorly served by social workers who, not surprisingly, often feel ill-equipped to tackle the plethora of problems which may be associated with dissatisfaction with the educational system (Swann, 1985; CRE, 1985(a)), with massive rates of unemployment, all manner of discrimination and harassment by the police (Smith, 1981; Small, 1983). Social workers are right to make it clear that structural problems of British society and the behaviour of other departments and institutions are not their responsibility to solve. They cannot, however, escape dealing with their consequences; nor can they opt out of making very clear the effects of certain policies, and of challenging and trying to change them. In Chapters 14 and 15 Pitts and his colleagues argue this case strongly in respect of the juvenile justice system. These responsibilities may entail various kinds of positive action which take account of special needs or which try to ensure that existing problems are not further exacerbated by social work policy and practice. The plight of young black offenders demonstrates this well. Approximately 14 per cent of West Indian origin young people are aged between 16 and 19 compared with six per cent of the general population. It is in this age group that the highest levels of offending are found. With no other intervening factors it could therefore reasonably be expected that services for young offenders would cater, certainly in areas of concentrated black settlement, for quite substantial numbers of young black people. However, as Taylor (1981) and Pitts and his colleagues in Chapter 14 demonstrate, these services are not working equally for young black and white people. Quite disproportionate numbers of black offenders are found in penal institutions while the community-based provisions for young offenders, supervision and probation orders, intermediate treatment and community service, do not adequately cater for young blacks. The reasons for this pattern are complex. It may reflect in part discrimination in sentencing. If so, this may in turn be a consequence of reports for courts which, by conveying negative images of their background, behaviour and attitudes, imply that young black people do not need or are beyond help (Pinder, 1984). Such reports are unlikely to contain positive recommendations for community-based sentences, thus making it more probable that young black people, relatively early in their offending careers, will receive custodial sentences. It has been argued (Parker et al, 1981; Morris et al, 1980) that intervention by social workers with young black people actually or apparently involved in delinquency may stigmatize them and draw them prematurely into the net of welfare serices, not always to their advantage. Unfortunately, this argument has been too easily and uncritically seized upon by those who want to explain away social workers' relative lack of involvement with young black people in trouble with parents, school or the law. This lack of involvement does not seem, as it was hoped would be the case with white children, to delay a young black person's entry into the criminal justice system or into residential care. On the contrary; the absence of explanation, advocacy or offers of help by social workers speeds young black people's journey through the tariff of sentences. We must not assume that intention or intervention work similarly for black and white people. In this case apparently benign intent may have malign consequences for young black people because of the other discrimination and deprivation to which they are subject. We must also question whether lack of involvement is in fact benign or based on racist beliefs that black people, for cultural reasons, do not need or cannot or will not respond to social work help; on a too ready acceptance of claims that white social workers cannot help black people; or on despair in the face of massive discrimination and multiple disadvantage.

Pitts and his colleagues pose the hard questions that need to be asked about the operation of the juvenile justice system, and the educational and political work that needs to be done with influential decision makers by social workers and administrators. These issues go well beyond the important task of examining the content and style of projects to ensure their attractiveness and relevance to young black people, and of preparing people to work competently and confidently in a multi-racial group where racial tensions may come quickly to the surface. Fears of this lead some projects to admit only small numbers of young black people or to rest content with the fact of few applications for their admittance. Arguments about racial issues which can commonly be found among adolescents make many people uncomfortable; overt racial antagonism is certainly frightening. Intermediate treatment groups can, with properly trained and supported staff, be one context where racial matters are dealt with honestly and positively.

 The final important point to be made about social work with black children and their families is that their needs cannot be seen in isolation from the rest of British society. Education and welfare services which take account of ethnic diversity enlarge and enrich everyone's understanding. Combatting racism may reduce inequalities; it also puts flesh on the principles of justice and fairness, so equipping all citizens for life in a society which should be committed to maximizing the life chances of all its members.

## References

ALLEN, R., and PURKIS, A., *Health in the Round*, Bedford Square Press, 1983.

ARNOLD, E., 'Finding Black Families for Black Children in Britain' in CHEETHAM, J., ed., *Social Work and Ethnicity*, Allen and Unwin, 1982.

ASSOCIATION OF BRITISH ADOPTION AND FOSTERING AGENCIES (ABAFA), *The Soul Kids Campaign*, 1977.

ASSOCIATION OF DIRECTORS OF SOCIAL SERVICES (ADSS), *Multi-Racial Britain: the Social Services Response*, 1978.

BAGLEY, C. and YOUNG, L., 'The Identity, Adjustment and Achievement of Transracially Adopted Children: a Review and Empirical Report' in VERMA, G. K., and BAGLEY, C. *Race Identity and Education*, Macmillan, 1979.

BALLARD, C., 'Conflict, Continuity and Change: Second Generation South Asians', in KHAN, V. S., ed., *Minority Families in Britain*, Macmillan, 1979.

BANTON, M. and MILES, R., 'Racism' in CASHMORE, E., ed., *Dictionary of Race Relations*, Routledge and Kegan Paul, 1984.

BARNARDO'S WORKING PARTY, *Racial Integration and Barnardo's*, Barnardo's Homes, 1966.

BATTA, I. D., and MAWBY, R. I., 'Children in Local Authority Care: A Monitoring of Racial Differences in Bradford', *Policy and Practice*, vol. 9, no. 2, pp.137-150, 1981.

BHALLA, A., and BLAKEMORE, K. *Elders of Ethnic Minority Groups, AFFOR*, 1981.

BRITISH ASSOCIATION OF SOCIAL WORK (BASW), *Social Work in Multi-Cultural Britain*, 1982.

BROWN, C., *Black and White Britain: the Third PSI Survey*, Heinemann, 1984.

BRUNTON, L., and WELCH, M., 'White Agency, Black Community', in *Adoption and Fostering* Vol. 7, no.2, 1983.

CENTRAL COUNCIL FOR EDUCATION AND TRAINING IN SOCIAL WORK (CCETSW), *Teaching Social Work in a Multi-Racial Society*, 1984.

CHEETHAM, J., *Social Work Services for Ethnic Minorities in Britain and the USA*, DHSS, 1981.

CHEETHAM, J., ed., *Social Work and Ethnicity*, Allen and Unwin, 1981.

COMMISSION FOR RACIAL EQUALITY (CRE), *Report of the Formal Investigation into the Allocation of Council Houses in Hackney*, 1984.

COMMISSION FOR RACIAL EQUALITY (CRE), *Report of the Formal Investigation into the Suspension of Black Pupils in Birmingham*, London, 1985(a).

COMMISSION FOR RACIAL EQUALITY (CRE), *Report of the Formal Investigation into the Immigration Service*, 1985(b).

COMMUNITY RELATIONS COMMISSION, *Who Minds?*, 1975.

CONNELLY, N., *Social Services Departments and Race: a Discussion Paper*, Policy Studies Institute, 1985.

CORNWELL, J., and GORDON, P., eds.,*An Experimentation in Advocacy: The Hackney Multi-Ethnic Women's Health Project*, King's Fund Centre, 1984.

COSTIN, L. B., and WATTENBERG, S. H., 'Identity in Transracial Adoption: a Study of Parental Dilemmas and Family Experiences', in VERMA G. K., and BAGLEY, C., *Race Identity and Education*, Macmillan, 1979.

FITZHERBERT, R., *West Indian Children in London*, Bell, 1967.

GILL, O., and JACKSON, B., *Adoption and Race : Black, Asian and Mixed Race Children in White Families*, Batsford, 1983.

GREGORY, E., 'Childminding in Paddington', in *The Medical Officer*, 5 September, 1969, pp. 135-9.

HOME OFFICE, *Racial Attacks*, HMSO, 1981.

HOOD, C., et al, *Children of West Indian Immigrants*, IRR, Oxford University Press, 1970.

HORN, E., 'A Survey of Referrals from Asian Families to Four Social Services Area Offices in Bradford', in CHEETHAM, J., ed., op.cit.

HOUSE OF COMMONS SOCIAL SERVICES COMMITTEE, *Children in Care*, Vol. 1, HMSO, 1984.

JACKSON, B., and JACKSON, S., *Childminder*, Routledge and Kegan Paul, 1979.

JENKINS, S., *The Ethnic Dilemma*, The Free Press, New York, 1981.

JONES, C., *Immigration and Social Policy in Britain*, Tavistock, 1977.

LADNER, J., *Mixed Race Families: Adopting Across Racial Boundaries*, Doubleday, New York, 1978.

LAWSON, P., *Black Children in Approved Schools*, DHSS, 1977.

MAYALL, B., and PETRIE, P., *Minder, Mother and Child*, University of London, Institute of Economics, 1977.

MAYALL, B., and PETRIE, B., *Child Minding and Day Nurseries*, Heinemann, 1983.

MILNER, D., *Children and Race*, Penguin, 1975.

MORRIS, A., GILLER, H., et al., *Justice for Children*, Macmillan, 1980.

OSBORN, A. F., BUTLER, N. R., and MORRIS, A. C., *The Social Life of Britain's Five Year Olds*, Routledge and Kegan Paul, 1984.

OUSLEY, H., *The System*, Runnymede Trust, 1981.

PARKER, H, CASBURN, M., and THUMBALL, D., *Receiving Juvenile Justice*, Oxford University Press, 1981.

PINDER, R., *Probation Work in a Multi-Racial Society*, a Research Report for the Home Office Research Unit, 1984.

PITTS, J., 'An Eye for an Eye: Young Black People in the Juvenile Justice System', in MATTHEWS, R. and YOUNG, J. (eds). *Black Youth*, Sage, 1986.

RAMPTON REPORT, *West Indian Children in Our Schools*, HMSO, 1981.

RAYNOR, L., *The Adoption of Non-White Children*, Allen and Unwin, London, 1970.

ROWE, J., and LAMBERT, L., *Children Who Wait*, Routledge and Kegan Paul, London, 1970.

SCARMAN REPORT, *The Brixton Disorders*, HMSO, 1981.

SMALL, S., *Police and People in London 2*, Policy Studies Institute, 1983.

SMITH, D., *The Facts of Racial Disadvantage*, PEP, 1976.

SMITH, D., *Unemployment and Racial Minorities*, Policy Studies Institute, London, 1981.

SWANN REPORT, *Education for All*, HMSO, 1985.

TAYLOR, W., *Probation and Alternatives to Custody in a Multi-Racial Society*, CRE, 1981.

VOLUNTARY ORGANISATIONS LIAISON COUNCIL FOR UNDER-FIVES (VOLCUF), *Unequal and Under-Five: A Background Paper on Ethnic Minority Under-Fives*, 1984.

YOUNG, K., and CONNELLY, N., *Policy and Practice in the Multi Racial City*, Policy Studies Institute, 1981

# PART ONE
# UNDER-FIVES AND THEIR DAY CARE: WAYS OF ASSESSING AND IMPROVING PRACTICE

## Introduction by Shama Ahmed

The introduction highlighted the crucial contribution day care can make to the welfare of black under-fives and their families. Part 1 focuses on methods of tackling its inadequacies and fulfilling its potential. The different chapters, reports and training documents cover issues of policy and practice. They link with each other and we hope the section will be read as a whole.

Part 1 begins with a chapter by Asrat-Girma based on research conducted in day nurseries. She has clear notions of day care practice which is sensitive to children and parents from minority-ethnic groups and enhances their dignity. It is from that standpoint she approaches her study. She shows clearly how much practice needs to improve, at least in some day nurseries.

The following chapter concentrates on ways of improving practice. Our aim is to identify what needs to be done and how this might be achieved. We do not offer blueprints but we hope the material will stimulate further discussion, debate and experimentation. It concludes with sample papers, guidelines and checklists. These have been variously used to identify day nursery training needs, as an approach to assessing racial attitudes, in job interviews, and as guidelines to methods of challenging racist remarks. There are also policy papers on the development of day care for black children and proposals for specialist training. The proposals outlined in these papers would, of course, need to be adapted according to circumstance, but we believe they are examples of existing good practice, with much to offer people searching for practical and immediate methods of improving the day care of black under-fives. The section continues with an account of practice in a community nursery managed by black people and new ventures in the training of nursery nurses, and concludes with a policy statement.

# 1 Afro-Caribbean Children in Day Care *Asrat-Girma*

In recent years the issue of day nursery provision has become particularly emotive. A government committed to cutting welfare provision has turned its face against any expansion of this kind of care for under-fives, while the left, and women's groups in particular, have tended to regard the issue as part and parcel of the wider struggles of women's liberation. From a black perspective, this latter view has superficial attractions; it is well known that black women suffer disproportionately from the social and economic disadvantages which necessitate full-time day care. But on closer examination the issue is not so clear-cut. Day care cannot be seen simply as 'a good thing' of itself without regard to what it actually offers children. It is through examination of the content and procedures of their care that the merits or otherwise of day nurseries can best be evaluated. The quality of day care is of course vital for all children, but for black children and their parents the process of day care has particular ramifications. In this chapter these implications will be discussed and recommendations offered in the context of my own research on black children in day care[1].

Readers should bear in mind the prevailing day care policies and their problems discussed in the introduction, and in particular the fact that social services provision is not regarded as a service for working mothers, but rather as a method of providing for particularly needy groups of children something considered to be lacking in their own homes (DHSS, 1976; Mayall and Petrie, 1983). The staff in day nurseries have therefore for the time the child is with them the role of substitute parents. State day care is a service for a specific group. In many inner-city areas this group, which represents the most economically and socially disadvantaged, is predominantly black. Because many inner-city day nurseries are centres for black, underprivileged children, the impact of day care upon them is

[1] The research discussed in this chapter was funded by the Commission for Racial Equality and conducted under the supervision of Goldsmiths' College, University of London.

a burning issue, not least because black people have limited access to other forms of day care (Hughes, et al 1980).

## The Research Methods

As a black woman and mother it became obvious to me from the outset that my research was not going to be entirely neutral. If this is a weakness of the findings then so be it, although I question many research projects which at one and the same time claim objectivity yet rely on batteries of ethnocentric tests for their results. The use of the first person, whilst seldom acceptable in research papers, is again something for which I make no apology. The use of 'I', because I became so involved with the subject matter, is essential in giving a true picture of what happened.

The research centred upon an intensive study of six local authority day nurseries in one London borough where a large proportion of the population in one-half of the borough are of Afro-Caribbean descent, and where there are also considerable communities of other ethnic groups such as Moroccans. In addition a further six nurseries were studied for comparison, mainly in adjoining boroughs, including one community nursery which was accountable to the local authority, but operated by a local management committee and accepted children on a geographical, rather than a priority basis.

The number of hours spent in the nurseries, 258, greatly exceeded those spent by other researchers in this field. The methodology too was different from other studies. As in much qualitative research, the approach was to make initial explorations into the subject, to follow up promising leads, and to let the research be guided by what emerged from the data. Thus the investigation went far beyond the walls of the buildings. For example, I began by assuming I would find much of what I was looking for by examining the effect of the everyday work of the nurseries on black children, but it soon became clear that the research would have to include as well the views of the children's mothers. Then I found that I could not simply ask what they thought of day care; the facts of day care had to be set in the context of the mothers' own experiences of childbearing, their upbringing, pregnancy, childbirth, and their economic and social circumstances. In other words, the whole biography of the black women had to be understood to make sense of their experiences of day care.

Information was gathered in a variety of ways; from case reports and official papers and during many hours in the nurseries as a participant observer interviewing staff and writing up notes immediately afterwards. Mothers too were interviewed in whatever settings they chose, in cafés, on the streets, and on several occasions this meant striking a bargain whereby I could interview in return for simultaneously doing their hair in African style! By these means I managed to uncover a great deal of information which would not have been available to white researchers using more formal approaches. Cottle (1978) gives a similar account.

> Because we reveal so many sides of ourselves to so many people, the truth of conversation seems to lie in the situation defining the relationship between those engaged in that conversation. A woman interviewer would have elicited other information from the families with whom I spoke. A black interviewer would have had still other impressions and experiences. (p.11)

The nature of my research required a high level of engagement with the interviewees, particularly the mothers, so that I as the researcher and they as the informants could embark on a dialogue of opinions and ideas, rather than my being simply a recipient of answers to questions. This will become clear when I give specific examples to support the conclusions. Even the racism to which I was subjected on occasions, both overt and unconscious, became part of the research findings. For example, many of the professionals with whom I had to deal were visibly thrown by the fact that a black woman had come to question their very professionalism. 'But who is supervising you?' was a usual question, often followed by a level of interrogation to which in my view no white researcher would have been subjected. Within the day nursery itself, once my presence had become established and less obtrusive, and racist remarks had become common, staff would realize later and say 'Of course we didn't mean you! You're different.' Being a black woman researcher had therefore a definite effect on the research, and a beneficial one. It produced many insights into white perceptions of black people, and I was left pondering on the fact that the reception I had from many white professionals was experienced in a greatly magnified form by black women users of day care.

### Conclusions

These conclusions cannot reveal the whole complex picture to emerge from the many different kinds of involvement in the life of the nurseries, but I will give examples to highlight their meaning. First, both in the main sample and in the neighbouring boroughs, the study confirmed a very high over-representation of Afro-Caribbean children. In the sample nurseries Afro-Caribbean children constituted around 50 per cent of the total. They, together with other ethnic minority children of black and white parents, made up about 90 per cent of the main sample nursery population. It was disheartening to discover so few black care staff employed, only six out of 71, although black women were employed in low-grade domestic jobs.

Those black staff who are employed often have a difficult time making their voices heard and had generally to conform to the prevalent norms. One who had tried to introduce West Indian foods, for example, was overruled by the majority white staff. Again, the only black officer in charge tried to introduce multi-cultural books and play materials but eventually bowed to the white staff who objected for fear of losing them. Most of the staff were in the 18 to 24 year old age group, which suggested a constant turnover once this upper age is reached. An incidental, though enlightening, point is the finding that none of the staff would consider placing their own children in day care.

Second, efforts to reflect the cultural traditions and the racial identities of the day care users were minimal. The vast majority of the nurseries had no policy of meeting the needs of any of the ethnic groups represented in terms of play, reading materials, music, storytelling, food, and so on. In fact, books were found such as *Little Black Sambo* which are downright offensive to black children. The kinds of food on offer, alien to several of the ethnic groups in the nursery, were given on a 'take it or leave it' basis or, worse, were forced upon children. A particularly vivid example of this is a Filipino child who consistently refused to eat boiled vegetables, had been force-fed, and vomited constantly. She missed out on her desserts in an effort by the staff to make her eat the undesired food. This continued during a whole year I visited this nursery, with the same negative effects.

Children were never allowed to use their fingers to eat with, irrespective of the cultures from which they came. A typical reaction to such a suggestion was 'They would need to get used to eating with knives, forks and spoons. Everybody uses them in the next group . . . and it's very important when they go to school.' (Asrat-Girma, 1983, p.41.) Nursery officers generally disapproved of the idea of introducing ethnic foods with such remarks as 'The other children couldn't stomach the hot food' or 'What's wrong with what we're giving them? Anyway the council couldn't afford it.' The fact that much food was thrown away was ignored.

There was much basic prejudice against and ignorance of 'non-standard' food which illustrated how other aspects of black and ethnic minority cultures tend to be devalued or abused. For example, one senior worker with experience of working with Asian women in an intensive care unit suggested that the babies she was dealing with were underweight because their parents ate curry! (Asrat-Girma, 1983, p.77.)

Third, there was little effort to communicate with parents, and staff had particular problems communicating with black and other ethnic minority parents. Parents had no say in the running of the nurseries and most had no idea about what was happening to their children during nursery hours. Little or no encouragement was offered to any parents, black or white, to become involved in nursery life.

Fourth, the nurseries were invariably dominated by inflexible routines and standardized views of child care and child development, which were often at odds with those of the parents and yet which were never open to negotiation. A classic example concerns sand play. West Indian parents had often tried to explain the difficulty of getting sand out of their children's hair, yet the staff reaction typically was 'Coloured parents don't like their children to get dirty . . . some of them even ask that their children be not allowed to play with sand or water . . .' 'Shame this is. Some go up the wall, you'd think some awful crime had been committed.' (Asrat-Girma, 1983, p.55.)

Another example was of an Asian child whose parents had put a certain type of cream on her hair which was promptly washed off by the staff when she entered nursery, on the grounds that it was 'smelly'.

Fifth, there was tremendous ambivalence on the question of race which often manifested itself in the avowed 'love' of the children, coupled with deep resentment of black parents who were frequently identified as having 'abused the system'.

In one nursery, typical though of the rest, the Robertson's jam gollywog was greatly in evidence. My questioning of this eventually opened up general issues concerning racial stereotyping and other forms of conscious or unconscious racism which might affect black children in day care. There was a defensive air amongst the staff group. The deputy, for example, told me that in her previous job 'West Indian parents never said a thing, and in fact a black member of staff bought the Little Black Sambo book which all the children enjoyed . . . and another parent came dressed up as a gollywog at a fancy dress party we had'. One of the staff group also accused me of upsetting a child of mixed Irish and West Indian race by calling him West Indian, 'I have had him since he was a baby and he always thought he was an English child. I told him that too.'

(Asrat-Girma, 1983, p.66) Another nursery worker justified the golly-wog on the grounds that she as a white person had always loved the toy as a 'nice, friendly creature'.

Opening up such issues as a black person was often an emotional experience both for me and for many of the young white staff, and the atmosphere on quite a few occasions became heated. One worker, shaking and in tears with anger shouted that it was up to 'them' to adapt, otherwise they would always have the problem of not being accepted. 'If you don't like it' she said 'what are you doing here? And if other black people don't like it then why don't they go back to their own country . . . but you *must* like it here . . . you're given accommodation, jobs . . . we're friendly towards you, you *must* like it. If not you should go back!' This was by no means the only occasion documented in the research when anger was directed through me at black parents generally. The whole question of preserving cultural traditions and racial identity was almost universally dismissed as 'rubbish'; one deputy, seeming to speak for all, said, 'Couldn't you forget it and live like one of us?' – 'You should, you should', came the chorus of approval (Asrat-Girma, 1983, pp.67–78).

Whilst most nursery workers declared a lack of prejudice, that all children were 'the same' to them, they often followed up as the research continued with strong comments about the black mothers: 'You know I'm not colour prejudiced, but the blacks do live up to the image they're given . . . backward, don't care for their children . . . they change men like they change their shirts. Look around all the nurseries and you see more black children than any other.'

One nurse, after assuring me she wasn't racist, went on, '. . . the way the blacks go is disturbing. They come in, don't even say "let me settle the child", they just push them in and go off. If they *had* jobs to go to it wouldn't worry me. But all they do is hang around shop windows or walk about in groups . . . they have no future.' (Asrat-Girma, 1983, p.54)

Amidst all this there was an undercurrent, almost of envy, that black mothers were apparently obtaining a whole range of benefits without earning them. 'These parents are living on subsidized housing, claiming benefits . . . can't meet their financial commitments, gas, electricity, rent or HP etc . . . and they can't even look after their own children; they have no time for them at all.' (Asrat-Girma, 1983, p.48.) My own evidence from 20 in-depth interviews with black single mothers totally refutes the perception held by the nursery staff that they were lazy, backward, and merely exploiting the welfare state. On the contrary, and to be illustrated later, these women had tremendous difficulty in obtaining even the most basic rights.

The major point is that from countless examples of the kind of language used by nursery staff, and the things they do within the nursery, it is clear that there is an insidious, underlying racial ambivalence which pervades the attitudes and assumptions of the staff, and which inevitably affects the way children are treated.

Sixth, and very much linked with their preconceptions, many staff felt ill-prepared to deal with the problems of parents generally, and of black mothers in particular. Many staff openly admit this: 'While we're on training we're nothing. But the day we qualify we're able to give advice to mothers and also be an inflated social worker.' (Asrat-Girma, 1983, p.46.)

When in-service seminars were organized (and these were infrequent), many staff seemed hostile: 'I'm willing to learn about other cultures – I know plenty of West Indians and Africans, but whenever there's a seminar or something it's always run by blacks and they just get up and insult you.'

### The Mothers' Stories

Outside of the nursery, my interviews with black women told depressingly similar stories. Far from obtaining their rights simply by asking, they have all experienced enormous difficulty in acquiring the minimum resources to sustain them and their children; a host of obstacles were perpetually placed in their path by the state agencies whose actions were perceived by the women to be racially motivated.

> I went up the social security . . . they question you and question you; for every penny they give you, you have to have an answer for it. They wanted to know how many men I knew, how many times I'd gone out with them. Unless I tell them everything they say they won't tell me anything, but they just say it might be 'delayed'. Because I live with my mum, she had to feed me and clothe my son. They didn't give us any rent. The housing didn't wanna know . . . I had to live with my mum until my son was fifteen months old. (Asrat-Girma, 1983, p.118.)

> The social people came to find out who I was living with. They expected him to support me and my child, but the money he was getting was for studying. These people really fucked him about; they took away my book . . . it was hell. (Asrat-Girma, 1983, p.132.)

These are very typical, not the most extreme, reactions to the 'welfare' system from the women I interviewed, all of whom had felt degraded by the endless suspicions and questioning which arose, they felt, simply because they were young black single mothers.

Similarly their experiences of birth and pregnancy were experienced negatively rather than as a celebration. The attitudes of many health service workers was perceived to be at best patronizing but more often to be offensive and degrading.

> It's like this. When they're filling in the form in the hospital you tell them your name is so-and-so. Married? . . . you say 'No'. I think they must be putting something on it that you got the baby on the side, so everyone on the line knows what you been up to. When they ask me what I was going to do with the baby when it got born, I say 'You better ask my dad, he's outside.' They do have dirty minds, this nurse said 'It's not from your dad is it?'. (Asrat-Girma, 1983, p.102.)

> Went to the hospital. You know what they ask me up there? Do I want to keep the baby! You know how I felt? These people think black people are animals. I was so upset, I couldn't stop crying all day. And I keep saying to them 'Yes I do'. They never listen to you. You know, I'm beginning to think black people *are* no good, because deep down nobody want us to be here . . . they make you say all sorts of things you don't want to say in the first place. They put ideas into your head . . . You know what this doctor say to me? 'I know you won't believe me but the child would be better off not being born.' They love to see blood. Especially black people's blood. (Asrat-Girma, 1983, pp.97-8.)

In hospital the common experience was that to be poor, young, black and single sparked off in the staff a whole host of assumptions and petty degradations. In this context the offer of a nursery place was something for which the women were expected to be grateful. The life histories obtained show above all else that young black women share the common experience of being devalued and 'deskilled' since their early school life and through to young adulthood. Nowhere in the entire process was encouragement given to trust their own skills and capabilities. Health visitors and social workers frequently criticized the young black mothers for their failure as 'good parents'; 'The community nurse comes in and talks to me. I try to grasp what she says but it is always, ". . . probably you are not fit yet." When she leaves I say, "Maybe I'm not fit, maybe I'm not well" so I stay home stewing. It rings in my ears "Maybe I am not *fit*" – you know what I mean?' (Asrat-Girma, 1983, p.125.)

From the constant criticism, overt and subtle, to which these women are daily subjected, self-doubt has itself 'deskilled' them, questioning their competence as mothers and indeed as human beings.

The final stage is putting the child in day care which seems to confirm their own 'inadequacy' and denies their contribution to the care of their children, since, as we have seen, there is little connection between parents and day nurseries and no communication about the children's lives.

Nurseries were 'given' as a kind of panacea for the many difficulties black mothers were facing, often from the hands of that same system of which the nursery is itself a part. When asked, nearly all of the women would have preferred to have some other arrangement whereby they could be with their children at least some of the time, rather than place the child in full-time day care from one year old until school age. They felt they had no alternative to this 'panacea', that indeed, like rich parents putting their child's name down for Eton, they had to 'get in quick' or else be left out in the cold with absolutely nothing. The message studiously and systematically conveyed over the years and totally confirmed by the nursery regimes is *black women and black culture are inadequate*.

### Recommendations

Clearly, the scale of the problem goes far beyond the nursery walls. There are, however, fundamental inadequacies in the present system of day care which can and should be tackled immediately, and which require not so much increase in resources as radical changes in attitudes and the will and determination to face and to do something about the problems.

As the system is presently organized there is no point in increasing this form of nursery provision. Whilst recognizing the increasing demands from many quarters to increase the number of day nurseries, 'more of the same' would, given the above findings, be illogical until a thorough going overhaul of the system takes place.

First, recruitment to nursery nursing courses must be widened to open up the career to ethnic minorities, and to take positive steps to attract Afro-Caribbeans in particular into the work. One of the ways this might be done is to accept trainees from Youth Training Schemes with experience of working with children on to courses, though they may be without the minimum academic qualifications. Recruitment of more mature people whose life experience might equip them for the work could also take place, as might the active recruitment of men. This recruitment would have to be accompanied by a thorough revision of the content and structure of the courses to reflect the multi-cultural nature of modern Britain. The last chapter in this section explores these ideas further.

Given that many of the nurseries in this study had so high a proportion of black children, it was astonishing that local authorities had barely discussed the subject, yet alone acted upon important issues. Many things could be done immediately. It could, for example, be ensured that there are play materials, books, and so on that reflect the cultures within the nursery. It should be commonplace that staff read stories from other countries, with black heroes and heroines perhaps. Songs and music could also be multi-ethnic. Musicians, storytellers, and indeed parents and other members of the local community could be invited in to contribute, thus benefiting everyone.

The kinds of food on offer could also, at little cost and inconvenience, be varied to include ethnic foods, and to introduce some element of choice in consultation with parents. If the staff feel inadequate to provide the kind of environment in which the cultures of the children can be nurtured rather than denied, then perhaps this is where parents can become advisers and real participants. Although this should go without saying, local authorities should see to it that racist toys and books should be excluded from nurseries.

Local authorities could also appoint in each area nursery-based advisers whose task would include staff training on racism. Far more in-service training in, for example, welfare rights could be offered to the staff to enable them to offer something positive to the parents.

All this could happen now and would have some impact on the black users of day care. More is needed, however, if the root of the problem is to be effectively tackled.

One of the major recommendations of my research was the establishment in certain areas of *black women's advice centres*, the purpose of which would be to offer support and practical help to young black women, and in particular, black mothers and expectant mothers. Such centres would be organized locally by community groups already working in the field, or by women's collectives established specifically for the purpose, and funded either by local authorities or by central government through urban funding programmes. These centres would be independent, so that critical stances could be taken on all of the issues discussed above which prevent black women from obtaining their rights, and from contributing to the running of day nurseries. It was envisaged in my report that collective child care arrangements would evolve out of such centres, which respected women and children. If the charge of creating a 'ghetto' is laid, then it can only be said that the white-dominated system as it stands today has failed miserably for black children and black women, and that it is hard to see any alternative to an independent stance.

Following directly from my research, I was fortunate to obtain funding from the Greater London Council to establish precisely the form of centre described above which, at the time of writing, has been running for ten months. The three staff and the management committee are all local black women and constitute the collective. There is presently a crèche, and as well as acting as advocates for black women with the agencies of the State, we will soon be opening a craft workshop and other self-help schemes whereby black women can begin to take control of their own lives.

Radical changes within the state system of day nurseries, particularly concerning training and recruitment, will take years to filter through, even if the decisions were taken today. The immediate funding of a network of black women's advice centres could perhaps go some way to alleviate the current pressures upon black women and their children, of which the present system of state day care is so clearly a part.

## References

ASRAT-GIRMA, *The Use of Day Care Facilities by Children of Afro-Caribbean Parents*, unpublished research report, 1983.

COTTLE, T., *Black Testimony*, Wildwood House, 1978.

DHSS, *Low Cost Day Care Provisions for Under Fives*, 1976.

HUGHES, M., et al, *Nurseries Now*, Penguin, 1980.

MAYALL, B., and PETRIE, B., *Child Minding and Day Nurseries*, Heinemann, 1983.

## 2 Black Children in a Day Nursery: Some Issues of Practice  *Shama Ahmed*

Britain is now a multi-racial society, and the implications of this for the work of nursery officers and other care staff are wide-ranging. Different communities have diverse ideas of childhood, parenthood and the family. Different communities are also under different pressures. Many people claim that all children, in fact all people, are the same. Caring for black children, that is children of Asian and Afro-Caribbean origin, is no different from caring for white children. But there *is* a difference. Growing up black in Britain where policy making and practice is largely influenced and controlled by white people who may often be unaware, indifferent or antagonistic, poses many social problems for black parents.

Of course there are compelling arguments which suggest that racial differences are ultimately class differences, that poor white parents also get a raw deal. But the difference is that black children and families suffer racial disadvantage over and above class disadvantage. For instance, a central issue facing most black families, regardless of class and wealth is how to prepare their children to deal with their devalued racial status in a way which will be most beneficial to their overall emotional and social growth and development. Socialization of children is now doubly challenging for the black family, for now it must teach its young members not only not to dislike white people, the dominant group, but also how to be black with pride.

This chapter is based on a questionnaire used to examine in-service training needs of nursery staff in one nursery. (Appendix 1 p.58). The questionnaire examined such questions as the particular needs of black children, how these needs were currently being met and what could be done in future to ensure that young children in multi-racial areas are given appropriate care. The chapter highlights only a selection of the issues which emerged.

To begin with it is important to look at a nursery through the eyes of a small black child. As the child pushes through the day nursery door what will the child find – a somewhat familiar or an alien world? Will the child see itself and its home reflected there in any way? Will any of the adults in the nursery look like its parents and carers at home? Will the human images on the walls reflect him or her? Will the food smell and taste like the food at home; and what about the sounds and tones and words that the child will hear? What hidden and silent messages will the nursery transmit?

In developing a policy for the London Borough of Hackney, Headley describes day nurseries he saw as alien environments for black children:

> They are staffed predominantly by white workers whose knowledge base and child caring norms are essentially eurocentric, which inhibits the development of a necessary cultural continuum between the home and the day nursery. (Submission to Under-Fives Sub-committee, 24 July 1984.)

The acid test of a good nursery must surely be: has the nursery the sensitivity to build on anything from home? Will the culture of the child be regarded as a treasure? Will the nursery seize on the opportunity to add richness and variety or will it lose it?

### Dietary and Physical Needs of Black Children

An obvious need is food. Children from minority-ethnic groups may be used to a different diet to the one traditionally offered in a nursery, and it would seem that once recognized and understood this need will be relatively easy to deal with, or at least will not seem controversial to most nursery staff. But as Asrat-Girma demonstrates with graphic illustrations of controversy and conflict, an obvious need such as food can also be an area fraught with emotion.

During my interviews on how the day nursery staff experienced black children, it emerged that very great care was needed on the part of staff to discuss diet and food with parents when the children were first admitted. Parental attitudes were not always predictable, and there were surprises for the unwary staff. Some children were forbidden certain foods, but other Afro-Asian children were reared on sausages and chips. Meals could be problematic with children who wanted to eat the same as others but whose parents' beliefs required them to eat a special diet. How to handle this situation sensitively is more than a question of technique. It spreads into the realm of attitudes about cultures, and care is needed to ensure that a cultural-difference model does not unwittingly become a *cultural-deficit* model. Carers who wish to be sensitive need to know something about the pain that black children can suffer through lack of awareness. The issue of food culture and identity is developed further in Appendix 2 (p.59), and suggestions are offered for dealing with some negative and hurtful comments about black children's food and style of eating.

There are also certain physical differences, for example afro-hair and skin care have different principles of grooming to prevent dryness and flakiness. Asian parents may apply particular oils and creams which can attract negative comments from nursery staff and devalue the parents in the eyes of the child.

### Differing Notions of Routine, Discipline and Play – Who is Right?

Notions of routine, discipline and play vary greatly in ethnic minority communities. For instance, in certain Asian communities, though not in all, a young child may always be close to mother. She or he may sleep beside her at night. Strict attempts may not be made to control the time when a child goes to bed. Children are seen as participants in family events along with everyone else, and it may be considered a harshness and deprivation to separate them from adult activity by sending them away to sleep too early in the evening. Similarly, ideas about weaning and many other things vary in black communities. The important point is that in such discussions the tendency to compare the behaviour of black people with Anglo-European norms should be resisted. These do not necessarily represent the most desirable way of life. Most of the normative statements about children's behaviour now current in nurseries are little more than ethnocentric projections.

There are, of course, many obvious dissimilarities between black and white groups and within them, and these should be explored with confidence. We should be ready to take cognisance of such differences without necessarily seeking to change black parents and children. It is not necessary that everyone should bring themselves as quickly as possible into step with the white world.

In interviews conducted with nursery officers, a recurring issue was the vexed question of parental attitudes towards play. Some black parents also expected the children to receive some formal education in the day nursery. This was an area where the aspirations and true concerns of black parents could easily be misunderstood. Nursery staff can learn to appreciate the black viewpoint by understanding it. The account of the black community nursery by Morgan in Chapter 4 shows how this concern was legitimized and actively addressed in that project. More generally, the development of nursery centres combining care and education has endorsed this form of provision and vindicated black parents' educational concern.

Turning now to the issue of play materials, parents who fail to provide toys and books, at least of the approved educational variety, which nurseries and 'good parents' use to stimulate cognitive and language development, are labelled 'culturally deprived'. But there are other explanations. In some nurseries black children may have parents who come from rural areas in their countries of origin. As children they had little formal play equipment, but this does not mean that they necessarily suffered a lack of stimulation or were culturally deprived. In a rural setting, although the child had little play equipment and there may not have been complex mechanical toys or books, there was play with sticks and sand, pots and pans. Above all, the child in the village had the opportunity to find out that the most satisfying things available are small animals and other small children. This form of play required the cooperation of other children, and the child could soon begin to develop a concern about relationships with others. In addition the child in the village had grandparents and other adults who would pass on the cultural heritage of folk tales and folk-lore. Motor skills, mental concepts and linguistic ability were all stimulated without the unique material of a Western nursery. The first generation of parents of some (though not all) black children in an urban industrial environment may not appreciate that children are not receiving the stimulation they would have naturally received in a village context. Here, particular efforts are needed and the value of certain play activities for the child's development communicated.

Stories were also told of parents who took great pride in how their children looked and sent them beautifully dressed. The difficulty is that well-dressed children could be inhibited in their play for fear of a telling-off if they get their clothes messy or torn. Some Asian parents did not like to arrive in the evening to find their children in nursery clothes. Sandpits too could bring surprising problems to unwary staff. It could take a parent hours to remove sand from afro-hair. It is unwise and somewhat ludicrous to equate parental resistance to particular activities with a general restriction on play. Again Morgan illustrates in Chapter 4 how this is patently untrue. Staff attitudes in comforting and relating with black parents are often the key to how such issues are resolved. When parents are welcomed and can spend time in the nursery where they can observe their own and other people's children, they begin to find a way into that world and enjoy it.

## Psychology and Identity Needs

All children have certain psychological needs and without the fulfilment of these they cannot achieve contentment, self-reliance, and good relationships with others. Children need affection and continuity of care. They need security rooted in stable personal relationships, in familiar environmental conditions and in a feeling of belonging. They also need a secure sense of personal identity and self-respect, and need to be valued for what they are.

The interviews with nursery staff considered how conscious children were of their differences of colour and hair, and one senior member of a nursery conducted small exercises to test a child's feelings about himself and his colour. (Appendix 3, p.60.) Many staff acknowledged that, contrary to popular belief, small children were intensely aware of their differences; for example, if children were asked to paint pictures of themselves and their mothers and incorrectly painted themselves white, they could become quite upset and start to cry if it was pointed out to them that they were black or brown and not white. Some black children had covered themselves with talc or chalk and declared 'We are white now.' One black child said to his nursery nurse, who was well tanned after a holiday 'I like you because you have arms like me.'

The academic research on black children's self-esteem and self-image has also established that race and colour awareness in children starts early (Milner, 1983). Children not only learn to distinguish colours, they also learn to attach values to them and, unless positive steps are taken, black children may, in the most formative years of their lives, grow up devaluing themselves.

## Linguistic Needs

In multi-racial work, educational and language matters also assume special significance. Should Afro-Caribbean children's English be corrected? Should the teaching of a second language to Asian children wait until they have acquired some competence in their first language? How can staff learn to respond positively to a child's bilingualism so that they can say to a child who speaks little or no English 'Ranjit speaks two languages – I only speak one'. This may help little Ranjit to become less mute and withdrawn, to act more confidently, sensing from a changed approach that he is not always experienced as a problem.

### Contact with Parents

Staff attitudes towards black parents' involvement in the nursery seemed to vary greatly, and many found the idea attractive in theory but difficult to practise in a conventional day nursery. Again, the chapter by Morgan casts a different perspective, of a caring relationship between a community nursery run by black people primarily for black parents and their children.

### Conclusion

The theme of this chapter, the special physical, psychological and linguistic needs of black children, is large and complex and only a few aspects have been discussed. How can the psychological dislocation for the very small child from a racially and culturally different home be minimized? Why must the black child's background be reflected in the nursery activities? Is it harmful to teach English as a second language to very young children? Sometimes staff reaction to children's activities can unwittingly reinforce black children's feeling that they and their origins are not quite right. One example is that of the Asian child playing at making tea to whom the nursery nurse said, 'No dear, don't use the saucepan, here is the tea pot.' This child was only imitating her mother making Punjabi tea; it is easy for the child to conclude that ways of doing things at home – mum's way – are not valued by important and significant adults in the nursery. Building Blocks, the special training project for the day care of the under-fives, described in Chapter 3, makes this point powerfully:

> Afro-Caribbean and Asian children are all too often on the receiving end of negative comments about language, hair, food and play behaviour. This situation results in cultural repression: the black child censors his or her experience, is often reluctant to admit to any knowledge of his or her culture, shows withdrawal symptoms and seems slow to learn. This process is severely damaging to black children's emotional, social and cognitive development, affecting their ability to grow into self-loving, confident and purposeful adults.

If the aim of the nursery is to be as supportive as possible to the small child, then clearly the conflict between the child's home and the nursery must be minimized and the world of the home reflected, and therefore valued, in the nursery activities. The home corner, packets of food, vegetables in the play shop, the dressing-up box, the books and visual displays, music and movement, the celebration of festivals, the presence of black staff, parents and visitors, and the use of the child's language are some of the ways in which the importance and value of the child's racial and cultural heritage can be communicated. In the following pages training strategies by Building Blocks suited to anti-racist work with all under-fives are offered. Before that two further points must be stressed.

First, what is the speediest way to sensitize a nursery? It is my contention that although training has a role to play it can achieve little by itself. Training needs to be seen clearly as part of an overall strategy for non-racist work. The most essential element of that strategy is employment of black staff, particularly staff who have retained a real sense of identity with their community of origin. They are needed not just for their cultural knowledge and skills but for their racial knowledge also, their experience of what it is like to be black in British society. Shortages of staff in any field are rarely insurmountable problems. Witness the emergency training schemes of the 1960s to produce qualified staff. Similar initiatives can be launched to train black workers in fields where they are under-represented. In my experience, even a modest programme of talks among black fourth and fifth form students, together with approaches to the local nursery nurse training course, can lead in a matter of three or four years to some changes. O'Hagan describes such initiatives in Chapter 5. No doubt more spectacular results could be achieved in agencies where there is political and professional commitment to redress the consequences of past disadvantage and discrimination.

Of course, trained staff are not the only solution. Unqualified but appropriately experienced black adults have an even bigger role to play as carers, support workers, and language aides. For white children the introduction of caring black adults is also one way to counter some negative black images so popular in their culture.

Needless to say an anti-racist approach has enormous implications for staff attitudes. Training can rarely act as a solution when attitudes towards a particular type of work are negative or motivation is low. In such cases training programmes do not reach staff who need them most; and when such people have supervisory responsibilities, others below them also remain uninformed. Selection should try to ensure that there is a seed of personal and professional motivation for transcultural and anti-racist work. Some guidelines are offered on assessing racial attitudes of candidates in job interviews in Appendix 4 (p.61)

This brings me to my final point: the need to practise non-racist work with *all* children. The project described in this chapter had narrow terms of reference and was specifically concerned with establishing the style and content of work being done with black children. This should not distract attention from the essential need for the caring professions to intervene for change in all areas of mainstream child care.

A positive policy and practice on the issue of racism is as relevant in all-white groups of under-fives as it is in racially mixed groups. It is essential that the development of multi-racial and anti-racist practices should not be confined to nurseries with a black presence. When working with young children, whatever their ethnic background, and when the nursery is all white, it is important that nursery staff counter in all children the development of negative and racist attitudes. According to this view it is the bulk of white British children who are the most educationally and culturally deprived by the monocultural, parochial and anglocentric approaches of conventionally-run nurseries.

## References

LONDON BOROUGH OF HACKNEY, Submission to the Under-Fives Sub-committee, 24 July 1984.
MILNER, D., *Children and Race*, Penguin, 1983.

## Appendix 1 Sensitizing the nursery to the needs of black children

The questionnaire set out to identify training needs of nursery officers working with Asian and Afro-Caribbean children in a multi-racial day nursery. Time was also spent in observing play materials, wall displays, dressing-up box, books, music, diet, visitors, contacts with parents. The questionnaire was divided into three sections and used as a discussion document.

*Section 1 Information about the respondent*
This obtained information about the respondent's position, training and experience.

*Section 2 Basic information*
This dealt with the objectives of the nursery, and the duties of the respondent.
Content of this discussion could vary. For example, with the senior staff, their supervisory training and staff selection responsibilities were discussed: how the

budget was spent, what type of materials were purchased and from where. With other staff a detailed description of their day-to-day tasks was requested.

## Section 3 Specific needs of black children

This section raised particular questions concerning black children's presence in the nursery; their behaviour and perceived needs; how these needs were currently being met and what could be done in future to ensure that young children in multi-racial areas are given appropriate care.

Questions were asked to assess respondents' knowledge and understanding of psychological, especially racial, identity needs of Afro-Caribbean and Asian children; knowledge and attitudes towards child rearing and socialization practices in different cultures; linguistic needs of minority children.

Questions were also raised about views and skills in communicating with black parents; their awareness of such parents' perceptions of the nursery and its objectives; contacts in these communities; racial composition of volunteers and friends of the nursery.

Content of their qualifying training on these matters was discussed. In reflecting on their training, respondents were encouraged to distinguish between course teaching (if any) in black cultures from inputs on racism in the majority culture, and its effects on black children and on their own personal development.

## Appendix 2 Food, culture and identity

Introducing Asian and Afro-Caribbean foods for under-fives should not be viewed as a temporary fad or trendy fashion. It should also not be equated with the largely discredited anthropological approach which treats the cultural background of black children as exotic and sometimes marginal. Much more is implied by the adoption of a coherent food policy. It is a practical way for a nursery to communicate respect for the child's home and background. There are psychological aspects of feeding which should not go unrecognized. But the issue of food is not without contention and controversy; typical of the food related questions and statements that are heard are the following:

'Our black children eat everything, they don't really want to appear different. Should one force them to be different?'

It is important for carers to establish how children really feel about breaking parental instructions and family taboos. For example, Roksana, a nine year old Muslim girl in care, ate meat contrary to parental injunction. She did not wish to be different and this suited the staff greatly. Yet, when she had confidence in our relationship, she expressed anxiety and feelings of guilt, she worried about betraying her mother and wondered about punishment from God.

Frequently identification with core culture is interpreted as positive indication of cultural assimilation, but some superficial interpretations could be avoided if there was more awareness of subtle racial pressures on children of all ages.

Rejection of a minority ethnic culture is not an unusual first response among children who are in a small minority. In such cases it is probably best to ask what might the staff be doing to turn off a small child's confidence in identifying with its home? Could it be that the carers are failing to communicate that to be

different is not only acceptable, it is desirable?
'*White children reject Asian foods as smelly Paki foods. Should one react to that?*'
Isn't it a fact that many foods smell? Curry may smell but so does cauli, and ham and bacon . . . What is acceptable is a question of what we are used to.

It is true that when ignorance is shown or blatantly racist attitudes are expressed, we may have difficulty in finding the right words and phrases to respond with the immediacy, accuracy and honesty that the situation demands; but hurtful things need to be responded to and handled in anti-racist ways.

Carers should build their skills and confidence in tackling racism and create an atmosphere that supports black children's cultural identity, one which promotes the child's acceptance and recognition by other children.
'*We do not allow Asian children to eat with fingers; we teach them table manners and how to use knives and forks. Is there anything wrong with that?*'
Whatever the aspirations of care staff, the quality of work is greatly affected by ancillary staff, and none is more important in this than the cook. Cooks need to understand their therapeutic contribution in supporting a child's self-image and identity. They should be accessible to parents' requests and encouraged to try out different recipes and presentations.

Management will need to ensure that cooks have adequate time, space, tools and contacts with helpful black parents and volunteers who can assist them to do the job properly. An active policy of recruiting cooks from Asian and Afro-Caribbean communities should also assist in the learning process. The outline of one training programme is described as follows:

### Food, Culture and Identity

Course description:  This is primarily a practical course in cooking Asian and Afro-Caribbean food for cooks of day nurseries and other establishments who are keen to vary their cuisine. However, the course will aim to relate the provision of food to the issue of identity, and the objectives of the course reflect this concern.

Learning objectives: 1 To develop skills in identifying ethnic origins and religious backgrounds.
2 To examine and relate the significance of food to emotional issues and the issues of racial identity.
3 To examine the significance of religions, particular customs and beliefs affecting diet.
4 To be able to shop and cook for a variety of dietary needs.

Intended for:  Cooks and heads of day nurseries and other establishments.

## Appendix 3 Some elementary exercises for testing a child's sense of racial identity

All children need to understand their own identity. They have to find the answer to questions such as: who am I? Am I the sort of person they say I am? Am I the sort of person I want to be?

1 Children are asked to draw a picture of their mother. If black children portray their mothers as white and get the colour of hair, skin and eyes wrong, the significance of this is discussed.

2 Children are asked to draw a picture of themselves. The significance of their response and perceptions is discussed.

3 Children are presented with a series of dolls, drawings or photographs and asked questions such as 'Which one looks most like you?'; 'Which one do you like best?'; 'Which one would you most like to play with?'

Answers can give clues to a child's self-perception, colour and race preferences, likes and dislikes. When too much ambivalence, or dislike of self is evident, it is a cause for concern and ameliorative action is called for.

## Appendix 4 Notes for interviewers

*Assessing racial attitudes of candidates for day nursery work – some guidelines*

From: *Perspectives on Asian Social Needs*, Report of the DHSS and Coventry Social Services Department.

1 All candidates applying to Coventry Social Services Department receive, along with a job description, a paper on the department's equal opportunity policy.

The paper provides the context in which racism awareness questions can be legitimately raised.

2 *The Background*

A recent departmental report made the following observations on staff selection.

Training programmes, however well devised, will not manage to educate or modify the stance of those with strongly held antipathetic views, and when such people are of senior grade those whom they supervise will tend to remain uninformed.

The project team would therefore urge Social Services Departments when appointing staff in multi-racial areas to look for readiness to work with all client groups and some understanding of the issues arising in the provision of social services to ethnic minority groups. Appointments made with these considerations in mind would be subject to additional safeguards if departments have a systematic approach to the induction of new staff in matters relating to multi-racial social work.

The project team would make the further point that selection of Asian workers entails consideration of equally sensitive factors which need to be recognised. Simply to be Asian is no guarantee that social workers can work effectively with a local Asian community. Some are highly assimilated and westernised, and thus may be unable to relate successfully to the Asian working class. At selection it is important, therefore, to establish that an Asian applicant has retained a sense of identity with his or her community of origin.

## Suggested approaches to raising questions on racial attitudes

### Using the Application Form

The application form should be studied carefully as this could provide leads, for example if the candidate attended an inner-city school or worked in an inner-city agency or establishment the interviewer may wish to use that as a launching pad for assessing candidate's views on a multi-racial society and on racial equality.

Alternatively, the interviewer might point to the candidate's application form and say something like 'This department pays some importance to multi-ethnic experiences. Do you have any experience of living or working in a multi-racial or multi-ethnic environment? If so, what was the multi-ethnic setting? Which ethnic group did you work with? Were there any particular opportunities, issues, anxieties arising from that context?'

### Using the Equal Opportunity Statement

This could be used with heads and deputies of nurseries and co-ordinators of day care services.

The interviewer could begin by saying that the candidate must have received details of the city's equal opportunity policy and could then go on to describe the policy briefly and raise questions on it. For instance, 'The department has an equal opportunity policy which applies to jobs as well as client services. Have you any views on this? Have you any experiences in implementing such a policy with regard to employment of black staff and/or with regard to allocation of places to children from minority ethnic groups? If Asian children are under-represented in the nursery, what could be the reason?'

### Candidates applying to work as nursery officers

Some suggested approaches are:

1 Have you any experience of working with children from different races and cultural backgrounds?
2 What do you think of a 'colourblind' approach to work with small children? (A colourblind approach, seemingly a liberal position, denies children's ethnic and racial identity. Black children may be regarded as white and their particular situation and stresses may be ignored.)
3 How do you think a nursery can support black children's racial identity?
4 Interviewers can pose hypothetical problems, for example: if white children refuse to sit with black children or call them names what would you do; what do you think should happen; how would you deal with it?
5 Interviewers may say something like: there are no black children in this nursery but the staff are interested in promoting positive attitudes among children towards all people. How do you think we can work towards this goal? I would be very interested in your response.

6 Have you any experience of black community organizations?

*Assessing candidates' interests and willingness to attend racial equality training for nursery staff*

Interviewers could make a general point about the department providing such training to new staff within the six months induction period.

1 Would you be interested? (Is it mandatory?)
2 Have you any experience of such training?
3 Did it help?
4 Were there any problems?

# 3 Cultural action for the under-fives: training strategies developed by the Building Blocks project *Judith Koetter, Patsy Anderson, Sandip Hazareesingh and Kelvin Simms*

Building Blocks is an anti-racist resource and education project for carers of children under five, set up by The Save the Children Fund and funded by the DHSS Under-fives Initiative and the GLC Women's Committee.

### The problems to be tackled

The problem, as we see it, is that in a racist society such as Britain there are two established patterns of dealing with the minority presence in mainstream society: cultural silence, that is the general absence of reference, images and representations, especially of Indian cultures, and cultural distortion, that is the existence of caricature and negative images, especially of Afro-Caribbean cultures. The absence of positive references to Afro-Caribbean, Indian and other ethnic-minority cultures, together with early exposure to negative stereotypes and distorted images, are particularly harmful in the initial stage of development when children are still in the process of forming clear concepts of themselves and others. Thus majority children who develop 'naturally' in a racist society and are brought up to believe that 'white is right' have their emotional and intellectual growth maimed and are unable to realize their potential in becoming caring and aware adults, or to experience and value the vast majority of the world's cultures. It is minority children, however, who experience the most damaging consequences, emotionally and culturally, of living and growing up in a racist society which systematically negates, silences, distorts, and oppresses their cultural heritage and values. They are often unable to feel and see themselves and their culture as they really are, which severely damages their self-esteem, cultural identity and emotional development, and their ability to grow into self-loving, confident and purposeful adults.

Over the past decade or so, educationalists and carers in the under-fives field have slowly begun to grasp the importance of children's play activities reflecting the multi-cultural reality of their everyday lives. Thus the topi, shalwar, kameez, dutch pot or wok have begun to make rather a timid appearance in the home corner, and in recent years there has been a notable increase in the children's books and play materials depicting people from different cultural backgrounds. However, these efforts, while underlining the fact of cultural diversity, have achieved little in terms of promoting an understanding of the real-life context from which these crafts, images and representations have sprung. The main stress has too often been on the 'exotic' and hence marginal nature of these materials which, used in isolation, are seen as belonging to 'alien cultures' and can thus reinforce the existing negative attitudes towards them.

Crucially, this cultural diversity approach has failed to promote either ethnic-minority children's positive self-image or majority children's valuing of ways of life from other than European cultures that are now an integral part of British culture. This is primarily because the use of multi-cultural materials has, so far, rarely been coherently linked to the practical perspectives of understanding and valuing other ways of life in Britain.

### Aims and objectives

Building Blocks' aims and objectives are as follows:

1 To intervene and work towards change in all areas of mainstream child care practice so as to bring about equal valuing of, and greater provision for, ethnic-minority children. We try to introduce innovatory work and practice, based on relevant research, consistent with our anti-racist objectives.

2 To foster, through the planned use of play materials reflecting a diversity of cultural experience, these children's recognition of and confidence and pride in their cultural identity.

3 To provide, at the same time, the white child with accurate and positive information about different ethnic groups so as to enable the child to *value equally* all the cultures of contemporary Britain.

4 To act as an anti-racist resource, training, and information centre of

65

cultural issues for carers of children under five and for interested community groups and individuals.

## Definitions

We believe that racism, at a fundamental level, attacks ethnic-minority children's racial and cultural identity, and consequently affects their emotional, social and cognitive development. A basic component of our educational work is therefore aimed at fostering ethnic-minority children's recognition of and pride in their racial and cultural identity.

From this perspective, the limitations of 'black' as an umbrella term become rapidly apparent. Its use would mean a confusing double identity for most ethnic-minority children, disastrous in educational terms. To call a Vietnamese child 'black', for instance, would be meaningless. Such a usage would also do little to enhance the self-image of children who are really, that is culturally, black. Black children are black not because they are oppressed, but because they are of African descent.

It is precisely because we recognize the importance of positive cultural identification in the fight against racism that our definitions also need to be anti-racist. For instance, in relation to South Asian children, the core cultural definition we use is Indian. The concept of 'Indian' does not negate language, religious or regional variations within South Asia, but represents a broader cultural definition, based on commonality of shared meanings, which the twin processes of imperialism and racism have sought to conceal from, and hence deny, South Asian communities.

To summarize: Building Blocks uses the term 'black' to refer solely to people of African descent, and the terms 'South Asian' and 'Indian' to refer to people originating from the Indian sub-continent. 'South Asian' refers to geographical origin; 'Indian' to cultural origin.

## Strategies and practice

Building Blocks addresses itself particularly to racism in the institutions that influence the quality of care and education of children under five. We accept the research findings that emphasize the importance of these early years in the values a child receives while developing his or her cultural perceptions of the world. We recognize racism in the under-fives' world is often unintentional, though this merely emphasizes the importance of raising awareness so that covert and hidden as well as obvious racism is identified and dealt with.

In order to meet our objectives Building Blocks employs three main strategies in its own practice.

## Partnership or 'Contract' work

On invitation the project team works directly with the staff, volunteers, parents and children within a variety of provisions concerned with the care or education of the under-fives in the London Borough of Southwark.

A 'contract' lasts three or four months or approximately a term. Commitment is made at the onset by signing a contract between the project and the provision. In consultation with the project, an initial training programme is designed to examine the effects of racism on individuals and within professional practice so that the provision can collectively begin the process of challenging such attitudes, behaviour and practice through its short and long-term strategies.

Building Blocks then works directly with the children using play and learning activities specifically designed to support a child's cultural and family identity, and help all children value equally how others look, speak, believe, and behave. With these purposes in mind, the staff are encouraged to develop their own multi-cultural activities and are further supported with resources (toys, books, visual and other learning materials) from the Centre.

The work is monitored throughout and at the end of the contract period an evaluation day, involving all those who participated, examines the effectiveness of the process and sets future targets within time scales. Building Blocks continues to monitor the work of the group and offer help and support, if requested, and if and when problems arise.

## Training

Building Blocks designs training packages to meet specific needs of other, London based, under-fives workers or nationally with organizations that have a specific under-fives brief, for example, National Childminding Association, Preschool Playgroup Association, National Association of Advisers for Under-fives, and so on. The purpose of this training is to examine critically under-fives practice in the context of a racist society; the support groups that often result from such training ensure a commitment to tackling racism at the levels of policy and practice.

Building Blocks is often asked to have an input in child care or educational courses within institutions of further and higher education.

Our main purpose here is to identify racist assumptions in textbooks and other learning materials and, by working with both students and tutors, to influence changes in the mainstream courses and syllabuses which provide the vast majority of under-fives workers with their basic training.

*Resource Centre*
Our project functions as an anti-racist education and resource centre, not only for under-fives carers and teachers, but also for tutors, trainers, advisers and health workers, as well as for parents and community groups. We welcome visitors and can provide issue-raising sessions on racism and early childhood, or give information, advice and support to individuals and groups engaged in similar work elsewhere.

# 4 Practice in a community nursery for black children *Syble Morgan*

Our community nursery was set up in November, 1976, as an early childhood learning centre primarily to provide black pre-schoolers with the basic skills they need for academic success, and as an alternative to the racism and destruction of black self-esteem found in mainstream nurseries and schools. Racism breeds chronic anxiety, self-hate, lack of self-confidence and lack of self-knowledge. It restricts black children at all levels. The vast majority of black children are also poor. It is these prevailing social conditions under which the child is reared that are responsible for many of the problems the child displays. Poverty and racist propaganda in the media and elsewhere discourages their development and has a negative effect on their self-image. We therefore decided to work with black parents in order to help children to acquire skills necessary for academic success; we recognize that school performance can be influenced by the child's pre-school experiences.

We needed an institution that would be accountable to us, black people in the community, to determine our own needs and to set our own policies for meeting those needs. We had to organize ourselves into a group and demand decision-making power over the expenditure of funds, the hiring and firing of all staff and the setting of educational policies and programmes.

We decided to have a totally black staff so that the children could identify with their own people, and be taught by someone who resembled their own parents from the very beginning of their school life. After they have been steeped in their own culture in the early years, they can mix with all the peoples of the world and still be proud of their identity.

It is very important that the black child should be exposed to situations where black adults exert authority, leadership, initiative and knowledge to counter beliefs that they are inferior to whites. To counteract this destructive notion, it is very important that black children are taught to love themselves and other black people, as the basis for a loving personality in general. The child must also be taught to respect and love other ethnic groups as well. It is important to note here that although our management committee and our staff are black, we have had white children at our nursery.

All our practice in the nursery is informed by certain principles which are part of our culture. For example, we value family support because it is the key element in our struggle to survive. When we say 'family' in the black community it is not confined to a husband, wife and children living in isolation; we have a more complex notion of the family which includes more distant relatives and close long-standing friends. We believe that were it not for the adaptability, resilience and endurance of the black family we would not have survived as a people.

Our nursery policy is different from a social services run nursery in many respects. Perhaps the most important difference is the criteria for admission. Although the majority of our mothers are single parents, who are charged the same fees in a social services nursery, we do accept married mothers, who are charged less in a social services nursery, whose family income is very low. Because we are a community nursery, we are much more involved with the children's lives. When they are ready for school, members of the staff take them there, if it is one of the local schools nearby, and also collect them in the afternoon. Throughout their time in the nursery we are actively preparing the children for school, teaching them numbers, and so on. Our programme is designed to provide practice in school-related skills, and to prepare children to learn reading, writing, arithmetic and spelling.

If a parent is ill, then a member of staff may go to the hospital with the parent or visit him or her. Our parents form a network, so that we are aware of any illness or crisis that arises in any family; a parent tells the staff and we then intervene in whatever way we think appropriate. For example, two mothers whose homes were burnt out were given financial help from the nursery fund-raising budget.

## Play

We do not subscribe to the myths about black parents' negative attitudes towards play. Play in our nursery, as in others, is used to develop language, social skills and body control. We use play materials which give black children a sense of pride in their identity; materials that show black people having successful experiences, black astronauts, black doctors, athletes and so on. Use of and respect for black art, literature and music are good experiences for the children. Positive interaction with black staff and parents is observed by them. Respect for black people helps children to be proud of their blackness in a very racist environment. It is important not to send contradictory messages, as happens when teachers hang pictures of famous black people such as Paul Robeson around the room, while everyone knows that they never speak to the parents of the children with any respect.

### Discipline

Some child care experts claim that black parents are too strict with their children. It is true that the excessive stress that black parents have to live with, because of racism, can sometimes result in 'too strict' behaviour. But parents can be strict without being excessively harsh or spanking their children, since spanking creates more problems than it solves. Talking with the child is more useful. Inconsistent responses, strictness at one instance and permissiveness the next for the same type of offence, will only create confusion, doubt and anger in the child. We communicate this understanding to our parents, many of whom are very young. We suggest to parents that when punishment is necessary, it is best to withdraw some privilege or other and that this is the most effective if it follows closely the offence, and gains the child's attention. It is important not to try to shame children when they are naughty. One must show that one likes and accepts the child, but not the behaviour.

In the past, because aggressive black males were more than likely to be in danger, and still are, some parents and teachers tried to crush normal aggressive behaviour in their children at this early stage. The children were taught to obey authority figures whether they were right or wrong. This produced too many black people who were afraid to stand up for their rights, who learned not to see injustice but to smile and comply with anybody in a position of authority. Sometimes this approach backfired and created the very behaviour it was supposed to destroy, as happens when children who are spanked and scolded too often without cause respond with the excessively aggressive and negative behaviour parents are hoping to crush.

### Language

Black children have to be bicultural and bilingual. They must be taught to function efficiently in both cultures, to respect equally and handle efficiently 'black English' as well as the school's 'standard English'.

There is a view that black children are poor in their expression of verbal skills. The black verbal style can differ from that of other children. This difference does not mean that black children have an inferior cognitive structure; it means that their experiences produce unique verbal skills which are found in a typically black community, skills which are not validated or accepted in classrooms, and which tests with white orientations do not measure.

Many studies have been done concerning standard and non-standard English (Baratz and Baratz, 1969). When these linguists refer to the word 'dialect' they do not limit themselves to the way that people in different regions of a country pronounce words. They refer to a total linguistic structure, the organized way that the language grammatically relates certain words to other words. A dialect is a fully-developed linguistic system. Unfortunately, the schools tend to regard standard English as 'right' and any dialects as 'wrong'. Instead of recognizing that black children are speaking a well-developed language, and then using that language to teach them standard English, the teacher defines her goal as that of stamping out the children's 'bad' language, which is related to their culture and basic black identity, and replacing it with standard middle-class English. The children cannot therefore bring their cognitive learning and expressive styles into the classroom; and when they take standardized tests, they are forced to leave their black culture and verbal skills outside.

### Food and nutrition

When we started the nursery, we were very concerned about nutritional education among our parents because the majority of them were vegetarians, and were having problems in planning a balanced diet for their families. For this reason we set up a workshop on food and nutrition.

With good nutrition as our objective, we carefully selected and adapted recipes from different Caribbean countries which included staple Afro-Caribbean dishes such as banana bread, made with whole wheat flour, cornbread, rice and peas, bean dishes, yams, plantains, green bananas, sweet potato pudding and so on. When we are short of staff parents who come in to help for a morning session will sometimes stay and help us prepare lunch. The cultural diversity of Caribbean cookery is not well documented, and should be more widely known, because what we eat and why is an important part of knowing who we are. Their ancestors placed great value on preparing foods exactly as they had done in Africa, in a conscious attempt to reinforce their identity through keeping alive the culinary part of their culture.

Several Caribbean dishes came directly from Africa and were adapted to local conditions. For example, Accra (the African name is Akara) is a Caribbean version of a West African dish, made from boiled shredded salted fish, mixed with a well-spiced batter and deep fried. In West Africa, dried beans replace the fish, otherwise the preparation is identical. In several Caribbean Islands there is also Foo-Foo, pounded plantain; the identical preparation of this can be traced to Nigeria.

Food and cooking illustrate cultural differences among ethnic groups and this can be used to incorporate information about the variety of cultural backgrounds, as well as to expose the children to a wider array of tastes and flavours.

### Recommendations

1 The training given to nursery nurse students needs to be changed to reflect the reality of our multi-cultural society. Because of institutional racism, most students taking National Nursery Examination Board (NNEB) certificates seem to have negative ideas about the cultural backgrounds of the children they will care for. They are not taught to respect different cultures and many do not understand how racism damages black children.

The failures of the training institutions to provide practical and realistic guidance is a real problem. For example, one commonly-used textbook perpetuates the usual myths regarding children of West Indian origin.

They may need special guidance in handling and caring for play materials or books as they are generally lacking in their homes. They find a great deal of choice bewildering, as they are not encouraged to be self-regulating at home. Strict discipline and sometimes corporal punishment at home can mean that soft-spoken restraints and explanations about behaviour limitations go unheeded at the nursery; sometimes the children even regard the adults as 'soft' or weak.

West Indian children can be lively, boisterous and responsive. Their feeling for music and rhythm often makes it physically impossible for them to remain still when music is being played. (Drain and Martin, 1983, pp.243-244.)

2 Students should know something about black hair and skin care. African hair is extremely delicate. To combat dryness, the hair needs to be washed with a mild shampoo and to be conditioned, after which it should be allowed to dry naturally. Over-oiling of the scalp can clog hair follicles and retard growth. Students must be taught that hair does not have to be straight to be beautiful. Also black skin tends to be dry and needs frequent moisturizing.

3 It is very important that black children in social services run nurseries are given Afro-Caribbean foods, and are taught respect for the value their ancestors must have placed on this part of their culture, so that through practice and oral traditions they pass it on.

In conclusion, the more realistic and practical the training of nursery nurse students the less harmful will be their contact with black children.

## References

BARATZ, S., and BARATZ, J., *Social Education*, National Council for Social Studies, Washington DC, April 1969, pp. 401-4.
DRAIN, J., and MARTIN, M., *Child Care and Health*, Hulton Educational Publications, 1983.

# 5 *Training responses* *Maureen O'Hagan*

## Introduction by Juliet Cheetham

There is often a lack of clarity in the objectives of training programmes for a multi-racial society. The most common confusion is to assume that a multi-cultural approach is also an anti-racist approach. The reality is that multi-cultural strategies may never confront racist attitudes or behaviour, and may perpetuate the notion of cultural hierarchies in British society. In other words, there may be a greater awareness of different cultural practices of minority-ethnic groups with regard to child care, but they may continue to be regarded as intrinsically inferior, odd or exotic.

The importance of this must be borne in mind when new learning initiatives are being planned and assessed. O'Hagan describes the scope there is for new training ventures. In taking up these opportunities trainers need to plan courses which do not simply increase knowledge and understanding, important though this is; they have too to address the problem of institutional and individual racism.

## Response of National Nursery Education Board courses to a multi-cultural society

The following views are the author's own and do not necessarily reflect the views of her employers, the Inner London Education Authority (ILEA).

### National responses

### The new syllabus

This contains a large section, referred to in the introduction to this book, on multi-culturalism, covering both health and education. This means that all course tutors have had to take account of the fact that the new syllabus represents the needs of the multi-cultural society in which we live. These curriculum aspects cannot be ignored, even if a course has a totally white clientele.

Ideally, the curriculum should be totally integrated so that the multi-cultural aspects are not taught as a separate specialist subject. This probably operates best in local education authorities where there is a strong multi-cultural or anti-racist policy. Ideally the multi-cultural aspects of the curriculum should also be approached from a perspective which views them as part of ordinary British society, and not the source of problems requiring special attention. In areas where staff are not adequately trained, a problem-solving and specialist approach may be the easiest way of beginning to include this subject in the curriculum.

*Flexibility of the Nursery Nurse Examination Board (NNEB).*
There have been significant moves by the Board to acknowledge the needs of a multi-cultural society. The examination can be taken in the Welsh language, and there is no reason why other languages should not be added in the future. The Board has validated a course for Orthodox Jews when women are unable to join mainstream courses because of religious codes preventing their mixing with males. It has also validated a 48 week course at Camden Training Centre for unemployed people where the emphasis is upon recruiting from minority groups; this includes males, who are sparsely represented in NNEB courses. The Board is considering validating a three year course, run for 21 hours a week, for those unemployed people who cannot obtain grants to attend the full-time two year courses.

The Board is only able to explore such initiatives if course tutors approach them with their local requirements. The scope for new initiatives is wide.

*Certificate in post-qualifying studies*
This very new pilot scheme by the Board has allowed a great deal of scope for colleges involved in this scheme to devise their own courses in response to local and national needs. They have exhibited their flexibility by allowing various methods of teaching, including lectures, seminars, distance learning and open learning. From the conclusions of research into the pilot schemes the Board will devise a definitive course which will probably come into being in September 1986. Colleges such as Leicester and North London have devised units which include multi-cultural,

anti-racist and anti-sexist components. One such unit is described as follows:

*Factors Affecting Contemporary Child Care*

The unit aims to make students aware of the factors which affect the development of normal children in a changing society. Students will examine methodology and current research relating to race and race relations, stress and equal opportunities and the effects these may have upon the child, family and child care workers. Students will acquire practical skills in affirmative action strategies and interventionist policies appropriate for working in problem areas.

## Local responses

### Short courses for qualified nursery nurses

North London College has run short courses for qualified nursery nurses for many years. One of these courses, *Understanding Children from Multi-Cultural Backgrounds*, has been extremely popular and over-subscribed. It is open to all under-fives workers and people working with ethnic minority families, not just nursery nurses. Residential social workers in child care, youth workers, peripatetic house parents and nursery nurses have taken part. More recently people from community nurseries and the less conventional centres have been attracted. The course is described as follows:

This course has been designed to aid greater understanding of the physical, social, emotional and intellectual development of these children by examining child-rearing practices in multi-cultural groups. It will also examine the effects of immigration on traditional lifestyles and child-rearing and identify areas where conflict with the host community may arise.

We aim to aid awareness and recognition of problems which may arise for such children and their families and to examine how these may be alleviated; also to increase the students' knowledge of facilities and agencies which are available specifically for multi-cultural groups and to examine how these may be used to their best advantage.

Although it is probably not ideal to run such specialist courses, they can be necessary in the transitional period as Britain moves towards a more pluralistic society, because many nursery nurses trained under previous regulations and syllabuses may not have learnt about work in a multi-racial society. They therefore need in-service training to enhance their knowledge and give them the skills to work appropriately in multi-cultural Britain. They also need the opportunity to examine their attitudes in the light of race relations legislation and the anti-racist policies of local authorities.

## Access to NNEB courses

In response to the local Race Relations Committee, North London College explored the idea of an access course to the main NNEB course. When ethnic-minority representation on ILEA NNEB courses was examined, it was discovered that in a quarter of the courses students were predominantly from the ethnic minorities, particularly Afro-Caribbean. The group which was under-represented was Asian. Given this strong representation of Afro-Caribbean students an access course for them, which had been the original intention, would not have been permitted by the Race Relations Act. An access course for Asians, who were under-represented, would be permissible were funds forthcoming. At North London College, and possibly nationally, another group which is at present under-represented on courses are males. There are cultural and other reasons why these groups do not now consider nursery nursing as a career, but it must not be assumed that these attitudes will endure forever. Depending on local circumstances colleges should be alert to the possibility of arranging experimental new courses for people beginning to show an interest in working with under-fives.

## Conclusions

The NNEB is moving with the demands of a multi-cultural society and would move faster if course tutors made the Board aware of their needs. It is not that the Board is inflexible; rather that the course tutors are tardy in making their needs known. The post-qualifying certificate offers further training in areas which individual colleges choose to meet their local needs. Once again, it is up to individual colleges to ascertain these, to plan the appropriate courses and seek validation for them. Ethnic-minority nursery nurses are being trained in some big cities. They are not sufficient in number to meet the needs of a multi-racial society, but enough to make it impossible in some areas to mount access courses within the parameters of the existing laws.

The Board is not inflexible or closed to suggestions, and this really does mean that colleges need to start talking to it and negotiating rather than viewing it as an unapproachable body.

# 6 *Policies for day care* Clifford Headley

**Introduction by Judith Cheetham**

All the initiatives discussed in this section will gain strength and coherence if they are part of a departmental policy for the day care of black under-fives.

The following proposals, prepared by Clifford Headley for Hackney Social Services Committee, provide an example of a nursery policy. It could be extended to incorporate policies for other forms of day care which take account of the issues of access and the type and quality of care discussed in the introduction.

## Outline proposals for a nursery policy

While agreeing that the care of black children cannot be seen in isolation, and must be considered as part of the care and education of all children, in order to achieve what all nurseries should be aiming to provide for all children in today's multi-racial and culturally diverse society, it is fundamental that a whole nursery policy on multi-racial and cultural care be formulated. Such a policy would contain the following objectives:

1  To promote the principles embodied in the UN Charter of Human Rights and EEC directives.
2  To prepare all children for life in a multi-cultural society in which there is social and racial harmony.
3  To counter the damaging effects of racism.
4  To counter the factors contributing to under-achievement of black and other groups of children.
5  To create a caring and social climate which promotes strong motivation and a positive approach to all racial and ethnic groups.
6  To prevent negative patronizing or stereotyped views amongst staff and others involved in the provision of caring services. To instill in

all children confidence and pride in their own cultural roots and language.

7 To extend social relationships across racial and ethnic groups and develop an appreciation of other cultures.

8 To show children that the nursery values them as individuals as well as members of racial and cultural groups.

9 To act as a positive agent for social change.

### Proposals for race and cultural sensitivity

In order to acquaint under-fives workers with the lifestyles and practice of other cultures there should be:

1 The incorporation of compulsory multi-cultural education courses in NNEB and CQSW training.

2 More emphasis on in-service training with respect to multi-cultural and racial care.

3 The appointment of more black workers at all levels in the day nurseries, and more emphasis in schools now that child care and community studies are being taught.

4 The value of the contribution which the parent can make in the nursery should be fully exploited.

5 The multi-racial and cultural nature of the community should be reflected in the books and educational and creative play materials used in the nurseries. This should also be reflected in the daily diet.

6 Black and ethnic minority activities should be fully incorporated in the daily routine, and not seen as special activities.

7 Some visiting should be undertaken before a child enters the nursery in order to share information and to discuss the expectations of home and nursery.

8 Staff should have a positive approach to dialects other than standard English and this should be reflected in the way in which they assess children's language development.

# PART TWO
# BLACK CHILDREN IN CARE

## 7 *Transracial placements: conflicts and contradictions* John Small

### Introduction

This chapter focuses on one of the most fundamental yet controversial areas of social work practice, namely, transracial placements. By this is meant placement of black children in white homes. The problems experienced by foster and adoptive parents who are caring for black children are qualitatively similar. Consequently the arguments presented here in respect of adoption practices are equally valid for fostering[1].

This chapter includes an examination of the concept of race and uses several frameworks to demonstrate how racial-identity confusion in black children is rooted in the family and society, and therefore cannot be separated from the power relationships within society in general and social work agencies in particular. Different groups of transracial adopters and their dilemmas are identified and the implications for their children illustrated. Gill and Jackson's research in 1983 will be critically examined, and in particular the failure to recognize the identity needs of black children in a racist society. If 'these black children have been made white in all but skin colour . . . have no contact with the black community and their "coping" mechanisms are based on denying their racial background' (p.137), we must surely question Gill and Jackson's conclusion, that 'they feel confident in using the term "success" to describe the experiences of the majority of these families and children and there is little evidence that a group of similarly aged white children

---

[1] This chapter is an extension of 'The crisis in adoption' which was originally published in the *International Journal of Social Psychiatry* vol. 30, nos. 1 and 2, Spring 1984.

growing up with their natural parents would not include a number of children experiencing similar or greater difficulties.' (pp.132-33.) Certainly white children in substitute white families, or their biological families do not deny that they are white, nor want to be black. For them the vital issue of racial-identity confusion does not exist.

Many white people do not understand the conflicts and the suffering experienced by those who are confused about their racial identity. Maximé discusses this in detail in Chapter 8 but the following brief accounts illustrate the dilemmas.

Many transracially adopted children are aware that the darker their skin colour the more undesirable they are to white society; and many feel it is better to be white than black. One adoptive parent of a black child heard the child saying 'I'm glad I'm not black, the black children get teased; but I don't want to be brown either, because everyone notices me because I'm different.' Mother replied 'But it is nice to be different; people are all different and it would be boring if we all looked the same.' Parents may understandably often try to deny the reality of their black children's unhappiness because they like to think that their children are secure and happy, thus reflecting their success as adopters. The denial of the reality of the visibility of the black child in a white family creates the pre-conditions for the phenomenon of identity confusion. Many, although black, will grow up believing or wishing that they are white. Yet '. . . they will be moving out into a society which is significantly racist in its attitudes and its distribution of opportunities. They will be moving towards establishing their own families and racial background will be an issue.' (Gill and Jackson, 1983, p.136.) These children will not always live in the protective arms of the family, they will have to make decisions about jobs, marriage, political and social commitments based on where in society they feel that they are able to find a place. Many of these children do not have skills to relate to black people and they will experience rejection by white society (Ladner, 1978).

Yvonne, placed transracially and now 24 years old, will never forget the day when she and friends were playing in the park and saw a black man passing by. The white youths began yelling 'Nigger, nigger, go back to where you come from.' The girls continued to play. One of the youths walked over to the group, looked at the black girl and said 'By the way, you are a nigger too.' That was the first knowledge that Yvonne had of being black. 'I was devastated. I really did not want to be black because it was different to what my parents and the other children were. It was something totally new to me. I hated being black.' To tell the child that colour in this society does not matter is to ignore the racism in the society.

## Transracial placements: a question of power

Transracial adoption, the adoption of children by parents of different racial origin, developed in earnest in the mid-1960s and has been on the increase since then. In part it was a response to the needs of childless white couples for whom white infants were no longer available for adoption. It gained momentum with the philosophy of the assimilation of the immigrant child into society. The black community thus became a 'donor' group for white society. This usually entailed placement at a very tender age, because it would be difficult for some parents to deal with the issue of race and colour if the child had developed a sense of racial identity and pride in his or her heritage. This could prevent the possibility of identification with, and integration into, the white family.

Transracial adoption was also encouraged by developments in child care practice designed to reduce dramatically the number of children living in institutions, of whom a disproportionate number were and still are black (Raynor 1975; Rowe and Lambert, 1970). There was too the erroneous belief that black substitute parents could not be found (ABAFA, 1976).

New Black Families has demonstrated unequivocally that black homes can be found for black children (Small, 1982). The choice for the children trapped in the welfare system is therefore not solely between white families and a life of institutional care as we are led to believe; there are black families willing and capable of opening up their homes to these children, but there have been policies and practices which have prevented this development. Paradoxically, Gill and Jackson's book appeared at a time when there was a great deal of activity in the black community directed towards finding black families for black children, thereby making it progressively unnecessary for transracial placements to continue. Nevertheless, finding more black adoptive families will necessitate more black social workers in the key agency posts that determine policy, more black social workers involved in family finding, and child placements and recognition of the strengths of black families.

The one-way traffic of black children into white families begs fundamental questions of power and ideology. It raises questions as to the type of relationship which exists between black and white people and, furthermore, the type of society that those involved in the practice are creating. Transracial adoption encourages the phenomenon of racial-identity confusion described in other contexts by Fanon (1970), Naipaul (1961, 1962) and Rushdie (1981). 'They did not . . . see themselves as black or show any real sign of having developed a sense of racial identity.' (Gill and Jackson, 1983, p. 139.) This often leads black children to deny the reality of their skin colour and to reject people of similar race and colour. White liberals have recognized the problem and made attempts to recruit black parents in the 1970s (ABAFA, 1976). The first black adoption agency, New Black Families, began to tackle the problem in 1980. While some workers believe that the best place for a child is within a family, and that it is better for a child to be placed transracially than to have no family, anxiety is increasing about the outcome of transracial placements.

It is of crucial importance that while social services departments, voluntary agencies, and professionals are adjusting their views and talking about issues relating to transracial adoption, the matter should be dealt with in a sensitive way. That is to say, when there is a shift from traditional methods in the placement of black children then careful consideration should also be given to the implications that this will have for black children, the black community and for adopters. It is certainly not the intention of the black community to undermine the good work being done by current transracial adopters and foster parents, who have opened their homes to black children.

### Transracial placements and the social environment

The social context of transracial adoption raises several fundamental questions. First, is the best place for a child with a family? If the answer is yes, should it be a family similar to the child's racial and cultural origin? If the answer is again yes and such a family is not available, should the child remain in institutional care, or should the child be placed transracially?

If we believe that the child should be placed transracially as an alternative to institutional care, then social workers must resist the massive denial or evasion of the negative consequence of some transracial placements for black children when the substitute parents have not been prepared or perhaps are very unsuitable to care for a black child. Out of the multiplicity of factors influencing the development of the personality of the black child the following are the major influences.

The first is the estimation and expectation of others; the majority of society and the 'significant others'. The latter, who have the most profound impact on the personality or the self of the child, are those individuals with whom the child interacts most closely and who give him or her security. These 'significant others' over time actually become a part of the psychic structure of the child from which develops the concept of self. Reality is usually defined by parents, as the most important 'significant others'. Children will adjust their behaviour to meet parental approval. This may not include positive valuation of black people or different ethnic backgrounds. Thus, at least until adolescence, the black child is likely to share these values. The most recent findings have highlighted some of the fears of the critics of transracial adoption; 'These black children have been made white in all but skin colour.' (Gill and Jackson, 1983, p.137.)

Curiously, Gill and Jackson are aware of the problem of identity confusion but believe that it can be avoided if black children are placed transracially when very young '. . . it is possible that older black children may, by the time a placement has occured, have already internalised a definition of themselves as being black and that this definition may jeopardise the possibility of integration and emotional identification within a white family.' (p. 138.) The argument seems to be that the world of reality and the concept of self are or should be structured by white parents and society. Thus children should be placed transracially at a very young age, so becoming 'white in all but skin colour'. If they already have a concept of themselves as black it will be too late to 'turn them white'. Bean, writing a year later in 1984, supported this view by saying that '. . . when the adopted child is an older child who has already acquired a cultural background and a set of cultural responses, these will have to be unlearned if he or she is to acquire a new cultural identity.' A crucial aspect of a child's interests is thus ignored. Jackson herself saw the danger in 1976: 'Unless you can accept a child's colour, you will always be rejecting a very important part of him.' (p. 4.) Sadly, this principle does not seem to have informed the later research.

As racial tension increases, social workers must adapt themselves to the prevailing racial climate. They must take a leading role in giving direction to families who have expressed interest in providing a home for a black child. For example, they must be helped to recognize that, in a society which is hostile and oppressively racist to black people, the black family has to develop coping mechanisms which allow the group to maintain dignity and self-respect and which help the family to survive in a psychologically healthy way. These survival mechanisms of the black family have to be extended to the black community generally in its economic life, education and social relations. These experiences are outside those of white society. Consequently most white families are ill-equipped to provide the environment to prepare the black child for the tremendous task ahead. It is these survival techniques which provide the cultural and psychological framework that gives energy and support to black children. The desperate wish to care for a child, however sincere, is not a guarantee that white adopters will provide such an environment.

If the black child is placed in an environment which is hostile, the inevitable consequence of this will be repeated attacks on the child's personality which will cause severe damage to his or her self-esteem. It should be clear that if a child is placed in an ethnically insensitive white community he or she will fail to develop the mechanisms necessary to survive in a racist society.

If Britain was not a racist society, transracial adoption would not be an issue; but as long as race relations continue their current path transracial adoption must be an area of concern. Since the aim of adoption must always be to provide a child without parents with an environment which will foster normal development the commitment must be to the child, not to the parents or to the agency.

### The characteristics of transracial adopters

The limited systematic study of transracial adoptive couples in Britain shows some general characteristics. First, transracial adopters tend to belong to relatively high socio-economic groups. Second, they often live some distance from the black communities and so their black children tend to be socially isolated from immediate relatives and from other black people. The literature further suggests that transracial adopters are often very self-confident people with a resilience to stress. They often approach agencies that have a policy for placing children transracially; they may prefer children who are racially different from themselves. Their motivation to open homes to black children appears often to have a strong moral and ethical base (Fricke, 1965; Roskes, 1963). These values, held usually with great sincerity, deserve examination because they may have unintended harmful implications.

Some parents only want to adopt a child of two black parents, that is of African, Afro-Caribbean or Asian origin. The rationale behind this decision may be to make it abundantly clear that the child is not the product of the adopters' relationship with each other or with anyone else. These adopters often see themselves as helping the 'poor blacks' with the fantasy or rescue mission born out of collective guilt. It is as though they are saying 'Look at us, we are not like others because we even adopted a black child'. They may feel responsible for the racial injustice which other white people have inflicted on blacks, and see these injustices as entailing all manner of pathology for the black community, with its strengths and survival denied or not recognized. These assumptions will be detrimental to the black child if he or she is seen as being rescued from a life of misery. Embracing such a cause does not ensure a black child's welfare and may, unwittingly, damage it.

This group of adopters may include those whose motivation is largely intellectual or political. They cannot become emotionally involved, and if faced with difficulties withdraw their interest because their motivation and commitment are often very superficial. It is possible too for some adopters to attempt to improve their self-image if they believe, perhaps subconsciously, that 'having a black child in the family confirms our self-worth because they are much less than we are.' Others may adopt because it is a dramatic way of rejecting what their family and society stand for.

A second group are the adopters who are prepared to adopt a child of two black parents or a child of one white and one black parent, and to accept the child as he or she is, recognizing the difference in racial and cultural origin. Some of these parents may also wish, through adoption, to protect children against the social order, but they are 'real' parents in that they are prepared to go beyond their own concerns and hold the child's interests as their priority. (The guidelines on page 95 can be used to identify this group of parents.) Many such adopters are anchored firmly in their beliefs; they are open-minded and not contented with stereotypes or a superficial view of society. They are also very confident people with a secure sense of their own identity, and are able to resist the various pressures brought to bear on them by friends, relatives and society. They eventually become black families in white skins.

A third group are the colonialist and the neo-colonialist with experience of colonial societies. They often feel they know it all and tend to give the impression that they are 'experts' on blacks. They are often the most difficult to assess since their experience usually lies outside that of social workers, who may be suspicious of such applicants' knowledge but uneasy about rejecting their apparently confident experience.

Some transracial adopters will only adopt a child of 'mixed race'. These adopters do not want society to say that they have a black child, that is a child of two black parents. A child of 'mixed race' is therefore seen by them as not black and not white, but closer to white than black. They perhaps feel that since there is a degree of whiteness in the child they will be able to identify with that. Some of these families may never be able to accept the blackness of such a child, but, at the same time, they know that he or she is not really white. It is often the children of such families who have the most profound racial-identity crisis.

### Colour and identity

If a healthy personality is to be formed the psychic image of the child must merge with the reality of what the child actually is. That is to say, if the child is black (reality), he or she must first recognize and accept that he or she has a black psychic image. There are several black children who have grown up in childrens' homes with purely white staff, and others who have been placed with white families who are isolated geographically and have no contact with black people (Gill and Jackson, 1983, p.134). Some of these children are saying that they are not black or that they do not want to be associated with other black people. What seems to have happened is that they have internalized the negative images that are attributed to black people and do not feel that they should identify with them. This can happen when an institution or family are racially sensitive, in the white sense, but ethnically insensitive to the child's background and needs. This may sometimes be the result of lack of information and reluctance on the part of the carers to take measures to correct this. Many families often feel that assisting the child to reinforce his or her identity in terms of colour and ethnicity will probably render the child unable to form a healthy attachment to them; the child may feel that he or she should belong to a black family. Many people also feel that there is no necessity to deal with racial issues since the child is seen as part and parcel of the family and 'a child is a child'.

Within my own practice, I have never met a white child who says he or she is not white; neither have I met a black child growing up in a black family saying that he or she is not black. It should therefore be clear that there are factors operating within the family and the society which contribute to this pathological state.

Gill and Jackson had the ideal opportunity to demonstrate how the phenomenon of identity confusion could be understood through the process of racial discrimination in society, a path whereby children of minority groups tend to internalize the values of the dominant society, and internalize derogatory values about themselves. Milner (1975) has summarized and contributed to the long history of research which demonstrates black children's denial of their colour (Clark and Clark,

1947), and their preference for white identity (Goodman, 1964). Social workers must recognize, therefore, that in racist societies they are working with a potentially vulnerable group. But that is not the end of the story. As black communities became aware of the effect that society was having on their children, they forged a conscious approach to provide a buffer between racism and the self-esteem and self-worth of their children by raising the level of consciousness of the strengths of black traditions and family life. They have fought against the pressures to make black people invisible and their efforts have, in part, been recognized by wider society (Milner, 1981, 1983). Black people have thus carved a social and political path more conducive to the psychological well-being of their children who do not now misidentify their ethnic origins. They have a sense of worth anchored in positive racial identity although they still perceive, correctly, that whites are the most favoured social group (Davey et al, 1980). It is curious and extremely unfortunate that this evidence has been ignored and the significance of racial identity minimized.

## Fundamental dilemmas in transracial placements

### The acknowledgement of differences?
Transracial adopters face the profound problems of defining their position as a family and in society. Should they see themselves as all other parents in the general population, or as different? If they decide on the former, then they may deny differences between themselves and their child but they must, in the interests of the child, differentiate the child and his or her natural parents from themselves in terms of race, colour and sometimes culture. Recognition of differences and the acknowledgement of attachment struggle together and are major difficulties. There are several ways in which this dilemma could be resolved.

The family may choose to minimize differences and emphasize the need to attach and integrate the child within the family network, perhaps from the moment the child enters the family, as part of the love, warmth and attention which a young child needs and which is the hallmark of good parenting. Others may try to steer a middle passage. Then there are those families who emphasize differences by their awareness of the racial origin of the child. Thus they try to help the child to develop a concrete sense of identity based on the child's race, colour or ethnic origin. All of these approaches involve acute dilemmas for the families.

Some families wonder whether they should request information about the background of the child and, if this is supplied, how it should be used. Should it be taken seriously, or should it be ignored? If the family should choose the first method, for example, ensuring that a life story book is provided, then the child has the option of an identity outside his or her adoptive family. If they choose to ignore the historical background of the child and feel that thus they will be better able to identify with him or her, then in times of crisis the child will have no solid racial and cultural identity and the family may not have the information to help the child in these crucial times. Some transracial adopters may prefer to isolate themselves from the cultural background and ethnic origin of their child because it is easier in the short run to escape conflicts.

Then there are others who are satisfied with superficial information because they feel that if more is revealed then conflict could arise in the family. In cases where a child is born out of wedlock, these families may struggle with their conception of what a normal family should be and various moral issues. Families with such children are sometimes in a moral trap. They fear damaging the child within their secure family relationship. Their dilemmas are similar to those of many adoptive families but exacerbated by the racial and ethnic issues already discussed. When it is difficult for the family or the child to attach themselves to each other, then at the end of the day the child will leave the family and become attached to the black community.

### The 'closed' family system as a contributory factor in racial identity confusion

Most transracial families operate a closed family system (Gill and Jackson, 1984, p.104). They are closed in the sense that the black child is cut off from the black community and all interaction takes place within a white social structure. In such a setting, all lines of authority descend from white society, all interaction takes place between members of the white society and there is no interaction which would enable a bicultural existence (Gill and Jackson, 1983, p.134). To protect the black child we need to develop strategies to enable the white family to become open so that there can be reciprocity between white and black society. The child's psychic structure must not only be that of his or her white parents and of white society. If a child does not know any other black people, he or she does not value them; all his or her values descend from the adoptive parents. The child may rationalize the situation by saying that the family is the only family he or she knows and thereby acquire a psychic balance. Creating links with the black community may not be easy, and some families will try to maintain their original form by blocking out positive responses from black people to the child and other members of the family. These positive responses are desirable and would indeed change the nature of the family and would be in the best interests of the black child and his or her parents, but may not be seen in this light by the white family.

To adopt or foster a black child means that the family is no longer white, if the interest of the black child is considered paramount. They can no longer live as a middle-class white family geographically isolated and alienated from other black people. The families cannot remain within the confines of the white world without serious psychological damage to the black child:

> White parents who adopt black youngsters must also be willing and able to identify not only with their black children but also with black people generally. They cannot be permitted to isolate their child and view him or her as different from other blacks; rather they must perceive their child to be an extension of other black people (Ladner, 1978, p.288).

Fortunately, some transracial adopters are able to speak for themselves and are therefore able to correct in some ways the folly of others.

> The black culture will have a significant, if not dominant, place in your family perspective because every other influence will be portraying and reinforcing the white culture – hence a token attempt with a few books and the occasional embarrassed conversation will not combat it. Think how it feels to be a black child looking at books, advertisements, films, TV, and hardly ever seeing a similar face – the message that comes across is that there is no place for black people in our society. (Parent to Parent Adoption Service, 1983, p.3.)

## Mixed race: its meanings and implications

The concept of mixed race, which has become part of conventional social work language, is misleading because it causes confusion in the minds of transracial adopters. It can lead them to believe that such children are racially distinct from other blacks. Consequently, they may neglect the child's need to develop a balanced racial identity and thereby a well-integrated personality. The term 'mixed race' should therefore not be used by administrators or professionals, and should be discouraged among people who want to provide homes for black children. Many black people find the term derogatory and racist because they feel it is a conscious and hypocritical way of denying the reality of a child's blackness. Certainly, mixed-race children are regarded as black by society and eventually the majority of such children will identify with blacks, except in instances where reality and self-image have not merged (Bagley and Young, 1982). Indeed, Gill and Jackson (1983) found no difference in racial identity between so-called mixed race and black children. It is therefore more appropriate to use the term 'mixed parentage' instead of 'mixed race'.

The term 'mixed race' is also inaccurate. The majority of the people from the Caribbean, and to a lesser extent from Africa, are of 'mixed race' although they are not regarded as such by professionals and transracial adopters. Their various racial mixtures, for example, African and Chinese, Indian and African, white and African, are the result of miscegenation under slavery and colonialism. Out of this process come the different shades of black people's skin colour which we see on the streets of London. These people and their children differ from the so-called mixed race children only in terms of time, and are only a few generations removed from the point at which the mixture occurred. If there is a need to ascertain the race of the parents of the child then this can be done by describing each parent.

For some prospective adopters, the lighter the skin, the more powerful the attraction; the darker the skin the more powerful the repulsion. We should constantly be aware that when most people use the term 'mixed race' they do not mean a child of Indian and African parents, nor a Chinese and a person of African descent, they generally mean the child of a white person and any other person who is not white. Nevertheless, in this society any child who has the slightest taint of black is seen by the majority as black. This is indeed unfortunate, but in a society where race and colour has been made into such an issue, for those children there are no 'in-betweens'. 'Mixed race' children are cemented in their blackness.

Many families who are misled into believing that 'mixed race' children are not black will go on to think that their children are capable of becoming culturally assimilated colourless Europeans. As a consequence, the child will be given a white mask (Fanon, 1970). The child in such an environment is given maximum protection from exposure to his or her real self, or from those who will act as a mirror to reflect the child's racial image. But can the child transcend the blackness and wear the white mask with pride? I would suggest that in this society it is not only impossible but psychologically dangerous.

It may be that those parents do not consider colour to be important, but such a blind attitude towards the role of group differences in the society is unwise. It is possible that parents do convey to their children that they themselves do not judge and relate to people on the basis of their skin colour, but they should also tell the child that many people in the society do. Failure to do this will obviously leave the child unprepared to understand and deal with the first time he or she is called 'nigger', or some other racial slur . . . (Ladner, 1978, p.125.)

The trauma of experiencing racism is inevitable, and this experience will result in a sudden and rapid disintegration of the white mask with all the consequences that depersonalization brings. The majority of these children have not been given the tools to function as a black person. Consequently, they are likely to be equally rejected by some black people who may say that they are not black enough, not in the colour sense of the term but in culture and attitude. Some children may therefore adopt a black mask which they wear fiercely but weakly. Professionals must recognize this process.

### The development of positive identity

It is possible, but rare, for black children in white families to form a positive identity. Gill and Jackson (1983) found that five of the 35 children were to some degree proud of their colour but only a small minority of the children had positive feelings about their colour. The parents of these five children had made some effort to give the children pride in racial background. No such efforts had been made for the children who preferred to be white or by those parents who brought up their children 'entirely white'.

Gill and Jackson go on to identify eight 'black and mixed race couples', seven 'mixed race' children and three black children, and use this sample to demonstrate that racial-identity confusion, as they found it in the transracially placed children, could also be found in black children in black families and 'mixed race' children in 'mixed race' families: 'They provide an interesting comparison . . . because . . . same race placements are increasingly regarded as the ideal by social workers . . . and it is in the black and mixed race couples that (it is said) the child will come to develop a strong racial identity.' (p.129.) They report that, like the transracially adopted children, none of this sub-group used the term 'black' when referring to racial background. The parents did not have a policy of stressing racial pride or identity and these children did not identify with the black community. They regarded themselves as 'coloured' or 'half-caste' and at least one wished to be white; they had no sense of racial pride. Consequently, they are roughly equivalent to the transracially adopted children.

This argument highlights flaws in the study as a whole. First is the difficulty of depending substantially on parents' responses. Green and Shapiro (1974) caution: 'parents [are] usually the persons best informed about their [the children's] behaviour – [but] are also the most emotionally involved and usually the most biased in their favour. Case records, social workers' reports and teachers' evaluations all have inherited biases and limitations.' (p.90.) Second, the instruments used for white middle-class parents may not be equally appropriate for black parents because they may fail to take account of different subjective experiences and racial and ethnic backgrounds. Third, this sub-sample of seven parents is an inadequate basis for Gill and Jackson's major claim. Only three of the couples were black, and five of the children were 'mixed race' thus further complicating the analysis. Fourth, the two researchers were white and so handicapped in their assessment of black families and children. It is possible too that the black couples who were allowed to adopt in the period of the study were 'white parents in black skins'. The resistance then to black families adopting makes it likely that successful selections in the 1960s and 1970s depended heavily on identification and involvement with white society, with the neighbourhood, the school and friends being predominantly white.

### Towards the interests of the black child

Given our understanding of the dynamics of transracial placements what should be the essential ingredients of any substitute home for black children? In addition to the ingredients necessary to enhance the normal development of any child, such placements should be capable of:

(a)  enhancing positive black identity.
(b)  providing the child wth the 'survival skills' necessary for living in a racist society.
(c)  developing cultural and linguistic attributes necessary for functioning effectively in the black community.
(d)  equipping the child with a balanced bicultural experience, thus enhancing the healthy integration of his personality.
(e)  providing continuity of experience based on the reality of British society.
(f)  minimizing alienation from the black community.
(g)  enriching the environment of the child's cultural heritage by balancing the black community response to its heritage.

Many transracial adopters find it difficult to refer to the child as black, and moreover, they feel, as we have seen, that telling the child about his or her ethnic origin is potentially dangerous (Gill and Jackson, 1983, p.130). It is indeed the fear of those families which contributes to negative self-concepts in the children.

They should be helped to recognize that racism is a reality in society and that although they cannot protect the child from it, they can prepare him or her to deal with it when it is encountered. Consequently, helping the child to develop a positive racial identity and pride in being black is an essential component of good parenting in a transracial setting. It is crucial to good self-concepts and for the healthy integration of the child's personality.

White families who have adopted or who are currently fostering black children should be given training. These training sessions could be conducted along the lines of pre-adoptive and foster care classes (Small, 1982).

The outline presented below is in note form with issues which could be used in training.

### Guidelines for selection and preparation

1   The geographical location of the prospective family must be considered carefully since it is important for the child to see black people:
    (a)   to reduce the feeling of isolation.
    (b)   to mirror the blackness of the child.
    (c)   to provide black role models.
    (d)   to protect the child from racial attacks and abuse.
2   The family should be sensitive to the prevailing race relations climate and be cognisant of the possible effect of this on the child's identity formation.
3   The family should have clear concepts of what a multi-racial society is, or should be, and should be willing and able to provide the child with a balanced view of the different races.
4   The family must be prepared to have black friends to demonstrate to the child that blacks and whites do have common interests and can interact harmoniously.
5   The family must be prepared to develop contact with the black community in order that the child does not feel that he or she is being cut off from his or her roots, which often creates the condition whereby negative images emerge.

6 The family must be willing and able to carry the child's past into the present and sustain it into the future, thus linking the child with its ancestral past in a positive way.

7 The family must be able to accept the child as a black child in a positive way and not dismiss the child's colour as insignificant, because in society generally the truth is the opposite.

8 The family must be prepared to find ways and means of linking the black child with other black children.

9 The family must demonstrate that they have the capacity to work with their conscious or unconscious feelings of threat from blacks.

10 The family must be prepared to foster an awareness of the child's religious background.

### Life style of the family

1 Reality for the child is defined and controlled by the family. Consequently, the neighbourhood they live in, the interests they have, the lifestyle of their friends and colleagues will necessarily determine what is reality for the child. These issues must be confronted.

2 The attitude of the extended family and friends towards black people and to a black child being part of their family, must be ascertained.

3 The family must be able to demonstrate their willingness and ability to differentiate between different lifestyles, race and colour without inferring the inferiority of one and the superiority of the other.

4 The motivation for wanting a black child should be carefully examined. Is it ideological, is it guilt, is it to fight a political battle, or to make a political statement? Is it religious, or is it out of pity? Is it concern for over-population? Is it to resolve curiosity about black people, or is it an experiment? Is it a second best, or in line with current fashion?

5 Every effort should be made to discover whether the family have the ability to put themselves in hypothetical situations and conceptualize and deal with the difficulties that are likely to arise with the black child, particularly during adolescence. What, for example, is the prevailing attitude in the family towards the black child dating the neighbour's daughter? Can they deal with what may appear to be sexual threats, and the reality of mixed marriage?

6 If there are no institutionalized support systems, particularly in relation to adoption, can the family, friends and local community

help the black adolescent to overcome these difficulties?

7   Can grandparents accept that they have black grandchildren which will change the nature of their family?

### Identification with white adopters and the black community

1   Can the family provide the environment for bridging the gap in the interests of the child's personality?

2   Can the family accept what may not be the attractive child in terms of race and colour that they initially wanted?

3   Can the family help or allow the child to develop a black personality without feeling that a wedge is being driven between the family and the child; does the family expect the child to be a white person in a black skin?

4   Can the child or children of the prospective family accept and relate meaningfully to the black child?

### Socialization outside the family

1   The attitude of neighbours and parents to black children mixing with their own children should be ascertained.

2   What opportunities exist for relationships as either boyfriends or girlfriends?

3   What opportunities exist for socializing with two cultures?

4   What is the attitude of friends, neighbours and the community to mixed marriages?

### Adaptation of family and child to existing and future conditions

1   Can the family deal with conflicts about colour within and without the family? Is the family aware of the stresses and strains that will be brought about for the child and family if the child should experience rejection on the basis of colour; can they deal with this type of problem?

2   Can the family provide the child with the skills that the black person learns in the black community: the skills to cope with racism? Can the family provide the cultural and linguistic skills necessary for the child to relate to, and be accepted by, black people?

3   Can the family accept the fact that not all people in the UK are white, and those who are not white are, by definition, black?

## The school environment

1  Is the school multi-racial? If not:
2  What is the prevailing attitude of teachers towards black people generally?
3  What expectations do teachers have for black children?
4  What concept does the school have of a multi-racial society?
5  What is the attitude of pupils in the school towards black people?
6  What is the attitude of families towards black children attending the same school as their own children?

# References

ASSOCIATION OF BRITISH ADOPTION AND FOSTERING AGENCIES (ABAFA), *The Soul Kids Campaign*, 1976.

BAGLEY C., and YOUNG, L., 'Policy Dilemmas and the Adoption of Black Children', in CHEETHAM, J. ed., *Social Work and Ethnicity*, Routledge and Keegan Paul, 1982, pp. 83-97.

BEAN, P., *Adoption Essays in Social Policy, Law and Sociology*, Tavistock, 1984.

CLARK, K. and CLARK, M., 'Racial Identification and Preference in Negro Children', in NEWCOMBE, T. and HARTLEY, E., eds., *Readings in Social Psychology*, Holt, New York, 1947, pp. 169-78.

DAVEY, A. G., et al, 'Who Would You Most Like to Be?', in *New Society*, 25 September 1980.

FANON, F., *Black Skin, White Mask*, Paladin, 1970.

FRICKE, H., 'The Little Revolution in Social Work', in *International Adoption*, vol.10, 1965, pp.92-7.

GILL, O., and JACKSON, B., *Adoption and Race: Black, Asian and Mixed Race Children in White Families*, Batsford, 1983.

GOODMAN, L., *Race Awareness in Young Children*, Collier, 1964.

GREEN, L. J., and SHAPIRO, D., *Black Children, White Parents: A Study of Transracial Adoption*, Child Welfare League of America, New York, 1974.

JACKSON, B., *Adopting a Black Child*, Association of British Adoption and Fostering Agencies (ABAFA), 1976.

LADNER, J., *Mixed Families*, Doubleday, New York, 1978.

MILNER, D., *Children and Race*, Penguin, 1975.

MILNER, D., 'The Education of the Black Child in Britain: a Review and a Response', in *New Community*, vol. 9, no. 2., 1981, pp.289-93.

MILNER, D., 'Children and Race: Ten Years On', *New Society*, June 18, 1983, p.55.

NAIPAUL, V. S., *A House for Mr Biswas*, Penguin, 1961.

NAIPAUL, V. S., *The Middle Passage*, Penguin, 1962.

RAYNOR, L., *Adoption of Non-White Children in Britain*, Allen and Unwin, 1970.

RAYNOR, L., *Adopting a Black Child*, ABAFA, 1975.

RAYNOR, L., *Inter-racial Adoption*, ABAFA, 1970.

ROSKES, E., 'An Exploratory Study of the Characteristics of Adoptive Parents of Mixed Race Children in the Montreal Area; thesis submitted to the Institute of Psychology, University of Montreal, 1963.

ROWE, J., and LAMBERT, L., *Children Who Wait*, Routledge and Kegan Paul, 1970.

SMALL, J., 'Black Children in Care: Transracial Placements' in *Good Practice Guide for Working with Black Families and Black Children in Care*, Lambeth Social Services, unpublished, 1982.

SMALL, J., 'New Black Families', in *Adoption*, vol. 6, no. 3, the New Black Families research report in preparation, 1982.

# 8 Some psychological models of black self-concept *Jocelyn Emama Maximé*

## Introduction

The literature on self-concept or self-image is voluminous and very varied. Ruth Wylie in her compilation of self-concept research (1961-1979) listed at least 500 studies carried out on the self. On close examination of many of these studies, and studies in general of self-concept, one finds a variety of definitions of the self. Also apparent in the research is the lack of appreciation of the importance of race in the assessment of one's self-image. Few studies before 1970 included the race dimension, and most of them highlighted the black child's negative image of him or herself. However, as racial self-awareness is being more thoroughly researched reports, from American researchers especially, claim that black children do have a positive image of themselves, unlike previous studies. Nevertheless, they stress that immediate attention should be given to whatever techniques or methods seem useful in enhancing the black child's self-image.

This racial aspect will be examined, especially through various psychological models, to gain an understanding of the black child's concept of self. Also pertinent to this examination is the black child's community-life situation, since evidence by Small (1982), Gill and Jackson (1983) and Breakwell (1983) have shown that in the UK a black child's self-image varies, especially if that child has been institutionalized. A summary of a few cases is presented to assist in the understanding and appreciation of some of the problems social workers encounter. Alternative names will be given to all clients mentioned. Then finally, and most important, a collection of techniques for use in boosting black self-concept in children or adolescents with low self-esteem is given.

## Self-concept definitions

> In psychological terms, identity formation employs a process of simultaneous reflection and observation, a process taking place on all levels of mental functioning by which the individual judges himself in the light of what he perceives to be the way in which others judge him in comparison to themselves and to a typology significant to them; while he judges their way of judging him in the light of how he perceives himself in comparison to them and to types that have become relevant to him. (Erikson, 1968, p.22.)

Erikson rightly maintained like Goldstein (1939), Maslow (1954) and Rogers (1962) that identity formation is a continuing process of 'progressive differentiations and crystallisations which expand self awareness and exploration of self.' (Burns, 1979, p.25.)

Most of the literature devoted to the evaluation or examination of identity (Breakwell, 1983; Burns, 1979; Cattell and Dreger, 1977; Fransella, 1981; Hall and Lindzey, 1978; Harré, 1976 and Holland, 1977) admit that there is an unresolved definition of identity. According to Breakwell (1983) the terms, identity, self-concept, character and personality, are all used interchangeably and, on examination of the literature, refer to the same process and phenomena.

In a review of the research into self-concept Thomas (1980) concluded that the self-concept is the image or picture the person has of himself. He argued that this self-image is developed through childhood and adolescence under 'the formative influences of home, school and social environment and forms behaviour' (p.24). Breakwell (1983) on the other hand departs from the staticity of identity with its formalized structures and views the self-concept or identity as a process, a selective, active, adaptive process. As mentioned previously, the definitions seem infinite. However, for our purpose our operating definition could simply be the appreciation that black identity or black self-concept is an active developmental process which is exposed to various influences within and without, and can be selective and/or adaptive. It is now appropriate to advance into possible ways in which identity formation might evolve and be evaluated.

The following pages will focus primarily on black persons who experience difficulty in maintaining a positive sense of racial identity. It must be emphasized, however, that this is not an absolute statement on the condition of the entire black community, most of whom posssess the survival skills necessary for the development of a positive racial identity.

## Psychological models of black self-concept

Within the field of social work as well as psychology or any of the caring professions, major psychological theories are taught to aid professionals' interpretation of events. When many of these psychological theories conflict with our aims and interests, it is easy to reject them out of hand without a proper consideration of the elements which can be extracted and utilized to clarify and improve our understanding. In fact few if any critics of psychological models ever take time to assess the relevance of these theories to black people.

On a superficial level many theories seem to be clearly incompatible and contradictory. Freudian psychology and behavioural psychology are generally viewed as occupying opposite ends of a theoretical spectrum. This can be seen in the psychodynamic emphasis on the internal mechanisms of individual behaviour, and the behaviourist focus on the external stimuli and mechanisms.

On close examination, one is confronted with seemingly obvious answers to pervasive and daunting questions still unanswered. A look at various elements of these traditional psychological models will highlight the eclectic approach strongly encouraged in this chapter. Additionally, the following discussion focuses on the interplay of theoretical perspectives with race and the self-concept as outlined by Maximé (1983).

### Social learning theory

This approach claims that the child's behaviour is shaped by external reinforcements. Most importantly this theory propounds that the primary process of learning is via observation of what models do in the child's own environment. Thus, the social behaviour we observe emanating from that child is determined by his or her conditioning, and the reinforcements and models to which he or she is exposed.

Let us consider this approach in examining what often happens to the black child.

1  Most black children in this society are reinforced positively when they show signs of adjustment and acceptance to society and its values. This happens even when society is so often hostile and rejecting to black people.

A case in point is that of a ten year old girl, Cherry, who had been resident in a children's home for the last 9 years. I was asked for a second opinion about Cherry by a black social worker who was finding the young girl difficult to assess though other reports were clearly positive; Cherry was described as 'a well-adjusted, obedient little girl who will fit nicely into a family'. The family placement interview undertaken by the social worker, however, revealed an individual with difficulties in self-acceptance. Cherry spent much of her time in a make-believe world producing beautiful paintings, all of white people. Furthermore, Cherry insisted that she wanted a white family as black ones were all too poor.

In my work with Cherry, I discovered further that she refused to interact socially with black children and denied the label 'black'. The mechanisms involved in this preference for white people comprise a complex weave of reinforcements of Cherry's unquestioning compliance and continuous rejection of her black identity through her drawings. Cherry's rewards came clearly in the form of favourable description of her behaviour and an acceptance of her as a 'well-adjusted' child. Here we have a black child described as 'well-adjusted' but unable to accept herself and hold positive feelings about herself.

The case of little Morris aged five is even more interesting. I went to see Morris briefly as he was being considered for family placement and there was some concern about the seemingly conflicting reports that came in from the children's home and the school. Reports from the home stated that Morris was ready for family placement and was a cooperative and lovable child even though a bit boisterous. On the other hand, the school spoke of the little terror and bully who 'got into squabbles over racial name-calling by other children'. I then visited both the school and the home and found myself in the middle of a complex psychological situation.

The residential home offered less than adequate emotional and physical care to the black children who comprised the majority. Morris' hair was falling out from lack of care and he was told that he was not black. His maladaptive responses to his situation could be seen when he told me that I should not refer to him as black, after observing me speaking with the head of the home. However, he did not realize that I had come with a black social worker who was some distance away. Thinking she was a possible parent and not connected with the authority, he ran to her begging her to take him away, talking positively about black people and himself to her.

In both the above cases, these children were rated very positively by their white caretakers because they seemed to have adjusted well to the system. In the case of Cherry, it is obvious that she was not 'well-adjusted'. How could she be when she disliked herself? As for Morris, at five he had already developed survival skills and was into some complex psychological manoeuvring. As far as he was concerned, being docile in the home was about presenting himself as a well-behaved and acceptable adoptee. He had not however worked out the school's importance, so he fought whenever his pride, self-respect and image were under attack. The case of Morris highlights a normative experience for black children who struggle to secure and maintain a positive identity in the school and day care systems.

2 Researchers in the area of social learning theory have found that mere observation is sufficient for the acquisition of behaviours. Many caretakers forget that there is a strong element of dependency in young children who are thus vulnerable to the prevailing attitudes and behaviours in their environment. The result here is that the black child tries to imitate and even adopt the behaviours of the adults around him or her. It is important to remember that simply through observation a child can acquire a variety of verbal, emotional, tactile and physical skills. This point is amplified by another case with a very young child and highlights the central role that conditioning plays in the shaping of the self-concept of a very young child.

I was asked to see a six year old, whom we will call Leroy, to devise a behavioural programme on his eneuretic problem. While exchanging pleasantries about what we had each had for lunch, his response to my lunch of dumpling and saltfish was 'Yuk'. I paid no special attention to this as there may be many foods most of us dislike. However, when I took this child to a special library as part of his treat for being dry, to my surprise he dismissed all the black books for his age group, asking for books on 'real' children. I was dumbfounded and picked Buchi Emecheta's *Dr Sean* and handed it to him, beginning to tell him how much he resembled Sean. His remark to me as he dropped the book was 'Yuk, I don't want to know about jungle people'. When I asked him why he had made that remark, his exact words were, 'My key worker always says "Yuk" to them, they are jungle people, I don't want to be like them.' Here we can see the process of imitation through assuming the behaviour of a model to the detriment of the child's own self-esteem and respect.

## Object relations theory

Coming from the bowels of Freud's instinctive theory, Klein (1932) and later Britain's Fairbairn (1958) developed an extension to psycho-dynamic theory, which postulated that the child does not only react to the objects in its environment but is also constituted by its object-relationships. Fairbairn stressed that early mental internalization of the environment and its reproduction in the unconscious mind determines personality. If we focus on Klein's work on children, she showed that the young child's perception of external reality and external objects is perpetually influenced and coloured by his or her experiences. Thus, she claimed that it is impossible to separate completely the outer and inner realities as they overlap. What is even more relevant, Klein spoke of a child's inexperience of a certain negative external reality and the frustration the child experiences as it is beyond his or her comprehension. Thus the child stands unprotected against the blind interaction and projects that rage on to external objects while internalizing the same object in all its terror and fearfulness.

If one examines Klein's work closely, one discovers that insight is given into the problem of confused black identity experienced by some black children.

1    Some black children, and in my experience most black children being cared for by white caretakers, harbour negative attitudes either towards black people in general or to what they fantasize black people to be. Many of them are totally inexperienced in dealing with black people and for many the feedback received about blackness from their caretakers constitutes their main source of knowledge about black people. This feedback, in most cases, leaves a lot to be desired.

2    Thus the physical realization of self as 'black', which is not perceived to be good and right, becomes terrifying to many of these black children. What results from this, as Klein rightly says, is rage towards others in the environment so that aggression is expressed especially to negative objects, in this case, black people. Many black social workers have experienced comments such as 'I don't want a black social worker', 'You . . ., don't come near me', or a hail of verbal and sometimes physical abuse.

This theory therefore sheds some light on the understanding of black identity confusion. It evaluates the self-destructiveness which is often a direct result of all the rage and objective identity rejection going on concurrently with an internalization of 'badness' because of one's blackness.

*Structural theories*

Broughton (1975) postulated seven stages of self-concept growth. The first three levels are of particular interest to this chapter. From his extensive study he concluded that 'stage 0', the first stage, corresponds to that of the pre-school child in which thoughts and actions are indistinguishable, while self is viewed as inside and the world as outside.

'Stage 1, refers to ages five and six in which self is being seen as the physical body and the overall view of reality is naive. Of particular interest, 'stage 2' is reflected in seven to 12 year olds who see self as an individual person, including both body and mind. At this stage, knowledge is viewed as personal.

Early work by Murphy (1947) and Wylie (1961) emphasized that by the age of three, the concept of 'objective' self is fairly well integrated, and as the child grows there is movement from objective self to a conceptual self as experiences and cognitive maturity aid in the development of self-awareness.

Numerous researchers, such as Horowitz (1939), Minard (1931) and Carter (1968) have also found that children as young as three years old are aware of race differences. Interestingly, both Goodman, (1946) and the Clarks (1947) in their early experiments found that black children, although aware of racial differences, expressed some psychological inability to identify with black dolls and consistently chose white dolls. As early as 1952, Trager and Yarrow, in an elaborate study of black and white kindergarten children, emphasized 'the complex learning in the young children's reactions to race,' (p.150.) They concluded from their evidence that many of the black children at even those tender ages (three to five years) found the topic of race too painful to discuss freely.

Professor Arnez (1972) from her prolonged and continuing research also substantiated the finding that identity confusion is observed as early as the edge of three in many black children (Clark and Clark, 1947; Goodman, 1952; Trager and Yarrow, 1952; Landreth and Johnson, 1953, Morland, 1958; Stevenson and Stewart, 1958). Arnez (1972) reported that 'of special import in all these studies was the tendency of black children to prefer white skin, white dolls and white friends. They often identified themselves as white or were reluctant to acknowledge that they were black.' (pp.93-94.)

Piaget (1932) proposed that children transcend various developmental stages from which they develop their attitudes to rules and numerous interactional skills. If we view one particular stage called the 'concrete operational stage' which takes place roughly between seven and twelve years, we can further understand many black children's experiences. This is the period in which clarity of thought develops and an acute awareness of separateness from others. In this period, the child is constantly modifying his or her behaviour in the light of the perceived intentions of others and has a marked preference for socializing with other children.

With particular reference to the black child:

1 Research has shown that this is the age when black children are most sensitive to racial issues.
2 This is the age in which we find a prevalance of 'identity confusion'. Within the context of Western society many black children in this age group confess to being forced to live in two cultures simultaneously: the white predominant one which is sanctioned as legitimate and the black one which is usually conveyed negatively.

Thus for some unfortunate black children their sense of blackness is repressed or carried around as a big heavy secret. Many black children, especially those in care in this age group, are totally accepting of anything said or done by whites, while rejecting of anything and anyone black. Comer and Pouissant (1975) claimed that because of this dual exposure some black people realize the need for a heightened awareness of 'black pride', self-confidence and assertiveness. However, some quite sadly develop a 'clinging to blackness' or a glorification of blackness as an end in itself. This is unfortunate because a black identity needs a strong inner core of positiveness which if absent, leads to destructiveness of self and other black people. Furthermore, Semaj (1978, 1979, 1980), Cross (1979), Williams (1972) and McAdoo (1978) have all shown that for some black children who have developed without a sense of racial awareness, the result is a preference for identifying with whites or racial-identity confusion. Age categories have already been researched by Semaj (1980) and his conclusions show that at:

Age 2½ – 4 – The black child understands categorization into various ethno-racial groups, but does not yet understand the basis of these groupings.

Age 4 – 7 – As cognitions mature, the black child has a clearer understanding of racial groups.

Age 7 – 12 – The ability to conceive racial groups and a more profound knowledge of these groups is acquired.

These three psychological models provide useful insights into the problems of identity and so a better understanding of the difficulties experienced by some black children. These same problems can also be found in some black teenagers and adults as the following research will highlight.

### Psychological nigrescence

'Psychological nigrescence' refers to the process of the psychology of becoming black, a process for black individuals who deny their blackness and harbour very low self-esteem. Thomas (1970, 1971) and Cross (1971) have each developed a five-stage model of this phenomenon to enable understanding of the stages an individual goes through in his or her journey towards a secure and confident black identity.

A summary of Cross' model will be discussed here as it lends itself readily to understanding the problems of black-identity confusion. According to Cross (1971), and fully substantiated empirical research, a demoralized black person in the process of change is characterized by:

### The pre-encounter stage
At this level, the person's world view is white orientated (eurocentric). He or she will even deny that racism exists. Interestingly, this stage transcends class distinctions.

### The encounter stage
The person now experiences or observes a situation that brings him or her face to face with racism. The experience is so shattering that it forces the individual to reinterpret his or her world.

### Immersion – emersion stage
'This stage encompasses the most sensational aspects of black identity development' (Cross, 1971). This is undoubtedly the most sensitive of the stages as outlined by Cross. Within this phase the person struggles to remove all semblance of the old identity while intensifying 'blackness'. Unfortunately, because the identity process is not positively founded, typical behaviours include sometimes the disparagement of white people while deifying black people. As some of us have found in our work, individuals at this stage can be encouraged through therapy to emerge gradually from this heavily ego-involved state to a more rational position.

### Internalization stage
The individual has now managed to separate the old identified self and the new self, thus moving towards a positive black identity.

### Internalization – commitment stage
Here the individual advances on the previous stage by involving him or herself in black groups or community issues.

In order to appreciate these stages more fully, the following two cases, one of an adolescent boy and the other of a young woman in her late 20s provide relevant examples.

## Charles

Charles was a boy of mixed parentage whose mother was a white business woman, and father an African who had long departed to West Africa. Charles enjoyed the first 14 years of his life in Suffolk. He was loved and protected by his mother who made it her duty as far as possible to see that he did not come into contact with black people lest he began worrying over his unknown father. Charles was happy and saw himself 'like other boys', this being assessed in material terms (pre-encounter stage).

Then Charles' Mum was promoted to London and both moved house there, totally unprepared for the events which followed. To be close to business Mum bought a house in inner-city London and Charles was enrolled in the nearby secondary school. Breaktime was a shattering experience for Charles. He found himself on the first day in his new school having to identify himself racially for the first time in his life. He was asked by some white boys 'Whose side are you on?' to which Charles said he had never given the question serious thought. The black boys on the other hand, stood looking unsympathetically at Charles in his dilemma (encounter phase).

Charles tormented himself for a week with this problem, never mentioning it to his mother, whom he anticipated would be very grieved. Quietly, as Charles examined himself, he started asking himself questions and becoming frightened by the answers. Charles said that during this period he became terrified of interacting as he felt he was not sure who he was. He explained that a part of him viewed himself as 'white with a bit of black', while another part of him was predominantly black and responded painfully to negative images in the news media and in some books about black people. Eventually he started feeling that he was a fraud because he was communicating in 'proper English' while he felt people expected him to speak in 'dialect' now and then. Soon he started, according to him, speaking in dialect but being aware of his 'proper grammar school English' every time he opened his mouth. Charles still refrained from confiding in his mother.

Eventually, Charles felt he could not face people outside the home as they all knew he was pretending and were watching him. Consequently, he became housebound for the next two and a half years and was diagnosed agoraphobic by various psychiatrists. When I met Charles he displayed all the symptoms of an agoraphobic; even his curtains were not drawn, and when I drew them he panicked at the light.

Charles then went into the immersion – emersion stage as we started therapy. First he had to confront himself as others saw him as a 'black youngster'. Second, he had also to accept his English accent as a part of him as he was British by birth and schooling. Third, he had to engage in confidence-building work and acquiring communication skills, which took care of his seeming agoraphobia. Eventually, he re-entered the education system and interacted with peers of various races as well as staff.

During this period, Charles went through a great deal of self-hatred as he confronted his 'old self' more and more. His close relationship with his mother broke down, as she had become a symbol of the white establishment. Fortunately I had forewarned her of this stage so she was duly prepared for this painful experience.

After some months of reading only black books and black newspapers, Charles entered the emergent phase in which he started communicating with his mother once more and accompanying her to various places. Charles is still struggling into the internalization stage, although he no longer has any symptoms of agoraphobia. As he gains in confidence academically, socially and spiritually, hopefully he will be a more secure person.

### Jackie

Jackie was a 28 year old dark-skinned black woman who came to see me because of a relationship problem which she feared could affect her work and place her once more in contact with social services. When she came for the first session she explained that her fear of social services was connected to her being in care for ten years. After fifteen minutes of listening to her relationship problems, I felt it necessary to engage in a technique I often use.

I asked Jackie to imagine that we were meeting for the first time at Victoria Station, London. She was to describe herself to me as if over the telephone so that I would be able to recognize her. Jackie went into minute details about the clothes she would be wearing and even accessories. I complained that I still had difficulty as other women were also in blue dresses like hers as they were very popular. She then took pains in describing her handbag, but to no avail. I still professed difficulty in recognizing her. Finally when she had tried describing everything without success, Jackie screamed for nearly three minutes. Eventually she uttered that I wanted her to say something she had not said for nearly 20 years, that she was black.

Thus began nine months of very painful but rewarding work for Jackie. Briefly, our work was sub-divided into three main categories: the cognitive aspect, the socio-historical aspect and the behavioural aspect. I will summarize at least one example from each therapeutic category so as to convey the quality of work done.

1   During one of the growth game sessions in which Jackie had profound difficulty in admitting she was a black woman she was asked to imagine being a bird of her choice engaged in any activity. Jackie, who was very good at mental imagery and role play imagined that she was 'a white dove, clean, sweet and smooth.' She saw herself flying high and enjoying the heights. Although her eyes remained closed, Jackie became visibly uncomfortable. Then she said that she was afraid 'of being discovered to be not really white.' She then asked to stop the game as she was beginning to feel 'vulnerable and heavy and would not remain up there for long.'

2   Part of Jackie's therapy was for her to engage in some historical reading to help her place her life politically into perspective. At this stage I recommended certain novels which dealt with racism and the struggle for one's identity. Morrison's 'The Bluest Eye' had a phenomenal effect on Jackie. Pecola's experiences of racism which she had to dismiss because of her obsession with 'blue eyes' which she could not have, brought Jackie to the encounter phase. Jackie started being aware of many of the racist interactions she encountered and even invited in some of her emotional relationships.

3   After about three months of the intense immersion phase in which Jackie felt she could not even associate with her white colleagues at work, she then entered the emersion phase. Her flat was smartly furnished but one of the things that struck my attention on my first visit was that there were no reflective objects in sight. On further investigation I found a small mirror, a fraction bigger than those in wallets, high up on the bathroom wall which one had to stand on tip-toe to use. Not surprisingly, Jackie's biggest task was to view herself naked in a full-length mirror. This only came after six months of intensive work. However, from then on, Jackie entered the internalisation phase. Part of her therapy involved expanding her social network. She formed positive friendships with black and white individuals and above all, she started loving herself and accepted herself as a black talented woman.

At this point, one must ask what the caring professions can offer to individuals in such a situation who seem clearly to be in need of some psychological and, in a few cases, psychiatric help. From my experience in working with social workers and workers in the caring professions, I have found that their input can be an essential one, especially if their approach is in preventative care as opposed to the crisis intervention model. I would now like to share some techniques I have always emphasized to all working with black children and adolescents; my experience so far has shown them to be of assistance in the formulation of a positive black identity.

### Techniques with the under-fives

As previously discussed, research has shown that from about the age of two, a child is aware of racial differences. Therefore:

1   When bathing the young child, even if the child has no speech yet, talk to him or her pointing out parts of the body, for example 'You've got beautiful little black fingers'; when this is done by white staff show the child the difference by placing a hand alongside.

2   It is essential to have black images or models or at least black people in posters involved in a wide range of occupations and activities. Too many nurseries fall short in this respect. It is unacceptable to have young children being brought up without any exposure to a variety of cultures; and to aim to nurture a young black child's personality in all-white establishments with white models in posters is highly questionable.

3   It is important to refrain from statements like this one, even if in joke, 'Have you really washed your face and hands? I have no way of telling if they are really clean'. As simple as the above sounds, and it is said so often by some adults, this can begin the eroding of a young black child's identity. Many young children who view themselves as dirty and display a diminished self-esteem have associated dirt and blackness. These are seen as synonymous and to be bad.

4   In response to a direct question by a three or four year old, such as 'Am I white or black?' it is important to associate the answer with a positive black person in the child's life, for example, 'Yes, black like Mummy or Jean who looks after you'. A child exposed to positive references about him or herself from confident caretakers is more likely to develop a secure personality.

### Techniques for twelves and under

1   When working in children's homes with five or six year olds who

never mention race, it is possible that they have been turned off the subject through too heavy discussions making them more insecure. The environment may not lend itself to discussions about race. It is important to use natural opportunities to open a discussion, when black people are on the TV, in the theatre, in books, or a black issue arises.

2   Racial issues should be discussed whenever they come up or as appropriate. If a child reports some incident, activity or statement in which there is a racist element the racial implications should not be overlooked or diluted. This must be encouraged because these discussions could help the child realize him or herself in terms of the society.

3   Children in this age group should be exposed as much as possible to black literature and black history. This is the age group, as was previously mentioned, in which clarity of thought and the moulding of personality begin.

4   Once more, positive black models in the child's environment are essential. It is vital that these models should not only be selected from music and sport, but also from the fields of science, mathematics and medicine in which black people have always made, and are continually making, a contribution to civilization.

## Techniques for teenagers

1   2, 3 and 4 for the 12s and under.

2   Exposure to situations which will inspire pride in their racial origin and which will nurture a more positive sense of identity.

3   Language is an often misunderstood area which could have grave consequences for the academic progress of the child. It is important not to condemn dialect (patois), but it is essential to make the young person aware that standard English is required in written and formal communication.

4   Double messages like Black is Beautiful on one hand, and most things black are negative on the other, should be avoided. Children pick up discrepancies, and many become angry and confused when they witness this ambivalence about blackness.

5   Avoid harbouring 'low expectations' of teenagers and communicating this to them whether directly or indirectly. Many black youngsters are already exposed to low expectations of themselves within the education system; perpetuating this in their home and

social environment could be very damaging to their self-esteem.

These are a few techniques which can be useful in helping black children and young people retain and develop their sense of 'self-worth' and 'racial pride'. It is significant that the issue of racial-identity confusion does not arise for white children. It arises however for black children whose sense of racial worth is not publicly and positively encouraged by the media, literature and the various systems in society such as education and the law. It is therefore essential that all working with black children, and especially those caring for black children, ensure that racial issues and implications are not overlooked. Black families, of course, have the task of heightening their level of racial awareness, so as to provide positive ammunition for their children's self-esteem. The black family face the major task of enhancing and maintaining the positive self-concept of their young in a world that constantly negates their importance. Workers should draw on this information, and other useful strategies from the black community at large.

Of importance is the warning and message from Comer and Poussaint (1975). 'A positive identity . . . must be built on an inner core of pride and positive feelings . . . or it may fade away under the harsh light of life's realities.' (p.17.)

All caretakers and workers involved with black children and black youth have a positive contribution to make towards helping them nurture their positive racial identity. To make this contribution, one may be required to change one's ideas and perhaps be involved in a re-education process which requires sensitivity and receptivity to race.

## References

ARNEZ, N. L., 'Enhancing the Black Self-Concept through Literature', in BANKS, L., and GRAMBS, J., *Black Self Concept*, McGraw Hill, 1972.

ASSOCIATION OF BLACK SOCIAL WORKERS AND ALLIED PROFESSIONS *Evidence to the House of Commons: Black Children in Care*, 1983.

BREAKWELL, G., ed., *Threatened Identities*, Wiley, 1983.

BROUGHTON, J. M., *The Development of Natural Epistemology in Adolescence and Early Childhood*, unpublished doctoral dissertation, Harvard University, 1975.

BURNS, R. B., *The Self Concept: Theory, Measurement, Development and Behaviour*, Longman, 1979.

CARTER, T. P., 'The Negative Self Concepts of Mexican American Students', in *School and Society*, No. 96, pp. 2117-19, 1968.

CATTELL, R. B., and DREGER, R. M., *Handbook of Modern Personality Theory*, Halsted Press, New York, 1977.

CLARK, K. and CLARK, M., 'Racial Identity and Preference in Negro Children', in NEWCOMB and HARTLEY, E., eds., *Readings in Social Psychology*, Holt, New York, 1947.

CLARK, K., *Dark Ghetto*, Harper and Row, New York, 1965.

COMER, J., and POUSSAINT, A., *Black Child Care*, Pocket Books, New York, 1975.

CROSS, W. E., 'The Negro-to-Black Conversion Experience: Towards a Psychology of Black Liberation', in *Black World*, vol. 2, July 1971.

ERIKSON, E. H., *Identity, Youth and Crisis*, Norton, New York, 1968.

FAIRBAIRN, W. R. D., 'On the Nature and Aims of Psycho-analytical Treatment', in *Journal of Psycho-Analysis*, vol. 29, no. 5, pp.374-85, 1958.

FRANSELLA, F., *Personality*, Methuen, 1981.

GILL, O., and JACKSON, B., *Adoption and Race*, Batsford, 1983.

GOLDSTEIN, K., *The Organism*, American Book Company, New York, 1939.

GOODMAN, M. E., 'Evidence Concerning the Genesis of Interracial Attitudes', in *American Anthropologist*, no. 49, pp.624-30, 1946.

HALL, C. S., and LINDZEY, G., *Theories of Personality*, Wiley, New York, 1978.

HARRÉ, R., ed., *Personality*, Blackwell, 1976.

HOROWITZ., R. E., 'Racial Aspects of Self Identification in Nursery School Children', in *Journal of Psychology*, nos., 7 and 8, pp.91-9, 1939.

HOLLAND, R., *Self and Social Context*, Macmillan, 1977.

KLEIN, M., *The Psycho-Analysis of Children*, Hogarth, 1932.

LANDRETH, C., and JOHNSON, J., 'Young Children's Responses to a Picture and Inset Test Designed to Reveal Reactions to Persons of Different Skin Colour', in *Child Development*, no. 24, pp.3-80, 1953.

MASLOW, A. H., *Motivation and Personality*, Harper and Row, New York, 1954.

MAXIMÉ, J. E., *Psychological Aspects in Caring for Black Children*, paper presented at the Commonwealth Institute Training Day for Residential Workers, 1983.

MCADOO, H., 'Factors Related to Stability in Upwardly Mobile Black Families', in *Journal of Marriage and Family*, pp.761-76, 1978.

MINARD, R. D., 'Race Attitudes of Iowa Children', in *University of Iowa: Studies in Character, no. 4, 2, 1931*.

MORLAND, K., 'Racial Recognition by Nursery School Children in Lynchburg Virginia,' in *Social Forces*, no. 37, pp.132-7, 1958.

MORRISON T., *The Bluest Eye*, Chatto and Windus, 1979.

MURPHY, G., *Personality*, Harper and Row, New York, 1947.

NOBLES, W. W., 'Psychological Research and the Black Self Concept: A Critical Review', in *Journal of Social Issues*, no. 29, 1, pp.11-31, 1973.

NOBLES, W. W., 'Extended Self: Rethinking the So-called Negro Self-concept', in *Journal of Black Psychology*, no. 2, 2, pp.15-24, 1976.

NOBLES, W. W., 'African Consciousness and Liberation Struggles: Implications for the Development and Construction of Scientific Paradigms', in WILLIAMS, R. L., ed., *Selected Papers. Beyond Survival: The Practical Role of Black Psychology in Enhancing Black Life*, Association of Black Psychologists, Missouri, 1978.

PIAGET, J., *The Moral Judgement of the Child*, Harcourt, Brace and World, New York, 1932.

ROGERS, C. F., *Client Centred Therapy*, Houghton Mifflin, Boston, 1951.

ROGERS, C. F., *On Becoming a Person*, Houghton Mifflin, Boston, 1962.

SEMAJ, L., *Racial Identification and Preference in Children: A Cognitive Developmental Approach*, Ph.D. thesis, State University of New Jersey, 1978.

SEMAJ, L., 'Reconceptualising the Development of Racial Preference in Children: The Role of Cognition', in CROSS, W., and HARRISON, A., eds., *The Fourth Conference on Empirical Research in Black Psychology*, Africana Studies: Cornell University, pp. 180-98, 1979.

SEMAJ, L., 'Race and Identity and Children of the African Diaspora: Contributions of Rastafari', in *Caribe*, no. 12, 1980.

SMALL, J., *Black Children in Care: Good Practice Guide (Transracial Placements)*, presented to New Black Families Unit, February 1982.

STEVENSON, H. W., and STEWART, E. C., 'A Developmental Study of Racial Awareness in Young Children', in *Child Development*, no. 29, pp.399-409, 1958.

THOMAS C., 'Different Strokes for Different Folks', in *Psychology Today*, vol. 4, no. 4., pp.48-53, 78-80, 1970.

THOMAS, C., *Boys No More*, Glencoe Press, Beverley Hills, 1971.

THOMAS, J. B., *The Self in Education*, NFER, 1980.

TRAGER, H. G., and YARROW, M. R., *They Learn What They Live*, Harper, New York, 1952.

WILLIAMS, R. L., *Themes Concerning Blacks* (TCB), Washington University, 1972.

WYLIE, R. C., *The Self Concept*, 1, University of Nebraska Press, Lincoln, 1961.

WYLIE, R. C., *The Self Concept*, revised edition, vol. 2, University of Nebraska Press, Lincoln, 1979.

# 9 Reviewing black children in care: introductory note *Juliet Cheetham*

The periodic review of children in care, which must be carried out by law, can provide excellent opportunities for critical assessment of decisions already taken and for comprehensive and detailed planning of a child's future. Practice varies widely from somewhat perfunctory and formalized procedures to energetic scrutiny of children's present and future lives which includes contributions from social workers, parents, teachers and other important people in a child's life (McDonnell and Aldgate, 1984). Reviews may be an integral part of consistently high-quality social work with children in care but they also provide the chance to rethink and, where appropriate, remedy decisions which, for whatever reason, turn out not to have been in a child's best interests. Such reviews and the action they may lead to can be tricky and painful, since they may imply criticism of earlier action or the putting into practice of beliefs and policies about child care which may not be universally accepted. This may be especially true in the case of black children because so many questions are still contentious. Should account be taken of colour and race? Do transracial placements have any place in child care? How may the identity of black children in care best be fostered? In what circumstances should black children, isolated from any contact with black people and with no account taken of their ethnic identity, be removed to alternative forms of care?

All these questions are raised by the following account of Bradford Social Services Department's special reviews of black children in care and carried out in 1984-5. Very few social services departments have made race or ethnicity an issue to be explicitly taken account of in reviews, and Bradford may well be unique in its intention to take action when reviews reveal circumstances detrimental to a child's interests. This exercise was a product of the general determination of the local authority and the department to improve services for black people, an intention which is being put into practice in very specific ways including

117

the appointment of specialist workers. One of these specialists was crucial in this review exercise and its aftermath. Given the general uncertainty about accountability and responsibility in reviews and the special difficulties of working with issues of race and ethnicity, it is probably essential that when such a review exercise is being started workers are given specialist responsibility for it. Once questions of race and ethnicity are part of mainstream social work practice specialists and indeed specialist reviews for black children might not be needed.

The review procedure and its outcome are described in extracts from departmental documents. They are excellent examples of detailed planning and precise reporting of outcome. They were not written as general policy papers, but the following points which emerge from them have wide implications for social work practice in child care:

1 High standards in social work with black children may be achieved if existing good policy and practice are fully implemented, provided account is taken of race and ethnicity.

2 To ensure that some adaptation in procedures may be necessary and some specialist responsibility allocated.

3 Line managers and social workers need to be involved with the review and its aftermath.

4 Social workers, on the whole, welcome help that might be identified as necessary during the review.

5 Full and precise reporting of such a review is essential.

6 It is essential not simply to identify problems but to act upon them.

7 This action may be difficult when, for example, it means helping white foster parents link their black foster child more closely with the local black community. They may not have the contacts to do this and some may have no wish at all to make relationships with people to whom they may feel hostility. There are special difficulties if foster parents of mixed-parentage children or the children wish to emphasize their white backgrounds.

8 The hardest question of all to decide is in what circumstances a black child's identity is so threatened that removal to alternative care should be considered.

The review revealed some black children cared for in a variety of circumstances whose identity and ethnic background were firmly in the minds of the care givers and part of their agenda of good child care. It is reassuring and right that such practice is identified. It shows the potential of social work and the progress that has been made over recent years from 'colourblind' to ethnically-sensitive practice. But the review also revealed clear examples of black children inappropriately cared for who, if brought up as white, may well be destined for considerable disillusion later in life. It is to the credit of the review that specific suggestions are made for improving their care. Bradford Social Services Department is clear that establishing ethnic issues as part of normal review procedures and taking account of their importance in planning for black children in care cannot be done through an isolated exercise. Merely to check that recommendations have been carried out means a follow-up, and the department plans to continue the review process every six months for the foreseeable future. Reviewing the cultural needs of black children, making sure they have a positive racial identity and have the opportunity for contact with the black community is, unfortunately, still often seen as an afterthought and 'extra', and not as an integral part of the children's development.

Apart from written, pictorial and other resource material the Department can provide for black children, implementation of their plans has meant a strong commitment in words and actions from individuals and associations within the Afro-Caribbean community in Bradford. The social worker concerned with the review is convinced that all plans for these children must include black people in their implementation and the black community must also be involved in their formulation. To this end Bradford policy is that no plans that affect Afro-Caribbean children and their families can be put into motion without first consulting the Afro-Caribbean community, its associations and its individuals.

Many departments and social workers now acknowledge difficulties and deficiencies in the care of black children but are at a loss to know how to remedy this. The Bradford experience starts to fill this gap.

## References

MCDONNELL, P., and ALDGATE, J., 'Review Procedures for Children in Care', in *Adoption and Fostering*, vol. 8, no. 3., pp.47-57, 1984.
MCDONNELL, P., and ALDGATE, J., 'An Alternative Approach to Reviews', in *Adoption and Fostering*, vol. 8, no. 4, pp.47-51, 1984.

# 10 The experience of Bradford Social Services Department *Mike Mennell*

***Extracts from Bradford Social Services Department's Circular 'Reviews of Children in Care'***

This circular draws attention to revisions to the standard review form. It draws your attention to the need for an ongoing record of access arrangements to provide information to parents and carers and, for an interim period, to provide a central record of access arrangements.

The Directorate also needs to review the services offered to children from Afro-Caribbean, Asian or mixed parentage children over a full review period. The circular outlines the required procedure. Reviewing staff are encouraged to use the ethnic minority reviewing sheet for ascertaining the cultural and religious needs of children from other minority backgrounds, for example, Chinese, East European.

All children in care will normally be reviewed during a period of six months and there is no expectation that additional reviews be arranged to comply with the study requirement. The Reviewing Officer will normally be an Area Social Services Officer or a Senior Social Worker.

As far as practicable the child, the natural parents and the current care givers will be included in the review process. This means their participation in the compilation of information and discussion leading to this, rather than necessary involvement in a review meeting. Actual participation in the review meeting is, of course, encouraged.

Reviews must, as far as possible, include, as well as the child, the natural parents and current care givers, any relevant relatives, any recent care givers and any agencies with relevant information. Again such inclusion must be within the specific process . . . .

The detailed study on ethnic minority children and their needs will lead initially to an appreciation of the overall problem and will identify services which the Directorate should try to develop. There will also be a requirement that future reviews take account of the cultural and religious needs of these young people with a monitoring process by specialist staff from the appropriate ethnic minority background . . . .

Where any review is of a child from a non-caucasian background then a specialist worker must participate in the review process or in the provision of information leading up to the review . . . .

The social worker concerned should advise an appropriate specialist worker and arrange a meeting with that worker and the child's present carer, together with the child wherever possible . . . .

The pre-review meeting will examine all the circumstances surrounding the child's cultural and religious needs and background as contained in the review document. The ethnic minority specialist worker will complete the form and submit it in writing to the Reviewing Officer not less than three days prior to the date of the six monthly review, together with any additional comments that that worker feels appropriate for the child's cultural and religious development. It will be the responsibility of the Reviewing Officer to ensure that this information is considered within the full review.

Where the Reviewing Officer considers it appropriate, he may ask the appropriate specialist worker to participate in the review meetings . . . .

A copy of the completed review form will subsequently be forwarded to the ethnic specialist worker for information and for any feedback comments.

In any situation where, on receipt of the review form, the ethnic minority specialist worker does not consider that the child's cultural or religious needs have been properly considered she or he should advise the Reviewing Officer in writing of the reasons for this doubt and may require a further review to be held for this purpose.

The ethnic minority specialist worker will then submit the same review form as follows:

(a) for Afro-Caribbean children or where one parent is Afro-Caribbean to the Afro-Caribbean Children and Youth Social Worker; and

(b) for all other children to the Ethnic Minority Fostering Social Worker.

This will be done regardless of whether the child is home-on-trial, in foster care or in residential care.

When an analysis is complete, areas will be notified of the survey results and the generally identified problems.

There then follows a checklist of issues to be verified by the Reviewing Officer. These include questions about plans for the child's future and contact with parents, which are common in review exercises, as well as a specific question as to whether appropriate cultural and religious care is being given in the care of children from ethnic minority groups who are identified as:

1  children of Afro-Caribbean origin where either parent or both parents are of Afro-Caribbean descent;

2  children of Asian origin where either parent or both parents are of Asian descent;

3  any other child where ethnic origin is sufficient to identify the child as possibly needing special cultural or racial consideration.

Children of mixed parentage will be seen to fall into one or more of the above categories.

As well as requiring the involvement of the specialist ethnic-minority workers in the reviews, the circular also asks all workers from ethnic-

121

minority backgrounds to cooperate in the exercise, despite the extra work involved, so as to provide an accurate assessment of background needs.

The form to be completed includes paragraphs to be filled in on recent family events, school progress, current care, medical history, the child's, social worker's and parents' views about the future and access arrangements. The part of the form which relates specifically to ethnic-minority children includes the following questions, requiring both answers and comments.

- Has the child expressed any views, either negative or positive, verbally or otherwise, concerning his or her colour or cultural background?

- Has the child had the opportunity to discover, and discuss, his or her own origins and racial or cultural situation?

- Is the child in touch with his or her natural community or cultural or racial heritage?

- What plans are envisaged to keep the child in touch with his or her natural community or cultural or racial heritage?

- Does the child have particular needs in relation to diet/religion/language/ medical/physical/education/other?

- Does the child have access to, and availability of, resources that develop a continuing sense of belonging to his or her own culture *within* the care placements?

- (A)  Have intended staff or carers received help and guidance in practical matters?

- (B)  Have intended staff or carers received training or guidance in race awareness, or cultural differences?

- Is it appropriate or practical to involve outside organisations and individuals in planning for the child's future?

To help informants to give specific answers and to increase knowledge of resources available they are directed to these notes for children from Afro-Caribbean backgrounds.

1  'In touch with natural community or cultural heritage' could include links with Afro-Caribbean voluntary organisations, contact with family *or extended family*,, contact with religious or cultural organisations.

2  Access to, and availability of, resources within the residential setting would include provision of papers, magazines, posters, clothing, television and radio programmes, music, etc that are specific to the Afro-Caribbean communities.

3  Practical matters would include hair and skin care, Afro-Caribbean food, Pentecostal or Rastafarian religions, sickle cell anaemia, use of 'Patois' as a

child's means of defining his or her view of themselves, parental country or origin, information etc.

Resource lists are available to help with these questions.

The notes for caretakers of Asian children are as follows:

1 'In touch with natural community or cultural heritage', could include links with Asian religions or cultural organisations, as well as contact with family or extended family.

Muslim children who have been in a white foster home or children's home for some time may find it difficult to feel at ease in the religious classes held at the Mosque. There is a possibility of finding sympathetic teachers of the Koran, and of Punjabi and Urdu. Further information is available from the Fostering Unit.

If necessary the child's social worker can provide an interpreter to assist communication between the child, natural parents and yourselves.

2 Access to, and availability of, resources within the home would include provision of papers, magazines, posters, clothing, TV and radio programmes, video films, music, and so on that are specific to the Asian communities. Ask the child's social worker for further information.

3 Practical matters would include: use of ritually slaughtered meat from halal butchers, and of Asian recipes; parental country of origin information. Again ask the child's social worker or the Fostering Unit for further information.

### The report on the review

The report on the review was circulated promptly within a month of its completion. The report on Asian children is not yet available because there is no specialist worker at present in post.

### Introduction

What follows is an overview of the situation of the 50 or so children of Afro-Caribbean origins who were in our care during the review period. Both the terms 'Afro-Caribbean' and 'black' are used to refer to any child whose parentage includes an Afro-Caribbean element.

A total of 53 children were reviewed during this period. As far as we know this is the total number of Afro-Caribbean and mixed-parentage children in our care though caution in accepting this figure is urged; during the review period several children were 'discovered' who were not on the official lists. Similarly, we are aware of a number of cases where black children have been received into care towards the end of the review period who have not been reviewed, others who have 'come in and out' during the review period, and those who have been reviewed but whose orders have not lapsed or been discharged. In some cases the child's situation changed during the review period, that is they moved from foster parents to residential care. The social worker (Afro-Caribbean Youth and Families) was involved in 42 of the reviews. Four of the ethnic/racial questionnaires were completed jointly between social worker (Afro-Caribbean) and the child involved. There is no exact information available regarding how many other children were involved in this part of the review process, though indications are that though racial and cultural matters have been discussed with some children the review form was completed in their absence.

Of this 53, 16 were in residential establishments, 29 were with foster parents and six were home-on-trial. Of the 29 fostered, only eight were with black foster parents of which the majority were relatives. Only one mixed-parentage child was with black foster parents who were relatives.

Of the 53 children, 35 were of mixed parentage, that is, one parent of Afro-Caribbean origins and one parent white. Information of the racial origins of two children was not given. There were a number of children from whom the nationality or background of the Afro-Caribbean parent was not known or, wrongly in two cases, attributed to a particular island with no corroborating evidence.

Of the children reviewed the dominant initial reason for reception into care was:

| | |
|---|---|
| Abandonment | 4 |
| Parental inability to care/relationship problems | 20 |
| Abuse/NAI | 8 |
| Offences | 3 |
| Mental or physical handicap | 3 |
| Non-school attendance | 2 |
| Beyond control | 6 |
| Bereavement | 4 |
| No information | 3 |
| Total | 53 |

In only three cases was the social worker confident that screening for sickle cell anaemia had taken place.

Excluding screening for sickle cell, there are 36 cases where further action pertaining to racial or cultural issues was considered necessary by either the social worker involved in the case after discussions with the social worker (Afro-Caribbean) or by the social worker where there was a lack of information available and where he or she had not been involved in the review. 'Further action' covered a wide range of issues such as practical matters, hair and skin care, cultural or racial background information, contact with the black community or individuals, ability to understand and combat racism, and so on. Some of the further action had been put into effect following the review process but information regarding the effectiveness of this will not be available until the next review process.

*Specific areas of concern*

We must naturally look at areas of concern where the racial or cultural needs of the children are not being effectively met. However it must be stated that in the majority of cases, with some alarming exceptions, both fieldwork and residential staff were willing to consider the racial dimension and eager for support and information in this area.

Of particular concern were:

1   The review form was found inadequate mostly in not allowing space for other comments, not having a clear space for inserting the specialist worker's name and designation, and confusion over the question concerning what constitutes a child's natural community.

2   'In touch with their natural community' gave rise to numerous comments amongst the children of mixed parentage. The most common theme was that mixed-parentage children had two distinct cultures and that we should not ignore one at the expense of the other or, more significantly, that in the case of mixed-parentage children with white natural or foster parents their natural and only culture was that in which they had been brought up by the white carer. In some cases there were feelings expressed that suggested that an awareness of black culture or an emphasis on racial background would have a detrimental effect on their 'white side'. Such feelings may betray an underlying racism, as they ignore the fact that *all* children in our society are exposed to a dominantly white culture and a white view of history and achievements. It also sidesteps the issue of mixed-parentage children, by the nature of our society, being seen as black and that, in any case, the majority of black people in English society have in the past a mixed racial background. These questions are explored further by Small in Chapter 7.

3   A major issue for all children, with white foster parents and in

residential establishments, was identifying a particular area of concern and then implementing it. The most frequent problem in this area was where fieldwork and residential staff had clearly identified the need for the child to have contact with black organizations or individuals but the child, because of past experiences dominated by a white view of the world and contact only with white people, found difficulty in doing so or rejected this outright.

4 In a small but alarming number of cases, and significantly all in cases where specialist advice or inclusion in the review process by the social worker (Afro-Caribbean) was not included, there appeared to be collusion between the field social worker and the carers in allowing, even encouraging, children to grow up attempting to pass as white. Comments received were of the type: 'She has been brought up as a white child;' 'Her or his hair and pale skin are not noticeably Afro'; 'His culture is that of white English'; 'Allow her to identify with her white rather than black background'.

5 In other cases raising racial or cultural issues had been put off by fieldwork staff or carers even though seen as being important, usually 'due to child's age', or 'will raise when necessary'. Whilst the age of the child may have significance in the manner the issue is raised the introduction of resource materials, books or toys that reflect a positive attitude towards black people, and this includes contact with black people as positive models, can be done at almost any age. To postpone this can, and will, lead to greater difficulties later on.

One notable exception to both the above issues (4 and 5) was the case where a child fostered with a white foster parent, a child who would have no difficulty passing as white, was constantly reminded of his racial and cultural heritage by the foster mother's own lifestyle and her insistence on constantly combatting all forms of racism in daily living. This foster mother was exceptional in many ways, as, it may be said, was the social worker.

6 There was a far greater acceptance of the need to concentrate on practical issues such as hair and skin care than to confront racial issues, attitudes and stereotyping. This is probably because of fieldwork staff's and carers' own fears and uncertainties in raising these issues. However, the use of practical tools does allow racial issues to be introduced in a non-threatening way and should not be demeaned if it is part of the whole process. In the case of foster parents some fieldwork staff felt that the inclusion of practical matters was, initially, the only way in which race issues could be raised without threatening the placement.

7 Concerning practical issues it became apparent that residential staff, being the main point of the day to day contact with the children, needed greater and more intensive training in these areas. This would apply equally to many of the white foster parents.

    Some of the residential staff involved in these reviews had attended the week long course in Afro-Caribbean issues (sic) in November, 1985. However, the day spent on practical matters (hair and skin care), whilst heightening their awareness, had not properly equipped them for day-to-day care that they could carry out themselves with confidence and expertise.

8 The review exercise seemed initially to create anxiety in many of the fieldwork staff and carers. This anxiety may be seen as being natural, and in time consideration of children's racial and cultural needs should become a natural part of all reviews.

9 Our policy now is not to place black children with white parents. This should decrease the number of placements where white foster parents are resistant to racial or cultural issues and where, in some cases, they have been identified as holding racist views.

    However, if children of mixed parentage continue to be placed with white foster parents, though of course there are arguments for placing these children with black families, this problem will continue.

10 Throughout the review process there was an encouraging take-up of offers of practical help, either through the resource material available via the social worker (Afro-Caribbean), or in a few cases the use of volunteers.

    As far as can be ascertained, however, there were only two cases where the workers involved actually made use of, by their own efforts, black organizations' offers of assistance. There was a corresponding lack of effort in making contact with black organizations offering educational and social opportunities, though one can appreciate the difficulties, and time involved, that this entails.

11 Concerning the question on the review form concerned with diet, religion, etc.:

  (a)  Diet was only considered important as a tool to introduce a cultural element into the child's (or children's home) life.

  (b)  Religion, including Rastafari, was not an issue in any of the reviews, though this was probably an indication of staff's lack of knowledge and appreciation of the importance of the black churches in Bradford.

(c) Languages, that is the use of patois, was not an issue in any of the reviews though several workers mentioned that they had children who had used patois as a means of identifying themselves.

(d) Medical matters were generally confined to the lack of screening for sickle cell, though other medical issues, not confined to racial dimensions, were included frequently.

(e) Education was used mostly to include the possibility of supplementary or alternative education within the Afro-Caribbean community organizations.

12 Concerning both residential establishments and foster placements, there was a distinct lack of resource material within the home or establishment that constantly reflected a multi-racial society or the positive achievements of black figures in history, science and so on, other than sport or music.

13 In nine cases racism in an overt form was identified by the child and the social worker as causing unresolved problems. This is likely to be an underestimation as in many review forms the child had expressed no views in relation to this as the matter had never been specifically raised.

## Summaries

The report concludes with summaries of the information gained on all 53 children. The following , which have been especially constructed to preserve anonymity, give typical examples of issues needing attention and of circumstances which were more satisfactory.

### Joe

Joe is a 15 year old boy of Jamaican parentage who was in the care of the local authority for offences and non-school attendance. His parents also felt unable to cope with his behaviour within the home. Joe had a strong racial identity and contact with the black community whilst at home, and the care plan needed to ensure that this was not weakened.

Through his various placements the right to have constant contact with the black community should have been considered an essential part of the care plan but presented continual difficulties. At one placement he was expected to 'earn' by good behaviour his attendance at his local black youth centre, at another his previous lifestyle (he enjoyed sound systems) meant that the hours he kept at weekends caused friction with both staff and residents. At one children's home the actual physical distance from the black community meant that his ties and identity started to weaken, and he began to associate with white children heavily into petty offending and solvent abuse. His offending continued in his placements, and there was the feeling that the only sanctions that could be imposed were to curtail his contact with the black community.

However, his contact with the black community did not cease throughout his placements. He was encouraged and assisted to take part in education classes run by a black organization, he spent most afternoons and evenings in the black youth centre building a sound system with other black youths, and black supervisors paid for it out of intermediate treatment funding. Alternative schooling was arranged for mornings, where he successfully completed a project on black culture. On leaving care he was found temporary accommodation with a black youth leader whilst awaiting shared council accommodation with another youngster from the Afro-Caribbean community.

None of this cultural content of the care plan can be said to have affected his pattern of offending; nor was it supposed to. What it did successfully was to ensure that Joe's right to maintain his racial identity and links with the black community was upheld, and that coming into care, despite the difficulties inherent in the system, did not culminate in another example of an isolated black child with a confused sense of identity.

### Joanne

Joanne is a 13 year old girl of mixed parentage, in care for many years both in children's homes and with white foster parents. There is no contact with her father who was from St Kitts, and she was rejected by her English mother who had remarried a white Englishman. Joanne had no contact with the black community and had a poor self-image of her racial identity, preferring to mix with white children to the exclusion of black children. Racial identity and pride in recognition of black culture and achievements had never been considered a factor in her many reviews.

A black young woman volunteer, herself of mixed parentage, was introduced to the children's home purely to advise and assist Joanne in the care of her hair and skin. From this practical beginning developed a friendship that continued with Joanne visiting the volunteer's home. Through the social work and committed staff within the home Joanne, at first reluctantly, agreed to participate in the local West Indian Carnival and spent some time in a black community association's premises. Joanne now still expresses the desire to be fostered with a white family but was recently becoming interested in learning about her father's origins and culture.

### Joy

Joy is a 15 year old girl with a Trinidadian father and English mother voluntarily received into care at the age of five and subsequently placed with foster parents. Joy's father is of extremely light complexion and both Joy's mother and the foster parents, in conjunction with the social workers in the past, have encouraged Joy to think of and pass herself off as white. The concept of a positive racial identity and of exploring her roots on her father's side vis-à-vis the black community and her ability to combat racism have been rejected by the adults concerned in her life, and specialist advice not been asked for despite guidelines.

### Rosalind

Rosalind comes from a Jamaican family and entered care because of violent and disruptive behaviour at school. She is now 17, and throughout her care placements has strongly and violently resisted any attempts to return home or have any contact with individuals or groups from the black community, or even discuss her attitudes regarding her race. Inside the care placements she has abused black staff, and outside her peer group has consisted of exclusively white associates actively involved in crime and drug use not normally found in the black community. At present in secure accommodation, it is planned she will return to Bradford to live in her own accommodation strongly supported by a keyworker and the intermediate treatment section. Though her keyworker is strongly committed to fostering a positive racial identity in Rosalind and she has been introduced to the multitude of positive things on offer in the Afro-Caribbean community in Bradford, it would appear that she will continue to reject any contact with black people or black culture.

### Corine

Corine, aged ten and of Barbadian parentage, came into care because of an unworkable relationship with her mother, and at present lives in a children's home with only occasional visits from her family. Though the care plan is for her to return home, in the intervening period her physical needs in relation to her hair and skin have been met by outside members of the black community who have also organized Caribbean evenings within the children's home. She has been encouraged to attend a Bradford West Indian Parents Saturday morning supplementary school and functions at other West Indian community organizations. Two black Afro-Caribbean residential workers have recently been appointed to work in the children's home.

## James

James, five years old, and of mixed parentage, was received into care at 18 months because of his mother's lifestyle and inability to care for him and had been placed with a white friend of the family who was subsequently approved as a foster parent. Whilst James could easily pass as white or of Mediterranean appearance, his white foster mother had constantly introduced music, food, magazines and 'ethnic' comics into the home and had made extra efforts to ensure that her social life (and that of James) included black people. Living in a predominantly white area of Bradford, where racist comment is an everyday factor at play and at school, the foster parent constantly reminds James, in a subtle fashion, of his origins, and encourages him to counter racist taunting amongst his peers.

## Beryl

Beryl, at 18 months and of Nigerian parentage, had been received into care shortly after her birth because of her mother's mental ill-health. Mother's access had been terminated due to her bizarre and sometimes violent behaviour towards the child on visits, and Beryl was becoming accustomed to being cared for and loved by only white people in the form of care staff and foster parents. Freed for adoption she was waiting for a black family, but in the long intervening period the fostering and adoption unit arranged for a black woman parent to visit and provide care, play and affection, so that a positive black figure was constantly a part of her early life. Basic child play and story books were provided from local black bookshops that had a black or multi-cultural content.

# PART THREE
# WORK WITH WOMEN
# AND GIRLS

## 11  An Asian Mothers' Self-Help Group  *Samar Sheik*

**Introduction by Shama Ahmed**

It is commonly supposed that Asian mothers are hard to organize in groups and by many white social workers this area of work is seen as an impossibility. Here, a mother of a handicapped child describes her experiences which impelled her and others in similar predicaments to form an Asian parents' self-help group, a support group to combat the inadequacies of the system. She describes vividly the hurts caused to her and others, however unintentionally, by individual professionals and by policies pursued in the health service, practices which can often be found in social services departments.

It is not a contradiction to point out the important supportive role played by social workers, mainly white, who had the concern and imagination to become involved and stay involved. A commitment to self-help principles should never lead to abandonment of vulnerable groups in society. There is a role for social workers in offering social and material support, leaving members free to determine direction.

Above all, the work described in this chapter is a testimony to the achievement of women who work for the group and it is proof, where none should have been needed, of resilience and strength and of what Asian women can and will do.

**Samar Sheik's story**

My initial disillusionment with the National Health Service began with the birth of my child. Although the actual birth and initial examination were perfect, and I was told I had a perfect child, this was not so.

I soon picked up signs that a mother's instinct just cannot overlook, signs that were mentioned in all the baby books as something to take notice of. Alas, when I consulted the doctor I was told that the baby was perfectly normal and that I should stop worrying. On a second and subsequently on a third occasion I was given the same advice. With a mixture of frustration, anger and worry I then approached the doctor at the local baby clinic who duly referred my son to a specialist, 'if only', as she put it, 'to put your mind at rest'. At least it was a step in the right direction.

So, in short, nearly three months of 'toing and froing' to the doctor produced no results for me, apart from the anger and frustration that only a young mother with her first child can ever understand. I know my experience is not an isolated one.

### Communication problems

Lack of thought on the part of the doctors which prevents them even trying to explain or sympathizing with the shocked parents is not uncommon. I experienced such uncaring behaviour which was aggravated by their assumption that I could not speak English. Imagine a mother with her first child, who has waited six months for the initial diagnosis of her child's condition, and understand the nervousness and anxiety experienced on such occasions. Once as I stepped nervously into the doctor's consulting room I came face-to-face with a most bewildering and frightening scene; the room was crowded with about eight or nine student doctors, apart from the paediatrician, who were all busy studying my child's case history. After taking one quick glance at me the doctors proceeded to discuss my child's condition amongst themselves. After what seemed like eternity the doctor turned to me and asked, 'Can you speak and understand English? I see you are on your own'. The only reason I can find for him to question my comprehension was the fact that I was dressed in an Asian manner. It is hard to describe the mixture of anger and frustration at the callousness of the doctors, and the shock and desperation at overhearing words like 'weak muscles', 'brain damage', 'effect on brain', 'no treatment', 'no medicine', and the questioning as to whether my child will ever walk.

Unfortunately, the same problems have been encountered by parents visiting the local child development unit where slow-developing or handicapped children are assessed for eight mornings or afternoons. At the end of these sessions the doctor, speech therapist, ophthalmologist, child psychologist and every other professional involved sit around a table with their reports and, as we see it, decide the child's future for the next 16 years. As parents we feel banned from this conference; in some instances repeated requests to sit in on the conference have been turned down. The child's future depends on the reports given by the professionals in these eight short sessions. Understandably, the professionals' joint decision has to be taken into consideration when deciding what school would be suitable for the child, but the parents' presence could surely only help in providing vital information where there are gaps, such as when the child, being in a strange environment, has not 'performed' as he normally would in his home environment. The fact that the unit employs all-white professionals can be very upsetting for a child, who comes from a totally Asian background into a place full of white people who all speak English. The language difference can be distressing for a young child whose visit to the unit is his first contact with English people. My child, being shy and clingy, just clung to me throughout the two weeks and was not half as active as he would have been at home.

As parents we can go blue in the face trying to get across the fact that this child can do something at home, but the professional will not take this into account. How can any child outside his home environment, surrounded by as many as four professionals at one time, all peering and poking at him, be expected to act naturally? If parents were allowed to sit in on the conference, any incorrect statements or misunderstandings, arising because of the child's inability to cooperate could be corrected.

There are other examples which highlight the damage caused by the lack of communication between parents and professionals. When my son was having a simple hearing test and failed to respond to bells shaken behind him he was pronounced partially deaf, enough to require hearing aids. My objections that he could hear me at home when I spoke to him from another room were ignored. I was told I was being childish and selfish to refuse the hearing aids. Eventually, I was bullied into accepting them, having been told that my son's failure to speak was the consequence of my refusal. There was no improvement, but when he started to attend a special school for physically handicapped children the audiologist there totally disagreed with the decision to put hearing aids on my son. Believing them to be both unnecessary and detrimental she asked my permission to remove them.

For other parents, even when the diagnosis is clear, the way in which the news is broken is often callous.

'The devastating news about my son was given to us in the hospital corridor' says Mrs C., who had the added responsibility of explaining to her husband what was being said as he was unable to understand English. Just visualize for one moment a mother and a father walking through a hospital corridor where their child is being kept for tests when they are bluntly told 'Your child has brain damage'.

## The lack of interpreters

In such circumstances interpreters are clearly essential, but they frequently do not exist. This I discovered at a visit to the local ante-natal clinic with a neighbour who does not speak a word of English and who was at an extremely important stage of her pregnancy. She already had two disabled children and it was vital that she attended her ante-natal check-ups. As I was going away on holiday I asked for an interpreter on future visits. 'Interpreters,' said the receptionist, 'we don't provide interpreters'. On another occasion in the maternity hospital I was on bed-rest because of a threatened miscarriage. This meant I was not allowed out of bed, even to visit the bathroom, as I was told even a slight amount of movement could mean the difference between a miscarriage and a stable pregnancy. I was therefore surprised to hear my name being called. The nurses on duty could not understand what the lady in the next bed was saying, so I was summoned to help. Eventually, I did miscarry. I cannot blame the nurse as I could have reminded her of her previous insistence that I should stay in bed, but this incident illustrates two essential points. The first is the lack of an interpreter, when the nurse could not understand what a patient was trying to say. The second is the fact that a nurse can forget which of her patients is on bed-rest as soon as she is faced with another need. Would this have happened to white patients too?

It is wrong that the responsibility is on the patient rather than on the hospital to provide interpreters. Many Asian people frequently take their children to interpret. This brings its own problems. In the gynaecological department, taking your children of 12–16 to interpret would seem utterly shameful for most parents. A further problem is that these children have to miss school. Similarly, it cannot be assumed that people would wish to ask friends or acquaintances to interpret for them in highly personal and confidential situations.

## A social worker and parents respond

The lack of interpreters was just one of the reasons that persuaded our social worker at the local child development unit to look into the possibility of starting a self-help group for Asian parents of handicapped children.

Since so many Asian parents are not very fluent in English, how are they to find out what services are available? And because of cultural differences, even if the language is there, Asian parents feel barred from associations whose members are mostly white people. The problems Asians face seem unending but even the few noted above supply enough evidence of the need for an Asian group.

Our social worker at the time who had contact with Asian families of handicapped children recognized these problems and suggested to myself and a few other Asian mothers, all with disabled children, that we should get together and form a group. This started nearly three years ago. We found a large number of women whose inability to communicate in English had meant that their knowledge of services and of the nature of their child's handicap was practically nil.

The aims of the association, now constituted into a formal organization, are two-fold:

1  To provide a totally Asian self-help group in order to help Asian parents of handicapped children in any way possible; first, by providing a place where parents can meet frequently to discuss any problems concerning their handicapped children in complete confidence; second, by providing information about welfare rights and other services available for the handicapped child.
2  To inform relevant professionals about the particular needs of Asian parents and children.

Nineteen families have had contact with the parents' group over the past years. What has it meant to them? We list some reactions:

The group has provided moral support as well as practical help with day-to-day problems with my child: moral support because the feeling that you are part of a group provides confidence when dealing with difficulties with one's child. For example, I have become confident enough to stand my ground when I feel my point is plausible, however much the professionals may feel they are right. With due respect to the professionals' qualifications, I feel a mother's instinct can't always be wrong.

I come to the group to learn about benefits I'm entitled to and to meet people and make friends.

We share problems

Getting together is the main thing for me.

Before this group I was going mad, but this group helped me realize my son was not the only one.

I like meeting people and helping others.

I cannot speak English and therefore I come to find out things.

Throughout the group's existence we have had a social worker or social work student coming to most of our meetings. We can therefore readily get advice when our own knowledge is limited. Some of the group members speak good English so they can interpret between the social worker and non-English-speaking parents as necessary. Although the social worker is present it is the mothers themselves who make decisions about group activities and it is one of us who takes the lead each meeting.

The organization did not grow without problems. When the first six mothers got together at the beginning we all felt very shy and reserved. We were not used to sharing our worries with strangers. It took time to discover that we could trust each other as we did not all share a common language or religion. However, the fact that we all share the same worries and problems associated with our children helped to bring us together and bind us in mutual friendship and concern for our children in a relatively short amount of time.

There were also practical difficulties to be overcome. A meeting place was obviously the most important issue to be dealt with. For the trial period of 12 weeks transport was provided for all the members to a children's home on the outskirts of the city. When we realized we not only *wanted* a group but that it was a necessity in British society today where Asian people are considered a devalued 'ethnic minority', we wanted a meeting place of the right size in the area most highly populated by Asians. Luckily, we were offered two places quite centrally situated which were very convenient for most of the families. This has also enabled us to hold family get-togethers; the parties and summer outings we arrange mean that families can have fun together. They are a good way of involving the husbands, other children and friends.

After much discussion we decided on weekly meetings at a time which does not clash with religious commitments or the regular out-patient clinics likely to involve our children.

We also had to arrange transport for the few mothers who lived in the outer areas of the city. Once again, we called upon the help of the social services department which arranged a voluntary driver. It is especially important to provide transport for a group such as ours, because for some Asian women the thought of travelling long distances by public transport is enough to deter them from becoming involved.

Our meetings now provide a forum for parents or any other person directly involved with a handicapped child to come and discuss any of their problems. We found through the initial meetings that many Asian families were completely ignorant about the facilities and financial rights available for their handicapped children. Communication problems also meant that people trying to find out about their rights had been turned away. We therefore decided that our group should become a place where people could not only speak in confidence about problems but also find out important information relevant to their needs. A few members have provided a voluntary interpreter service to other members when required. We have also helped members fill in forms and answer letters relating to their children. Sometimes we have invited speakers to our meetings to tell us about their services, for example disability rights, speech and occupational therapy, short-stay provisions and adoption and fostering services. Some of these professionals have kept in touch with us, visit the group from time to time and put new parents in contact with us.

Because all of the original six mothers had found the group so helpful we wanted to advertise so that more people could benefit from our meetings. We therefore publicized the group through leaflets and posters aimed particularly at potential referrers, social workers, doctors and health visitors as well as at the consumers, the families themselves. We displayed posters in doctors' surgeries, special schools, social services department district offices and in the local child development unit.

We have also given talks to social work students who are, after all, some of the most important people to be educated on the issues of physical and mental handicap in Asian families. In so many families the social worker is the person the homebound mother has most contact with, and therefore the more conversant the social worker is with cultural values and problems of racism and discrimination the more able he or she can be to help the mother both emotionally and practically.

The local television centre filmed a group meeting and interviews with parents and professionals. This also helped publicize the need for such an organization. This was an exciting occasion for the group members, although it brought its own problems. Most husbands were supportive of their wives' involvement but for a few it was felt to be against their religious and cultural expectations and they did not take part. We were also interviewed by the local press which provided another helpful outlet for our views. It is not always comfortable to draw attention to oneself, to one's problems and fears, but because we are doing these things as a group it is less stressful than doing them alone.

Because we are not ashamed of our handicapped children we hope that slowly other Asian people will become more accepting of handicap and will not see it as a punishment for some possible wrongdoing. Our long-term aim is to promote better understanding of disability in the Asian community, but our first priority has been to push for a better deal from the health and social services.

As we are becoming better known as a group we are becoming aware of other groups with similar aims to our own, and are beginning to make contact to see if by acting together we can bring about changes in order to make services more accessible for the special needs of Asian families. The difficulties of finding time to do this in addition to caring for a handicapped child should not be underestimated; and it is hard to have to criticize 'the hand that feeds'.

# 12 Cultural racism in work with Asian women and girls

*Shama Ahmed*

This chapter has two principal objectives: the first is to illustrate by means of case examples the dominant trends in conceptualizing the personal and social difficulties facing Asian women, that is women of South Asian descent. Second, it is intended to summarize systematically some pitfalls of relying too readily on cultural explanations.

It seems obvious that social workers will benefit from developing an understanding of their clients' cultural backgrounds. Clearly, in any interpersonal contact, but especially in a therapeutic relationship, it is important to understand and acknowledge the cultural dimension. This awareness is important but it is not enough. What I wish to do in this chapter is to highlight the significance of cultural differences but also to move beyond the acknowledgement of the importance of culture to an analysis of the dangers of relying too much on it. It is my contention that cultural explanations are not only be *used*, but also *abused* in current practice. They are far too frequently a way of disparaging other cultures.

Perhaps, to practitioners struggling to introduce into the work of their agencies a greater understanding of the culture of their clients this coolness towards the cultural dimension may come as something of a surprise. However, the argument is not *against* better cultural understanding but against an over-reliance on cultural explanations which distract attention both from significant emotional factors as well as structural factors, such as class and race. The important point is that for Asian clients the centrality of racism needs to be more explicitly acknowledged in the assessment process, and cultural explanations need to be considered in the context of racism.

Policy and action come out of the way we conceptualize things and concepts arise out of the material, historical and cultural matrix of a

hospital. The social worker found that Kamla had been seeing an Asian boy of 21 while her family thought that she was at school. When Kamla's elder brother discovered this, she got frightened and took an overdose.

In her discussion with the social worker Kamla quickly hinted at the prospects of an arranged marriage, which was distasteful to her; she rather hoped to marry her boyfriend. She made it clear that she wanted the freedom of her English contemporaries.

When problems are defined in such a way by young Asian girls, practitioners may fall for a 'victim' approach. This may lead to a flaw in the practitioner's thinking, an extremely dangerous flaw. We shall see how it can manifest itself.

Apart from identifying the problems of young Asian girls as a product of conflicting cultures, the status of women is also compared implicitly or explicitly in the two cultures. In this comparison exercise most practitioners regard the position of English girls and women as unconditionally superior, as something Asian women could aspire to. Indeed, many young Asians themselves may pass through a stage when they uncritically pose the English way of life as superior and desirable.

But such explanations and analysis often fail to take into account the young people's class and race position in society. Racially-aware practitioners can try to make their young clients conscious of the sources of their values and expectations. This can start by examining the notion of freedom in the context of the client's class position. What is the model of freedom working-class Asian girls carry in their heads? If it is the model of freedom internalized and experienced by working-class white girls then the social characteristics of this group need to be explored.

Broadly speaking, in an inner-city comprehensive school white school girls are a group of low achievers, whose lives are more or less entirely given over to the pursuit of boys, catching boys, going to discos to meet boys, following pop music to fantasize about boys, invariably with hopes of marrying early. Few girls in this social group have interests outside these narrow fields and white feminist workers have to strive hard to broaden their horizons. Can such dependence be called genuine freedom or genuine liberation? Furthermore, the problem is that for Asian girls to aspire to such a model of freedom could not be more at variance with the aspirations of their parents.

Asian parents may live in working-class areas but clearly their culture is not a manifestation of the English working class culture. In fact, the irony is that when Asian parents express high academic and career aspirations for their children, including daughters, these aspirations are discredited as unrealistic. It is seen as an unhelpful cultural value, rather than an adverse commentary on the British class structure and the stratified educational system which seems, on the whole, to 'cool-out' the aspirations of English working-class parents.

In working with someone like Kamla, one must also remain aware that the so-called crisis of cultural conflict may sometimes be masking a crisis of racial identity and self-image. Frequently, what the young client might know of Asian cultural traditions is only an adaptation of that culture to inner-city living and poverty in a foreign setting. Sometimes, the reaction is resentment towards one's own group which has been devalued by the outside world and a lashing-out at the values held most dearly by that group.

The social worker could start by trying to understand some of the cultural values and traditions of the Hindu community as well as the quality of relationships in this particular family. There were many loving relationships and after the overdose the family had become quite concerned.

Kamla's social worker also talked with Kamla about the implications of marrying her boyfriend. She found that Kamla barely knew him. All that existed was a surreptitious, clandestine relationship which had been very exciting to a 16 year old girl. Kamla's social worker asked to meet the young man and found a wide disparity between his intentions and Kamla's hopes. Very soon afterwards he disappeared. When Kamla had begun to overcome her grief her goal became the restructuring of arrangements with her family, and that became the social worker's task. Negotiations included college studies and looking for a Saturday job for which family help was enlisted.

The social worker's intervention was considered effective. In this case, the social worker developed a knowledge of the family power structure, identified the strengths the family derived from their particular culture and, by showing sensitivity to ways in which she might gain or lose acceptance of the family, she was able to resolve a number of problems.

### Case 3

The third case concerns a 16 year old Sikh girl who came to the attention of the social services. The girl was pregnant and wanted to marry her Muslim boyfriend against her family's wishes. She was received into care and although she miscarried she was successful in gaining the support of many white social workers, especially feminist practitioners. Her goal was marriage and freedom from parental influence. It took an Asian feminist worker to challenge the actions of her white feminist colleagues. She said that she would be relentless in dissuading any girl who wanted to marry at sixteen. White feminist workers involved in the case would usually be the first to condemn sexism in society which places young girls at a disadvantage, restricts their aspirations, idealizes romantic love and encourages early marriage. Indeed, this group of practitioners in a general discussion had no difficulty in describing marriage as a cage for young white girls; yet they had supported and helped the Asian girl of 16 in her desire to marry her first boyfriend. Is that not puzzling? What seemed to happen is that there was an over-identification with the young Asian girl because she was seen as Westernized and therefore naturally 'progressive'. Clichés abounded immediately: the 'plight of the girl', 'caught between two cultures', 'held down by tradition-bound parents'; she was seen as the main person worthy of sympathy and attention in the family.

In this form of analysis the oppression of Asian women is firmly located in the home alone. Yet a question that could be asked is: if a young girl wishes to opt out of parental domination, what is she opting for? In their desire for social and sexual freedom, girls have not always achieved genuine liberation; lacking in self- and social-awareness the young client sometimes drifts into a situation of sexual exploitation. Such double think, such simplistic over-identification with Westernized young people against their family can be attributed to racism; racism which manifests itself in a strong assimilative ethos. This ethos creeps in through the subterranean burrowings of the mind and clouds the thinking of well-meaning liberal-minded practitioners.

It is not suggested that such cases are easy. Such cases are very hard for a counsellor, even one from a similar culture, just as child abuse referrals from English families are very hard for English social workers. The important point is that when value conflicts are highlighted, premature stereotyping or labelling and devaluing of other cultures should be avoided.

What I wish to do next is to move beyond analysis of case material to a systematic summary of some of the dangers of relying too readily on cultural explanations (Ahmed, 1982).

First, deductions that are made about a culture to which one does not belong can sometimes be over-simplified and lacking in insight. For example, Sandhia, a one year old baby girl of Sikh parents was admitted to hospital with a fractured skull. At the case conference held by the health visitor, social workers and doctors there was a tendency to assume that, because of a traditional preference for male children in Asian culture, the female child must have been unwanted and therefore neglected. Later investigations showed that Sandhia was a much loved and long-awaited child of a somewhat slow mother who was unable to anticipate fully a growing child's activities and needs. This case highlights an important difficulty in cross-cultural communication: learning to differentiate between aspects of behaviour which are associated with consistent cultural patterns and those associated with individual personality differences.

Second, cross-cultural explanations pose the problem of knowing what is normal or abnormal within a culture. For example, an Asian referral from a social worker concerning a suspected incest case had a note stating 'This man should be told that this form of behaviour is unacceptable in our society'. Incest is not a norm in Asian society either.

Another example to illustrate this point is the outright rejection of an application from a single Asian woman to foster or adopt a small child. The application was not even considered worthy of investigation. This was justified on the grounds that single Asian women are stigmatized in Asian society; a typical instance when complex social phenomena may be reduced to grossly stereotyped cultural images.

Third, an over-dependence on simplistic cultural explanations is disturbing because the underlying emotional and psychological content in clients' problems may suffer relative neglect. This tendency is frequently apparent in work with Asian youngsters. It is interesting that, although the social work profession as a whole leans towards the psychological model in solving problems, the difficulties of young Asians are frequently seen as a feature of their traditional cultures. Thus there is a tendency to regard cultural clash as an explanation for most problems when working with Asian girls in difficulties, and 'culture conflict' has remained a favourite diagnostic label of social workers and others. It is not denied that the conflict exists between traditional Asian and Western values, but simplistic 'catch-all' cultural-conflict labels can impede a proper analysis of the client's psycho-social situation. It is noteworthy that, as a result of the diagnostic popularity of the cultural-conflict label, young Asians often present problems to white professionals in a way which experience has told them elicits a sympathetic response. For example, complaints of ill-treatment by parents and fears of an arranged marriage are now known ways to capture attention. However, the presenting problems may mask serious emotional difficulties or deep problems of racial identity. A more detailed analysis may show that cultural-conflict complaints may be a way of presenting other underlying problems, as physical symptoms sometimes are (Ahmed, 1978).

Fourth, a preoccupation with cultural-conflict explanations may lead to a denial of the crisis of racial identity and self-image. For instance, some Asian girls and young women, but by no means all, sometimes show a contempt for their parents, their colour and their culture. They may be ashamed to speak in their mother tongue or express a dislike of all 'Pakis', including a refusal to see Asian social workers. Why these Asian youngsters show a strong preference for the dominant white majority group is frequently insufficiently understood by white practitioners. Clearly, these are deep problems of racial identity not just instances of adolescents making a bid for more freedom. Yet this over-identification with white cultures is interpreted too readily by many practitioners as a positive indication of cultural assimiliation. Such superficial interpretations can mean that interventions which require supporting positively a client's cultural and racial identity are rarely identified. Furthermore, this type of thinking and assessment suggests that 'Asianness' and 'West Indianness' are conditions to be overcome, and that salvation lies in adopting white culture; and any white culture is deemed superior to any black culture.

Fifth, another pitfall of relying overmuch on simplistic cultural-conflict labels can be that the generation gap and family conflicts may never be related to young people's desire to resist racism. Yet a rejection of parental culture does not necessarily indicate identification with the dominant white culture but may result from a desire to forge a new black consciousness. Young Asian women (and men) may oppose certain family practices such as arranged marriages, but conflict can also exist between parents and children which is of a political nature. One criticism which the young Asians make of their parents, although historically it may not be entirely accurate, is that they have not stood up for their rights and forged a secure place in British society. Similarly, young women of Afro-Caribbean origins are developing new strategies to mark their presence in British society. In short, young women at work and even at school are not always passive recipients of Western values. Many Asian women quickly discover that white culture is equally hostile. Racism, white sexism, and work-place exploitation force them to be more critical. In fact, it is frequently the case that Asian women who fight oppression in the home also reject the social reality as it exists outside.

Sixth, no encounter is simply interpersonal or intercultural. All encounters are affected by the history of the relationship between the parties involved and by structural factors, that is the different positions they occupy in the social and economic structure of contemporary British society. Cultures are ranked in order of merit by the majority population, and practitioners' socialization as members of this society can rarely fail to give them a negative stereotype of non-white cultures as backward and under-developed. This is the historical heritage of a post-imperial society. Moreover, unlike other professionals such as teachers, a social worker's sole contact with members of minority cultures may be limited to people who are having difficulty in coping with life's stresses. A combination of these factors can result in the cultural-difference model unwittingly turning into a cultural-deficit model. Negative images of Asian and Caribbean family life have crept into social work analysis. Set against the test of white family and marital theory, the Afro-Caribbean family is often seen as a tangle of pathology, virtually non-existent as a unit or rapidly falling apart, with mothers too strong and fathers abdicating responsibility. On the other hand, the Asian family is seen as problematic because it is believed that roles are rigidly defined, with the mother's position weak and the father's authority all too pervasive!

Seventh, in multi-cultural social work there tends to be an uncritical reliance on cultural theories and culture-based explanations of behaviour, which frequently stop short of a more fundamental analysis which might be crucial in explaining the actions of minorities. It is significant that family disruption and breakdown are seen simply in terms of the innate deficiency of a culture, and the next critical step towards structural explanations is not taken. Yet a structural explanation might be more illuminating, because it would emphasize that culture is not static and that knowledge of the original culture in the countries of origin is not enough. The need is to know what is happening to a particular culture group here and now in this society and to understand the contemporary ethnic-minority experience in present-day Britain. Immigrants bring with them a culture, in terms of a set of beliefs and values; but as the social structure and material base of the receiving society are different, it may become difficult for them to achieve their traditional family goals. Life here may be dictated by the requirements of working in industry, which may lead to a need for substitute care of the children or to neglect of the elders in the community, despite cultural beliefs. Furthermore, foreign cultures the world over are no more homogeneous than white British ones. There are regional and class cultures within Asian and Afro-Caribbean societies, and people's differential access to resources clearly affects their behaviour and actions. For instance, opposition to arranged marriages is more common among middle-class women even in the Indian sub-continent and Asian women do not have to come to England to find their emancipation.

In considering the relevance of the material base of British society attention is drawn towards theories about the clash of values. But what is the nature of the values that clash? It could be argued that many Asians brought with them the values of a semi-feudal culture, while the value system confronting them in Britain was that of a white working class of bourgeois culture. Of course, if these cultures offered unhindered progress to their own women then there would be fewer obstacles in the way of a smooth transition. If this were really true, why then are white women fighting so hard against the sexism of white British cultures?

## Conclusions

It is in reviewing the pitfalls of cultural-based explanations of behaviour that the importance of majority and minority relations becomes apparent. It is in this context that we should examine the significance of racism and the dangers of seeing other cultures through imperial eyes.

There is no wish to deny that women are oppressed and subordinated in Asian society, as they are in white British society, in a few different and many similar ways. Resistance to sexism and other injustices in Asian and other minority cultures must continue inside the community; but it is imperative that in a society steeped in racism and with a deeply ingrained sense of Western superiority practitioners do not end up as collaborators acting against the interests of minority-ethnic groups, endorsing, however unwittingly, stereotyped racist beliefs.

## What can practitioners do?

First, practitioners should attempt to avoid comparing cultures because comparisons are invidious. They are offensively evaluative and seem invariably to be conducted from a white Western standpoint. It is becoming increasingly clear how difficult it is to approach the investigation of comparative value systems without carrying over deeply-embedded assumptions. In comparison exercises the tone of the argument is generally patronizing and culturally smug. There is usually a thick overlay of assumptions proclaiming the superiority of Western social relationships, and Asian women's resistance to traditional values seems always to be seen as Westernization. Invariably, Westernisation is equated with liberation, an assumption steeped in racism. We have different gender and kinship systems and therefore our analysis of exploitation must be specific and not deduced by comparisons with the European system.

I find myself having two distinct kinds of discussions. The one with Asian women is about sexism and oppression within our cultures. However, it seems impossible to have that same kind of frank discussion with white feminists because any acknowledgement of sexism in Asian society rapidly degenerates into realms of cultural racism, which proclaims the superiority of Western social arrangements. The white position, even the progressive one, seems to be 'Our culture may be bad but your culture is worse, it's thoroughly backward'.

The crux of the problem seems to be that use of a model drawn from one sex and gender system to talk about or evaluate another will produce a distorted picture which hardly aids understanding. Cultures reward, punish and extract casualties in many different and subtle ways, and there can hardly be a meaningful, incident-by-incident, comparison between two or more cultures. As an example one could look at the position of the older Asian woman from a lower-middle-class or working-class background. Such a woman may have started as an insecure bride, but at 60 as a grandmother and a mother-in-law, despite many social changes in the family, she is often quite a person. She retains status and some authority in the family which her English counterparts appear to lack. To Asian eyes an English woman of similar social circumstances and class does not seem necessarily better off; she can seem a graver victim of ageism and sexism.

Second, there is something practical we can do. At the very least developing guidelines for practice and routinely considering these is one disciplined approach in avoiding simplistic eurocentric explanations. Rhetoric is important but not enough. Our political beliefs and value standpoints must be acted out. We must not only say but also do something different. In short, we need to transform principles into practice. This can begin with the assessment process. In this much depends on the headings the practitioners are trained to hold in their heads in order to observe and organize data. Developing guidelines for practice which incorporate the centrality of racism is one disciplined approach to avoiding simplistic explanations. Agencies can be encouraged to produce guidelines and checklists for practice with Asian women and other minority-group clients. A checklist and instrument of analysis used by American social work practitioners is easily available and has been found useful in developing a broad practice (Cheetham, 1981).

There are urgent reasons why we need to develop alternative procedures. The 'system' seems only too keen to emphasize cultural studies which lack political analysis; as practitioners and especially Asian practitioners, we need to ensure that we do not fall into that trap. We should be calling the shots and we should be framing alternative questions.

## Case analysis

1   When analysing stress factors in a case check if there is a spread of these, or is there an over-reliance on culture-based explanation? (For example, watch out for over-simplifications such as culture conflict and use of extreme examples to describe cultural patterns.)
2   Is the notion of racial stress taken into account? (For example, racism at the workplace, or racist attacks on homes in the neighbourhood; racial stress is also experienced not only in its most aggressive forms but through unfavourable attitudes which pervade society.)
3   Is the notion of economic and class related stress represented? (For example, has possible status loss, job loss, discrimination or exploitation been considered; has poverty and low income been taken into account?)
4   Are other structural factors such as problems of Third World migration taken into account? (For example, incomplete and divided families including concerns about older relatives left abroad, or failure to achieve economic goals for which the hardships of migration were endured.)
5   Is the notion of emotional stress, that is emotionally disturbed family relationships, considered? (For example, incest or other forms of child abuse and long history of poor relationship with a parent.)

## References

AHMED, S., 'Asian Girls and Culture Conflicts', in *Social Work Today*, August 1978.
AHMED, S., 'Social Work with Ethnic Minority Children and Families', unit

16 of Open University Course no. E354: Ethnic Minorities and Community Relations, 1982. (Grateful thanks are acknowledged to the Open University for permission to use this section which has been expanded.)

CHEETHAM, J., 'Open Your Eyes to Strength', in *Community Care*, December 16, 1981.

JANSARI, J., 'Social Work with Ethnic Minorities: A Review of Literature', in *Multi-Racial Social Work*, no. 1, 1980.

WALWIN, T., *Black and White: Negro and English Society, 1555-1945*, Allen and Unwin, 1973.

# 13 An Asian women's refuge

*Surinder Guru*

## Introduction by Shama Ahmed

The previous chapter challenges the proliferation of simplistic and largely negative over-generalizations about the needs and circumstances of Asian women who come to the attention of welfare agencies. It is a matter of concern to us that our public image has been deformed and distorted; Asian women are perceived either as 'passive' or 'running away'. Such racist images obscure the strength and survival of Asian women. Nevertheless, we do not wish to deny that exploitation, pain and violence affect many Asian women and they have a right to be helped and supported. Many social workers are struggling to develop effective strategies which might enable battered and homeless women in Asian communities to achieve personal and collective goals.

In the following pages Surinder Guru presents three examples of her work with women at the Asian Resource Centre (ARC) in Birmingham, and argues the case for an autonomous Asian women's refuge. This chapter highlights issues such as access to help for Asian women, wider community and extended family involvement in problem resolution and the counselling approach which may be adopted. The situations described are extremely complex and there are obviously no easy answers. It may be useful when reading these cases to keep the following questions in mind:

*Access to Help*
1  How would a conventional social services team respond?
2  Are such women likely to be turned away?
3  Would assistance only be given if children were at risk?
4  Are the problems so overwhelming and complex that practitioners are likely to be paralysed by anger and hopelessness?
5  Would there be a temptation to hope only for political and

structural solutions leaving women and children without any
immediate help?

*Wider Community and Family Involvement*
1  Could practitioners in a conventional white agency become involved
   in negotiations with the extended family?
2  How can practitioners use the progressive aspects of Asian culture
   rather than relying on Western norms, so unwittingly giving the
   impression that these are being held up to the Asian community as
   superior and desirable?

*Counselling Approaches*
1  Can any distinctive features be identified in the counselling approach
   adopted?
2  Who can best undertake group work which relies on consciousness-
   raising techniques?
3  What insights and techniques would be needed for one-to-one work?

## An Asian Women's Refuge

*Azra*

Azra, an 18 year old woman, had been subjected to continuous and
severe violence from her husband since the time of her marriage. She had
been married three years and lived with her husband and two children, a
girl and a boy aged 18 and 9 months.

After the birth of the second child Azra could not endure any further
violence and confided in a nurse at her local clinic, who then referred her
to the ARC after consultation with the social services department.
Workers there felt that they could not get involved in the family because
the children were not at any risk and it was a marital matter. At the time
Azra was not quite sure that she could leave home. She wanted some
external pressure to be put on her husband that would dissuade him from
beating her. Relatives and friends had tried in the past but now did not
want to interfere any longer. She thought that somebody with authority,
for example a social worker, should talk seriously to her husband and
inform him that he would be imprisoned or fined if he did not refrain
from violence. She was sure that this would have a positive effect on him.
For approximately six weeks, the pros and cons of leaving home were
discussed with her. It was pointed out that such threats against her

husband could only be made by solicitors. The implications of involving a solicitor whilst still living at home were also discussed. She had also to think how she would cope with the pressures exerted on her by relatives if she took steps to leave the marital home. The financial and legal aspects of social security and legal aid were discussed.

During these discussions Azra was beaten again and this gave her the final impetus to leave her husband. At nine o'clock one evening she arrived at the ARC with her two children in a taxi. She was then placed at the refuge. The following morning she was accompanied to the DHSS and a solicitor. She settled in at the refuge and began to build relationships with other women there. She was quite shocked to see other Asian women in the same position. It was particularly comforting for her to meet other Muslim women at the refuge because she had said before that she found it hard as a Muslim to leave her husband. Her relationship with the Sikh women was also good. They shared in the day-to-day routine tasks of cooking, cleaning, shopping, sewing, and watching videos.

Azra learnt how to cut and sew salwar and kameez whilst helping another woman. She applied for her British nationality as this was, in her opinion, a means of securing her position. Her husband and relatives inquired after her several times but she did not wish to see them. At the age of 18 she found it difficult to manage two very young children on her own although she received some help from other women in the refuge.

At one of the women's groups run by the ARC and the social services department, a social worker discovered that Azra's daughter had a bruise on her cheek. When questioned Azra said that her daughter had had a fall. However, the bruising was very severe and her daughter had obviously been slapped very hard. The other women knew of the facts but would not say anything against her. Azra finally admitted that she had slapped her daughter. The matter was handled by the social services department and from thereon Azra's children were taken into care. They were fostered by a white middle-class family about 30 miles away from the refuge. The case was taken to court and during the procedures the department made contact with Azra's husband. The ARC sought to represent her interests and a solicitor was found for this purpose.

Previously Azra had refused to meet her husband, but the legal proceedings gave rise to new fears about losing her children. With the mounting pressure of the social services department's inquiries, more and more relatives wanted to see her. She therefore began to meet them on a regular basis, finding it supportive to discuss things with them. The relatives understood that Azra had been led to violence towards her child because of stresses in her life. They exerted a lot of pressure on her husband and blamed him for most of the incidents. They urged the couple to be reconciled in the interests of the children who would otherwise be brought up outside Islamic tradition. The husband held her responsible for the social services department's action but also took some of the criticism levelled at him by the relatives. Azra insisted that she would not be reconciled until she got her children back. There was a risk that she could go back into the marital home and be blamed not only for leaving her husband but also for losing her children. The women at the refuge sympathized with her, she was not ostracized. They understood her predicament and kept her mind off the matter as much as possible by keeping her busy.

Finally, the court decided that it would be best for the children to return to their mother. Azra was relieved beyond words and decided then to return to the husband who vowed never to beat her again and to provide sufficient money for the upkeep of the family. The ARC is still in touch with her. She is unhappy at home, her husband has not changed a lot, but he is afraid that she may leave him again. Every six months or so relatives get together to resolve the matter. There is peace for a few weeks and then conflicts resume, but Azra does not want to leave home again for she fears the involvement of social workers.

### Banso

Banso referred herself to the ARC after being at a white women's refuge run by the Birmingham City housing department. She went there from the hospital out-patient department. It was not the first time she had left home after being punched and bruised. She found the refuge lonely and unsupportive; she packed all her belongings and presented herself at the ARC saying 'They are all "gorian" (white women) there. I can talk to them for a bit but they have a different life, they don't know what I'm talking about.' Banso is a middle-aged woman. Her three grown-up children are living with their father. She had a long history of violence at the hands of her husband. 'Before I was strong, I'm too weak now, I can't take any more. He'll kill me one day.'

Before Banso came to the ARC she had a solicitor who acted for her for almost a year. She was advised by him to return to the marital home and continue legal proceedings from there to secure the marital property. She was also advised to contact the police immediately if her husband was violent. When Banso went home, her husband opened the door, slapped her face, threatened her with a knife, knocked her from wall to wall and again threw her out. She went to the police to make a report and returned to the refuge. An injunction was served against her husband to restrain his violent behaviour. It was at this stage that Banso came back to the ARC. She wished to take out legal proceedings to get her marital home from her husband but this could not be done until she could prove that her husband had been violent towards her. The police confirmed that she reported incidents to them on several occasions but stated that her husband had also made such reports. They maintained they had no proof that Banso was beaten by her husband or that he was responsible for the marital disharmony. The doctor's statement said that the wife had 'alleged' she was beaten, but he could not 'conclusively' say that she was injured as a result of any violence inflicted by her husband. So Banso could not prove that her husband had been violent. He had never beaten her in public; no one was willing to testify that they had seen violence being inflicted upon her; her children who had witnessed the violence refused to appear in court. Banso could not therefore acquire her property. When she tried to collect some of her belongings her local police escorted her home, but made it clear to the husband that he did not have to give them to her. Their presence was merely to ensure that no violence took place. Her husband refused her entry to the home. The police then advised her to go to court to secure any belongings she might have. She, however, could never prove that some of the belongings were hers. She had no receipts to verify that.

Now Banso is having to start building her life afresh, to save for things she already has but cannot acquire. She has made some close friends with women at the refuge, but she is still isolated and depressed, and they do not compensate for her children. Her depression is further accentuated by her ill health as she suffers from diabetes. She has to attend hospital regularly. She is also taken to see one of her children in a local cafeteria near to the marital home, some five miles away from the refuge. An application has been made to re-house her near her family so that she will be able to maintain close contact with them.

### Tara

Tara joined the ARC refuge in the winter after spending two weeks in the city's refuge. She asked if the ARC refuge could accommodate her with two children. She explained that the city hostel was very cold as she could not use the heating to suit her own hours, and that she could not cook her own food properly as there were no suitable cooking utensils. She was accepted at the ARC refuge that evening and her supplementary benefits and legal matters were attended to the following morning.

Tara's belongings were still at home with her husband. The local police were contacted who then escorted us to her marital home. Police explained, as usual, that the husband was under no obligation to allow Tara to remove her belongings, and that their presence was to ensure peaceful negotiation between both parties. The husband invited the policeman inside whilst telling us to stay out. After a few minutes the policeman returned and stated that the husband would not allow Tara to take anything away.

Tara made good friends with all the women at the refuge and was very active. She was a tremendous help in looking after all the children. She became very good friends with a Sikh woman and they performed all their daily routines together. She initiated discussions amongst the women about the relationships between men and women. On one occasion a discussion about sexuality took place and one of the women said that her husband boasted that when he visited white prostitutes they showed no grievance and let him do whatever he wanted with their bodies.

Tara's view was that these 'other' women get paid for their services, they get cash in hand. What do they have to be aggrieved about? Wives were treated by such men as slaves. Why should women be abused every day, do all their men's work, bring up their children, to get beaten, and yet not whisper a sound? Thus Tara was able to say that women have a right to raise their voices in protest; but she could not face her husband and relatives and confront them all the time.

During her stay Tara had a family wedding and funeral to attend. She did not feel strong enough to take all the pressures for reconciliation that would be exerted upon her by the relatives, together with insinuations that she had run away. She wanted somebody from the Centre to accompany her for moral strength on both occasions. So the women's worker went with her in order to encourage her to face relatives.

Later in the separation Tara's husband attempted several reconciliations, and meetings were arranged between the two parties and the women's worker. Tara insisted that she would not go back until the husband obtained a home apart from his sister. He promised to get his own property on several occasions, but Tara wanted these promises translated into action. In the end he did not agree to leave his sister.

Tara made her own applications for re-housing and was re-housed within the local community where she had the necessary support network. All her belongings were moved by the ARC to her new home and she was helped to settle in. The property was very dilapidated and Tara continuously had to ask the ARC to find volunteers to repair things. The frustrations of not having things done as and when required eventually led Tara to seek reconciliation with her husband. Since she had property of her own he only had to leave his sister and move in with her. The ARC again arranged meetings to discuss the situation and finally the husband agreed to live with Tara at her own property and to visit his sister regularly. This is the situation at present and its success remains to be seen.

### The response of the police, the courts and social workers

These examples illustrate the steps taken by women to resolve their predicament and take greater control of their lives. It is obvious that the single most important factor for women becoming homeless is physical or mental violence within the family. This is so for white women as well, but for Asian women violence can sometimes be exercised by other women, for instance, mothers or sisters-in-law. It is also working-class women who invariably find themselves in hostels and refuges. Middle-class women rarely come into contact with hostels because they have other financial and educational resources.

The cases described also illustrate how the depression of a battered Asian woman is further aggravated by the sexism and racism of white society. Police will often not act against a husband unless a woman can prove conclusively he has beaten her; and women may be frightened to report injuries to doctors and the police for fear of stigma or retaliation from their husbands. Furthermore, the police seem to assume that all property in an Asian home belongs to the man of the house, and they often advise the relatives of women who are trying to collect their property that they are under no obligation to allow things to be taken. Courts seem more interested in arrangements for children's care than in the violence inflicted on their mothers. When bruises and swellings can no longer be ignored women are often regarded as victims of mere 'domestic violence' which is left as a matter for the two parties to resolve. Injunctions are often not enforced.

Can social workers in white mainsteam organizations offer Asian women counselling to help them understand their own roles and bring about changes? It appears that the collective experiences of Asian women are rarely recognized. Groups where they could talk to each other about their own lives, build trust in other Asian women and understand their experience of violence and suffering are few. In the main, groups for Asian women concentrate on childcare, keep-fit and English classes. Such preoccupations suggest that Asian women are ignorant and need to learn to look after themselves and their children.

### The Asian Resource Centre refuge

Within this context the Asian Resource Centre in Handsworth, Birmingham, organizes its work. It is an advice centre which runs on the principle of Asian people organizing themselves independently. Its specific work is not subject to the direct control of the local council or any particular group within the Asian community. The Centre provides facilities such as accommodation for the elderly, advice on matters of immigration and nationality, welfare benefits, and also has a refuge attached to it.

In setting up a refuge for homeless women who have suffered violence from their families, the ARC has been instrumental in confronting an overt form of women's subordination: male violence, the strongest form of male domination. The workers do not doubt the women's version of the violence inflicted upon them, or the reasons for which they have sought to sever relations with their families. The refuge has six self-contained units and is based in Handsworth.

Leaving home is a pressing decision for any woman. It is more so for Asian women because the traditions of subservience to men exert pressure on women to remain in the family. This pressure is further increased by the racism they will encounter if they leave home.

The refuge is offered as a place where women can begin to communicate their ideas and experiences. This involves an analysis of relations within the home, together with the racism women have to confront. Within the confines of the family, most women have not experienced institutions such as the DHSS, housing departments, lawyers, social services, and so on. The act of leaving home will bring many black women face-to-face with the bureaucracy and the racism of these institutions for the first time.

At first the lack of support after leaving home causes severe depression, but as more women leave it becomes possible to form support networks through which women learn from each other's experiences. This provides some strength and courage and the knowledge that they are not alone. The act of leaving home brings many women together and gives a new outlook upon their lives. They now have to confront solicitors, the DHSS and housing departments on their own as women, not as appendages of men. By having to live with other Asian women a new identity develops amongst them. Women begin to see themselves more as women, rather than as Hindu, Muslim or Sikh. They begin to address such fundamental issues as a woman's right to live alone and lead her own life.

For the first time women talk about the violence inflicted upon them and the oppression they have experienced. They begin to understand how state institutions oppress black women when welfare benefits are continuously refused; when they are harassed into producing their passports as proof of their right to be in the UK; when housing departments refuse requests to be re-housed in the areas where women have their own support groups and where they will feel safer from racist attacks. Women talk too about how they are forced to retain their relationships with men when they are offered dilapidated properties which they cannot repair or redecorate without help. Women feel the impact of the racist and sexist immigration laws when they are separated from their husbands. They fear deportation because as a result of separation applications for the regularization of their status may not have been made by husbands. All these experiences make women unravel the connections between the racism of white people and the sexism of men.

### The need for an autonomous women's refuge

The new identity formed by Asian women living together is only possible when they can organize themselves autonomously with other Asian women. This identity cannot grow where women are placed in white-dominated refuges. Asian and other black women experience a lot of racism in such places and find that their cultures and values are constantly under attack. Managers and workers in white refuges often complain about Asian women not being able to understand English. Little attention is paid to the fact that the refuges are mostly controlled by white women and that no facilities exist for Asian women to pursue their own interests. Often there is no provision of proper utensils to cook Asian food, or for women to watch their own films, and so on. The request for specific facilities for Asian women can be met with the response 'We believe in treating all women the same'. The racism that black women receive from their white counterparts is ignored unless it reaches horrific and blatant proportions. Asian women have been told that they cannot use the same bath as white women, that their food smells (as though white people's food does not), and that their traditional dress is unacceptable.

At the ARC refuge women are not under the control of white people who define how they should conduct their lives. The only two requests women are asked to comply with are that they keep secret the refuge address and that they keep their rooms in reasonable condition. Women are therefore able to live their day-to-day lives as they please. The workers make every effort to ensure that the women stay within the community and that they are not ostracized from it. This enables women to maintain their old relationships and build new ones. In this way excessive disruption and total isolation is avoided so that women find the strength to challenge their roles. A vital development has been the support offered to the residents by women who have left the refuge and now live independently.

### Limitations of the ARC refuge

The limitations imposed on the refuge work are three-fold. The first and foremost limitation is the lack of sufficient resources and the refusal of the local council to provide funds. The refuge is not funded by any source, it is self-sufficient. One worker, whose responsibility is not only the refuge but also the main work-load of the ARC, is partly funded by the social services department and the Inner-City Partnership grant. Running costs for the refuge are not available, despite applications for its funding. The real potential of organizing women as a collectivity in refuges is severely handicapped by the lack of money.

Refuges need to be more comfortable and enjoyable places to be in. The ARC refuge offers a terrible physical environment to women in distress. It is poorly furnished; gas cookers, settees and beds are old and dilapidated. In winter the heating is insufficient. The interior of the building requires redecoration. Most important, the refuge does not have 24 hour protection by full-time workers. Women are put at risk without emergency help should the place be attacked by racists or male relatives. The lack of full-time workers also means that women are sometimes not accepted into the refuge if they require continual supervision because of illness or other risks.

Second, the charitable status of the ARC inhibits any political action. This has prevented women from becoming organized into groups which can overtly challenge their oppression. For example, women cannot go directly as a group to the old home of a particular woman and confront the family because of the violence that has been inflicted on her. It has been suggested that this would be seen as political activity.

The third constraint is imposed by the ideological context in which black women's struggles have taken place in Britain. These have of necessity been with the immediate survival of black communities in the UK. In the past few years the struggle against racism, rather than sexism, has assumed priority for black women. The fights have been against deportations, fascism and discrimination in employment, although women have sought to address within these contexts the particular oppression they face.

### The organization of Asian women for survival and strength

Asian women are increasingly organizing themselves to confront the issues that face them specifically. The anti-deportation campaigns on behalf of Manjit Kaur and Nasreen Akhter concerned women whose marriages had broken down and who therefore faced deportation because of the racist and sexist immigration laws. The Iqbal Begum campaign is currently fighting for Iqbal's release from Styal prison. She has been sentenced to life imprisonment for the murder of her husband who had been violent to her throughout her life. She was treated deplorably by the legal system which failed to provide her with an adequate defence, and sentenced her for life after a 20 minute trial. This campaign for the defence of Iqbal is struggling both against the sexism within the Asian community and against the racism of the State. Similarly, the black Women's Right to Benefit campaign is fighting for the rights of black women to acquire supplementary benefit when their husbands are abroad. The DHSS refuses women benefits in cases where their husbands are temporarily abroad, often to attend their parents who are not allowed into Britain, arguing that Asian women are dependent on their fathers, brothers, uncles and other relatives for their economic needs. White women rarely find themselves in this position as their menfolk do not usually have relatives who need their help and who are unable to join them in Britain. At the same time Asian families remain divided when wives and children of men settled in Britain are refused entry because their relationship to their sponsors is not believed (CRE,

1985). When married women are awaiting entry clearance for their husbands to join them in the UK they are refused benefits.

These are examples of how black women, Asian and Afro-Caribbean, have fought against efforts to institutionalize their position as dependants of men. This unity began with the Organization of Women from African and Asian Descent and now continues with groups such as Birmingham and Southall Black Sisters.

These struggles have been important in giving women political experience that has enabled black people to analyse their common oppression. Informal and autonomous groups are therefore an important and preliminary step towards organizing the resistance and fight against racism and sexism. Women must organize themselves in a way which promotes a consciousness based on their collective experiences and development. It is on these principles that black women's groups are being organized.

Despite these positive developments the struggles for women as women have been held back. Women live in fear of being accused of dividing the anti-racist struggle. Any critique of black institutions is inevitably used by racists who seize on the problems described here as examples of the inevitable 'pathology' of the Asian family in its control and authority over its women and children[1].

## References

COMMISSION FOR RACIAL EQUALITY (CRE), *The Report of the Formal Investigation into the Immigration Service*, 1985.

---

[1] For a further analysis of the 'pathology' of black families see: Lawrence, E., and Parmar, P., *The Empire Strikes Back* (Centre for Contemporary Studies), 1982.

# PART FOUR
# WORK WITH YOUNG BLACK OFFENDERS

## 14 *Developing an anti-racist intermediate treatment* John Pitts, Theo Sowa, Alan Taylor and Lorna Whyte

In this chapter we argue that if the disproportionate levels of confinement of black young offenders in child care and prison departments establishments is to be confronted by intermediate treatment (IT), then many assumptions about what IT is and what IT does will have to be revised. We attempt to identify the roots of the problem and elaborate a model of IT which could be effectively anti-racist, knowing this takes the practice of community alternatives to care and custody into new areas which require new skills. By racism we mean more than individual racial prejudice on the part of individual whites. We refer rather to institutions and practices which have the power, and use it, intentionally or otherwise, either to keep black people in a subordinate social and economic position in our society or to worsen that position. Our argument is that if we are to confront the racist practices which lead to excessive black youth confinement and imprisonment we must as workers develop a new practice of politics and a new politics of practice. IT in the late 1970s and 1980s has come increasingly to be defined as provision which does or should serve as an alternative to residential care or custody for young offenders. This is the definition of IT we use throughout this chapter and the next.

Our major purpose is to draw attention to the wider responsibility that IT practitioners and managers have in challenging the institutional racism of the juvenile justice system. This means being involved in politics and policy and changing the practices of key decision makers in the system. IT cannot therefore simply be preoccupied with programme content and methods; it becomes an activity analogous to community work.

We use the term juvenile criminal justice system to describe all the practices and institutions which respond to young people aged ten to 17 years. Thus it includes policing; the practices of probation officers and social workers; the practices of the psychologists and psychiatrists who advise the courts; the magistrates who sentence young offenders; the child care and penal institutions which contain young offenders; and the voluntary and statutory agencies which offer community alternatives to institutional confinement.

Workers within the juvenile criminal justice system in the larger British cities have been aware for some years that black young offenders are more likely to be incarcerated in child care or penal establishments than their white counterparts. It is only recently, however, that the real dimensions of this disproportionate incarceration have become evident. Kettle (1982) writes:

> In April this year, according to the Home Office, 50 per cent of Ashford Remand Centre was black. Brixton (another remand prison) and Aylesbury prisons were between 25 and 30 per cent black. So were Rochester, Dover and Hewell Grange Borstals and Blantyre House detention centre. Others with more than 10 per cent black inmates were Wormwood Scrubs, Parkhurst, Albany, Wandsworth and Reading prison and Wellingborough, Bullwood Hall and Feltham Borstals. (p. 535.)

Indeed, the Home Office, while unwilling to reveal exact figures, is concerned that the increase in the numbers of black people in prisons has led to changes in the relationship between the institutions of control and their black inmates. Cook (1982) writes of the Home Office seminar on ethnic minorities in prisons:

> The seminar heard that frequently superior physical and intellectual abilities of many black people have led to a growing black hold on traditional prison rackets like extortion and 'hoovering' – taking food away from weaker inmates . . . . But the department has failed to establish the point at which the growing proportion will become a danger to stability. (*The Guardian*, Wednesday 6 January 1982.)

Here once again we see the spectre of the black deviant who poses problems of control, containment and socialization to institutions which, it is implied, were quietly getting on with the job, the erstwhile white-dominated rackets notwithstanding, until they had to contend with this new and threatening phenomenon. As they have grown up, black British young people have been described as a problem for the schools (CRE,

1985), a problem for social workers, and they now emerge as a problem for the Home Office prison department.

The response to the 'problem' is similarly familiar. On the one hand the Home Office, in a spirit of enlightened pluralism, has ruled that Rastafarians will no longer have their dreadlocks cut off by the prison barber. On the other hand black 'ring-leaders' and potential 'sub-versives' are identified and dispersed around the prison system in an attempt to forestall the anticipated disruption.

Making a problem of a particular group of young people seen to present peculiar and unfamiliar difficulties makes it possible for the administrators and practitioners in the juvenile justice criminal system to avoid such important questions as: why do so many black young people enter the system in the first place? Do institutions and institutional practices routinely rather than inadvertently worsen the predicament of black young people when they fall foul of the law? The perpetuation of a notion of the black young person as problematic in a peculiar way has made it possible to ignore questions of institutionalized racism within the juvenile criminal justice system itself and amongst practitioners within that system.

### The response of IT

The early 1970s saw the development of IT. As the decade progressed the debate focused increasingly upon the question of whether com-munity alternatives to institutional confinement could make any impact upon the rapidly rising numbers of juveniles in institutions. The problem which perplexed the protagonists in this debate was that the growth of IT, the alternative, was being paralleled, indeed rapidly outstripped, by the growth of incarceration. What became clear was that this rapid rise in incarceration had little or nothing to do with levels of serious juvenile crime which remained fairly constant throughout the period (Pitts, 1982). The rise appeared to be attributable to changes in the system itself. Thorpe (1980) wrote:

> . . . . for it was the decision-makers – policemen, social workers, probation officers, magistrates and social services administrators – who effectively abandoned whatever potential for reform the 1969 Children and Young Persons Act contained. Quite simply cumulatively these disparate bodies of professionals made the wrong decisions about the wrong children at the wrong time.

The idea became established that effective intervention in the growing incarceration of youth meant eschewing considerations of the causes of juvenile crime, and turning to the decision makers and the institutions within the juvenile criminal justice system as the primary targets of intervention. Thus there developed techniques which strove to limit levels of confinement by developing within the social services departments 'systems of gatekeeping' in which social workers' recommendations to courts were monitored and vetted. Some Community Homes with Education (CHEs), the erstwhile approved schools, were closed and some of the savings were pumped into IT.

The appeal of these techniques to local authorities facing wave after wave of financial cut-backs was both financial and humanitarian. Speaking in 1977, Mrs Page, Chairperson of Islington Social Services Committee, asked:

What does this mean in terms of money and other resources? Councillors and officers were forced last year (1976) into some fresh thinking as we are faced with the horrifying cost of residential provision of all sorts. We concluded by agreeing to close two children's homes, change the character of two others and to transfer part of the revenue savings into increased votes for community-based provision of fostering and IT . . . . Our Intermediate Treatment project vote is increased to £10,000 which we hope will be our 25 per cent contribution to an Urban Aid Grant. (DHSS, 1977, p. 15.)

These approaches had their greatest impact upon social services departments but had little impact on the rising tide of young offenders entering penal establishments. As residential establishments closed the juvenile bench made increasing use of attendance and detention centres, borstals and prisons. The problem was that IT was born and grew up in a political climate in which law and order was emerging as an important political issue. As Millham (1977) noted:

. . . . if progressive movements require inherent tokens of appeasement to the forces of reaction, do reactionary movements similarly need to acknowledge the forces of liberalism?
Are those of you in the IT field merely symbolic? Are you merely cosmetic, providing a commitment to community care which in spite of government and local authority assurances we really do not have? (p. 22.)

IT has also failed to confront the fact that as the 1970s progressed it was the black community which emerged as a problem in the political rhetoric which accompanied government measures to control immigration, culminating in the 1981 Nationality Act. It was portrayed in this rhetoric as both an economic problem and potentially subversive of the nation's stability and cultural integrity (Hall, 1978). The increasing use, particularly by the Metropolitan Police, of military-style policing projected rapidly growing numbers of black people into the juvenile criminal justice system (Smith, 1982). The production in 1982 of the 'ethnic' crime figures by the Metropolitan Police as a vindication of SWAMP 81, and the enthusiasm with which the bulk of the British press made this dubious data front-page news all served to legitimize the assault upon the 'problem' of black young people. IT has been reluctant to grasp the fact that the growing incarceration of youth in general, but black youth in particular, during this period was not the consequence of a series of mistakes, but the logical outcome of government policies which emphasized the necessity to control, contain and discipline the beleaguered young people of the inner-city. These policies ensured that a growing and disproportionate number of black young people entered the juvenile justice system. The stage was set for a dramatic outcome, for this new wave of black offenders had already been identified by political rhetoric and professional opinion as presenting peculiar problems of containment, control and socialization.

Margaret Thatcher spoke of our culture being swamped; CHEs developed quota systems for black inmates in order to avoid such swamping. The police regularly reported that black youths on the streets were more antagonistic and challenging than whites and eventually developed their own 'swamp 81' in order to redress the balance. It was against this ideological backdrop that the juvenile criminal justice system dealt with the black young people who entered it.

Figures collected by probation officers in the Midlands indicate that the second highest category of offences for which young black people are charged arise out of confrontations with the police on the streets. These offences include 'criminal attempts', assaults on the police, public order offences and insulting behaviour, offences which had not occured until after the police arrived.

The new offence of 'criminal attempts' offers the police a more flexible law than the 1824 Vagrancy Act (SUS). The Criminal Attempts Bill was welcomed by the *Police Review* in an article entitled 'Let's Have a Loophole', and the *New Law Journal* explained that the new offence could be useful 'where firm dishonest intention cannot be established' (Dennington, 1981). The SUS controversy concerned the use of the law as a means of harassing black young people but 'criminal attempts' has other consequences. In Lambeth, for example, a young person charged with SUS would seldom, if ever, be offered the opportunity of being referred to the juvenile bureau which, if the charge is admitted, is empowered to issue a caution. Young people charged with SUS were normally charged immediately as a matter of course and so they had to appear in court. In court the complainant and the witnesses were almost invariably the police. Upon conviction the young person's name would be added to the 'recidivists' list, which meant that if at some future date he or she was apprehended for whatever charge no referral to the juvenile bureau could be made and the young person would be charged immediately. This has the effect of projecting those young people so charged deeper into the juvenile criminal justice system and further up the 'tariff' of penalties.

Landau's study (1981) noted that SUS was the offence for which there was the greatest difference between races, and also that white young people were up to 50 per cent more likely to be referred to the juvenile bureau than their black counterparts. This discrepancy could not be accounted for by the fact that black youngsters so charged had a larger record of previous offences. Landau shows that significantly more black first offenders were subject to an immediate charge decision than whites. He also noted that the police tended to see black young people as more antagonistic to them than whites and suggests that this may be a significant factor in the decision whether to charge immediately or refer to the juvenile bureau. In conclusion he writes: 'As to ethnic group, the main finding was that blacks involved in crimes of violence, burglary, and public disorder are treated more harshly than their white counterparts.' (p.146.)

In summary, young black people are subject to intensive policing (Smith, 1982); intensive policing generates further offences; upon apprehension young black people are less likely to be diverted out of the mainstream of the system to the juvenile bureau (Landau, 1981).

### Young black people and the welfare agencies

It is usually at the point of the court appearance that the young black defendant will encounter a social worker or a probation officer but the difference between white and black defendants continues, since many young black people who become involved in juvenile welfare or criminal justice systems do so at a later stage than white young people.

A distinctive feature of the background of many young black offenders is that they are not characterized by prior involvement with welfare agencies concerned with other social or family problems. Observations of black young people in borstals supports this view in that they appear to have a broader spread of academic abilities and tend in many ways to be more socially and academically able than white inmates. They are also much more likely to be drawn from 'respectable' rather than 'disreputable' families. We are not therefore seeing the apparently inexorable unfolding of a criminal and institutional career which may be traced back, sometimes over generations, but rather a rupture, a departure, from a previously conventional mode of existence by a group of young people, many of whom had until shortly before their first court appearance been successful conforming schoolgirls and schoolboys[1].

When social welfare agencies do intervene with younger black children in trouble, these children will tend to be made the subject of care orders, at an earlier age than their white counterparts (Pitts and Robinson, 1981). This is a further example of the tendency discussed in the Introduction of white social workers acting pre-emptively in their dealings with black families (Ousley, 1982). The imposition of a care order, under the offence condition of the 1969 Children and Young Persons Act, can have particularly serious effects if the child continues to appear in court. There is evidence that in the Crown Court black defendants are two or three times more likely to receive a custodial sentence than whites (Taylor, 1981). These custodial sentences have very little to do with the nature of the offence; they correlate more closely with whether the defendant is homeless, jobless or was previously the subject of a care order. Young black people experience extremely high levels of homelessness and they are much more likely than whites to be unemployed. Their predicament is seriously worsened if they have previously been the subject of a care order. The injustice is the greater because these defendants are also victims of structural inequalities which affect the black population in general and Afro-Caribbean young people in particular (Brown, 1984).

The probation service has also, by and large, failed to intervene helpfully in the lives and fates of young black offenders. They are substantially less likely to be offered the option of probation than whites. Most black offenders made their first contact with probation officers while serving detention centre or borstal sentences (Taylor, 1981). This contact is necessary because of the statutory responsibilities of the probation service for the after care of young offenders.

Why are black young offenders not being offered probation as a non-

---

[1] Pitts, L., 'Preliminary findings from research in progress', in Matthews, R. and Young, J. (eds.) *Black Youth*, Sage, 1986.

custodial alternative? There are clearly three possibilities; either the magistrate or the judge did not remand prisoners for probation reports; or the remand was made but the probation officer did not recommend probation; or probation was recommended and the offenders decided not to avail themselves of the option. The City and Handsworth Project in Birmingham was established to address these problems. It aimed to intervene with the courts and the probation service in order that they might both begin to use the probation order as a non-custodial alternative for black offenders, those offenders who by dint of their social circumstances were being condemned to custody. The project offered help with homelessness and employment and ran a literacy project. Project workers attended court and worked closely with probation officers in order that they should be aware that this support existed and that they would therefore be encouraged to recommend and offer the option of probation. The first year of the project revealed some perplexing results. Probation orders for black offenders increased by over 100 per cent but this was paralleled by a decrease in other non-custodial sentences, fines, bind-overs and discharges. More alarmingly, there was also a substantial increase in custodial sentences given to black defendants. In the second year of the project's operation the same tendencies continued. The behaviour of probation officers had changed; so had that of the magistrates and judges, but in the latter case the change has been paradoxical. The indications are that the increase in the use of probation means that offenders who would previously have been subject to lesser non-custodial sentences are now being made subject to the more serious probation order, thus pushing them closer to the gates of the prison if they are apprehended for further offences. Here we may be witnessing another sad example of an initiative which attempts to influence the functioning of the justice system being confounded by the apparently profligate and unfettered behaviour of the bench and the judiciary. Unfortunately the situation is likely to worsen since the 1982 Criminal Justice Act handed new powers to the magistrates to make a Youth Custody Sentence of up to a year. This resulted in the first six months of its operation in the numbers of young people subject to these or similar sentences increasing by 67 per cent. Given the association between unemployment and custodial sentences and the increasingly high proportion of young black people without jobs, we can conclude that magistrates' new powers of sentencing will significantly increase the likelihood of black offenders entering custodial establishments. Even prior to the enactment of the 1982 Criminal Justice Act, the black subjects of the magistrates court were wary of it. Taylor (1982) noted that whereas only 11 per cent of white people charged with indictable offences opted for trial by jury in a Crown Court, 43 per cent of black young people did. They claimed that the magistrates courts were 'police courts' and there you only get 'white man's justice'.

The Handsworth experience raised the question of whether young black people in trouble are offered alternatives to custody in the same way, and with the same frequency, as whites. A few years ago an investigation was undertaken into the ways in which intermediate treatment projects in an area of London with a large black population were responding to the predicament of black young people in trouble. It became immediately evident that although arrest rates for black youngsters were quite high very few found their way through the system to intermediate treatment.

Intermediate treatment workers interviewed said that the referring agents – social workers, probation officers, education welfare officers and the police – seemed reluctant to refer young black people, and as a result a disproportionate number went into custody. They also thought that many welfare workers seemed to assume that because of the influence of strict Afro-Caribbean child-rearing patterns, black youngsters would understand the detention centre in a way that they would not understand the more relaxed and 'person-centred' regime of IT. If this was in fact the process at work, then the possibility emerges that stereotypical, indeed caricatured, racist perceptions of a culture may seriously worsen the black young person's chance of being diverted from custody.

Projects which offer alternatives to custody have often failed to attract a black clientele, while there is considerable pressure for places at CHEs from social workers attempting to place black young people on care orders under the offence condition of the 1969 Children and Young Persons Act. Many of these institutions operate a racial quota system which attempts to prevent the proportion of black residents rising above 20 per cent. The quota system is, it is argued, necessary because of the problems of management posed by Afro-Caribbean young people when they are together in substantial numbers. This parallels exactly the complaints of the police, prison officers and, to a lesser extent, field social workers and probation officers and teachers: 'They band together'; 'They speak their own language'; 'They intimidate other residents, members or prisoners'; 'They are insolent to staff'.[1] This is not the

---

[1] West London Institute of Higher Education First Year CQSW project *Black Young People in Care*, unpublished, 1982.

universal experience of those who work with young black people so we must ask what seems to be the root of the problem. While this is not the place to examine institutional dynamics we know that when people feel threatened, devalued or misunderstood in institutional or group settings, they will often develop collective defences around common experiences and beliefs. In such circumstances what is individual, special and unique about people becomes obscured. This is as true of those in positions of authority as it is of their subjects.

The quota system has created a log-jam of black people in remand, observation and assessment centres. Indeed in Stamford House, a large remand and assessment centre in West London, 60 per cent of the population is black. The economic and other pressures to substitute community-based provision for residential care has been effective in delivering many white young offenders from the CHE. It will be a major task, however, to tackle the demonstrable reluctance of white-dominated welfare agencies to develop or use similar alternatives for black young people.

## Anti-racist practice

An anti-racist approach differs from those of integration and pluralism. The integrationist approach sees the problem as one of assimilating alien cultures into the British way of life. In this approach tolerance on the part of individual workers is seen as the major means whereby the 'aliens' will eventually merge and therefore become truly British. Pluralism requires a multi-cultural approach in which all cultures will be given equal status and value in contemporary Britain. Workers must have more knowledge of more cultures.

We do not argue that sensitivity to different cultures' needs is unnecessary; simply that it is insufficient as a response to the institutional racism which generates many of the social problems and much of the distress among Britain's black populations to which social welfare agencies are required to respond.

An anti-racist practice must shed light upon the structural, economic and social factors which generate both the predicament of Britain's black citizens and the attitudes and practices of Britain's white political and economic power holders. When power, enshrined in institutions, perpetuated by bureaucratic practices, always defines a situation to the detriment of the black people in it , it is racist and must be challenged by anti-racist practice. Anti-racist practice strives to redefine those situations, to make explicit the links between racist ideology, institutionalized racist practices and power, and to re-assign that power. The juvenile criminal justice system is one of the starkest examples of institutionalized racism in modern Britain. We argue that IT may be one base from which an anti-racist initiative in the juvenile criminal justice system might be launched.

## Developing an anti-racist IT

Until now IT has meant a range of groups and projects for children and young people in trouble and, to a lesser extent, an administrative intervention geared to the monitoring of decision making in the juvenile criminal justice system which attempts to divert some young offenders from residential care (Thorpe, 1980). Its problem in establishing itself as a major response to youngsters in trouble has been the lack of power that derives from being an 'optional extra' in the system. IT has lacked both a political analysis of the reasons for the disproportionate arrest rates and confinement of black young people in penal establishments, and policies to confront these problems. Practice which addresses questions of institutional and individual racism in the juvenile criminal justice system remains undeveloped. For change to occur political strategies, administrative structures and practitioners capable of, and willing to, challenge racism in their work are required.

## Political strategies

At present it is difficult to identify any pressure group or lobby making a sustained assault upon government juvenile justice policies. There is certainly no group which acts on behalf of black young people in the juvenile criminal justice system. There is disagreement within IT about the reasons for its failure to stem the high rate of custodial sentences for young people (Thorpe et al, 1980). The disagreements tend to focus upon administrative and practice issues and do not address the politics of juvenile justice in the mid-1980s. Intermediate treatment from its inception has been regarded by governments as a safety valve for a residential and penal system which could not provide institutional accommodation for offenders fast enough. It has thus become a holding operation for this system, not an alternative to it.

This suggests to us that if IT is to confront the problem to which it wishes to be a solution then it must engage in the politics of juvenile justice. A political campaign focused on the plight of black young people could confront both the racial and the socially discriminatory nature of the juvenile criminal justice system. While there is no identifiable alliance or lobby as yet, there are stirrings and possibilities.

The Runnymede Trust is studying the sentencing patterns of black defendants. The National Association of Probation Officers has completed a similar small enquiry. The National Association for the Care and Re-settlement of Offenders has established a project concerned with ethnic minorities in the penal system. The GLC Ethnic Minorities Unit produced a document on race and imprisonment. The Commission for Racial Equality is showing some interest in the issues. Two regional IT associations have organized study days on racism in the juvenile criminal justice system. Radical Alternatives to Prison (RAP) recently devoted an issue of its journal (*The Abolitionist*) to the levels of incarceration of black people and their tratment in penal establishments. For the first time the 1984 National Intermediate Treatment Federation annual conference had a workshop on Racism in the Juvenile Criminal Justice System as a result of which a national working party was established to formulate ideas about training and campaigning. There is also a growing number of academics and journalists who are researching and writing about the policing, judicial processing and imprisonment of black people.

Should an alliance emerge from these and similar organizations it would have to devise a strategy for change, a problem which has dogged many would-be penal reformers. Mathiesen (1974) argues that the populations of mental hospitals, prisons, children's and old people's homes are defined in political rhetoric as the unproductive and troublesome members of society. He argues that industrial societies routinely generate human waste and their continued legitimacy requires that those outside these institutions are not reminded of this substantial but largely invisible social by-product. These people are expelled to the archipelagoes which surround the mainland of civil society. He sees the task of abolitionist penal politics as that of reuniting those expelled sectors of the working class with the mainstream of the labour movement. Thus he commends the establishment of links between the populations of the institutions with activists, trades unionists, ex-prisoners, political pressure groups, academics and journalists on the outside who can together articulate an abolitionist alliance. These ideas have clear strategic implications for people trying to challenge and change the custodial sentencing of young black people.

How would such an abolitionist alliance, were it to come into being, approach the question of reform versus revolution? In demanding the abolition of imprisonment reformers are invariably asked to suggest the alternative. These alternatives can never meet all the objectives of the prison system the reformers aim to replace. They are then driven back to working upon piecemeal reforms of parts of the penal system. The irony is that working for positive reforms, better educational facilities, better treatment programmes, better colour TVs and so on, rather than hastening the demise of the prison merely serves to give greater legitimacy and credibility to it, thus making its eventual abolition even more difficult. IT practitioners must recognize the dangers of helping to create a multi-cultural prison. If we follow Mathiesen abolitionist penal politics must not pursue positive reform; they must not be trapped into the impossible task of helping the Home Office to avert racial conflict and antagonism in its prisons. The profound causes of these problems and their solutions are not to be found or dealt with within the prison. Effective positive reform will merely emphasize the appropriateness of black youth imprisonment.

Negative reforms, by contrast, are those which contest the power of the penal apparatus and attempt to diminish the credibility and legitimacy of the penal system. Thus the demand for the abolition of solitary confinement in prisons, youth custody and detention centres and CHEs, the cessation of enforced drug therapy by the prison medical service and the gaining of full legal and civil rights by institutional populations would all constitute legitimate negative reforms requiring the system to relinquish some of its power and control over its subjects.

This suggests a policy of attrition, a gradual process of wearing away in which the realities of the brutality and lawlessness of our penal system, which is nowhere clearer than in the case of black young people, are juxtaposed with the rhetoric of penal policy. The National Association for Young People In Care, which has been successful in organizing groups of young people in care and developing a charter of rights, has shown how strong and vocal alliances can be made between institutional populations and activists outside these institutions. It has pursued causes and taken up cases. In doing this it has used the media and adult help in the form of local support groups; but it has taken much of its strength from young people who are or were recently in care themselves. IT, probation officers and social workers are in contact with black and white young people in penal or residential establishments and those who have recently left them. Increasingly, these services employ ex-inmates as professional workers in the juvenile justice field. We have reached a point where there are sufficient people with a personal experience as subjects of the system to make an abolitionist alliance a reality.

An abolitionist anti-racist IT would contest the absurdity of penal policies which continue to create more and more penal and institutional places for less and less problematic black children and young people. It would demand a moratorium on the construction of new custodial institutions. It would campaign for the freedom of those who could be safely released, usually estimated as between 70 and 80 per cent of the population in custody. It would demand that IT's expansion must be firmly linked with a reduction of places in prison departments and child care establishments. In other words it would insist on IT as an alternative, not as an addition, to custodial measures. In all this it would underline the fact that it is black young people who are treated most harshly and most unfairly by a juvenile criminal justice system which is among the most severe and most inequitable in Europe. An abolitionist alliance which worked on behalf of black children and young people would have to recognize that the kind of casework and campaigning undertaken by police accountability groups is a necessary pre-requisite for effecting change in the ways in which black youngsters are policed. Local IT associations have a great deal to offer police accountability groups on these issues and vice versa. Such an alliance would need friends in Parliament, in Fleet Street, in universities and polytechnics and in local authorities. These friends exist but they have yet to be approached.

Where should the impetus for an abolitionist alliance come from? IT's equivocal position in the juvenile criminal justice system is in part its weakness. The relationship between IT and the police, the courts, social workers, probation officers, schools and prisons has never been clear. Each of these other agencies, services and institutions has a clearly defined role in the system. IT has, by default, been given the freedom to develop whatever relationships with these agencies it wishes. To this extent IT has considerable room for manoeuvre; as both a problem finder and a problem solver it can take fresh initiatives based on a new or clearer understanding of the problems with the juvenile justice system. We argue, therefore, that IT through its regional associations and its national federation, using its links with the parent professions of its practitioners – social work, education, the youth service and the law – is best placed to initiate the necessary political strategies which could contest racism in the juvenile criminal justice system.

What has been said thus far about political strategies is utopian in the sense that we write of something which does not yet exist. We write to sketch the possible shape of an urgently needed political initiative which will attempt to prevent the criminalization of a generation of black British children and young people.

## Administrative strategies

Like most other elements of social welfare provision, IT has developed on the basis of speculation about the existence of a problem and about the effectiveness of certain, sometimes not very clearly understood, techniques to counter it. Only recently has IT become concerned with information about what actually happens to young offenders in the juvenile criminal justice system and as yet, this concern has not been extended to the fate of black young offenders.

The first step in any administrative strategy is to ask the right questions and this requires collecting the appropriate information. To confront the predicament of black young people in the juvenile criminal justice system the following data is needed.

## Twenty questions

### Policing

1  Numbers and types of offences committed by juveniles apprehended by the police; their ages and race.
2  Numbers and types of offences committed by juveniles charged immediately by the police; their ages and race.
3  Numbers and types of offences committed by juveniles referred by arresting and station police officers to the police juvenile bureau; their ages and race.
4  Numbers and types of offences committed by juveniles cautioned by the juvenile bureau; their ages and race.
5  Numbers and types of offences committed by juveniles about whom the police juvenile bureau takes a 'no further action' decision; their ages and race.
6  Numbers and types of offences committed by juveniles who are referred back to the juvenile court for prosecution by the police juvenile bureau; their ages and race.
7  The number of occasions upon which any juvenile is offered the option of referral to the juvenile bureau; his or her age and race.
8  The number of times juveniles are cautioned; their ages and race.

9    The offences which a juvenile must have committed if his or her name is to be included on the recidivist list.

10   The names, race, ages and offence histories of juveniles on the recidivist list.

*Juvenile Courts*

11   Numbers and types of offences committed by juveniles appearing in juvenile courts; their ages and race.

12   Social workers' and probation officers' recommendations to the Bench with reference to the information provided by question 11.

13   The numbers of previous court appearances and the severity of offences committed by juveniles who are the subjects of a recommendation for care or custody; their ages and race.

14   An analysis of the correspondence between recommendations made by social workers, probation officers, educational welfare officers, psychologists, psychiatrists and remand and assessment centre personnel and disposals handed down by juvenile magistrates. This might include an analysis of the use of racist stereotyping in court reports.

15   The stage in a juvenile's progress through the juvenile justice system at which IT is offered. For example, is it offered as an adjunct to supervision, as an alternative to custody, or after a previous period of care or custody?

16   The use of remands in custody and disposals by magistrates after such remands. Is the remand being used as a way of giving the juvenile a taste of custody without the imposition of a custodial sentence?

17   The use or otherwise of bail by the juvenile bench; the ages and race of the young people.

18   The granting or denial of legal aid by the juvenile bench; the ages and race of the young people.

19   The identification of particular members of the juvenile bench with a preference for (a) the use of institutional or custodial disposals and (b) the use of institutional or custodial disposals for black juveniles.

20   The correlation between homelessness, unemployment, truancy and institutional and custodial disposals; the ages and race of those sentenced.

This is not an exhaustive list but such information would make it possible to establish whether, as is often suspected, black juveniles are pursuing a different trajectory through the juvenile criminal justice system from their white counterparts. It is on the basis of such information that administrative intervention in the juvenile justice system might be initiated. It would require both the establishment of juvenile justice policies by local authorities, and personnel to ensure that these policies are adhered to. Collection of data is not an end in itself, and the organization and use of such data must be carefully negotiated with the local black community.

Few local authority social services departments have a juvenile justice policy. None, as far as we are aware, have a specific policy on black young offenders. Any such policy would have to specify at the outset its opposition to institutional or custodial confinement for juveniles. It would require changes within local authority practices but also in the practice of other agencies. Personnel would have to be appointed whose job description requires them to tackle, together with colleagues in IT, the juvenile justice system, and in particular the effect it has on black young people.

For this to be a reality these workers would need support at a number of different levels. Firstly, they should have access to the social services directorate, since from time to time it will be necessary to mobilize senior administrators and the social services committee to negotiate with, and bring pressure to bear upon, other agencies and services. Secondly, these workers should be able to exert some control over the development of residential and community-based services for young offenders; this suggests that they would act at assistant director level. Thirdly, if they are to act on behalf of the black community, they would need to work with a support group made up of representatives of local black organizations and black young people with personal experience of the juvenile justice system. These workers would need legal, political and campaigning skills and experience in community action and organization.

Systematic collection of the kind of data outlined above would make it possible to identify areas in which black young people's treatment is discriminatory or unjust. This might require interventions with the police on such issues as the use of cautioning and particular modes of policing which generate further offences, such as stop and search. The worker might well discover that certain schools were supplying reports to juvenile courts which ensured that black children identified as problems in the school were being presented to the court in a way which put them at risk of heavier sentences. A particular court, or indeed a particular magistrate, might emerge as racially discriminatory and this could require the worker to adopt informal or sometimes formal means in order to contest particular practices.

It is important to stress that we are not advocating the appointment of race-relations or ethnic-minorities advisors in IT. The role we envisage involves intervention, and requires that the personnel have the authority and seniority to effect administrative and practice changes within the department and a negotiating role beyond it. The problem is not primarily to make the workers in the juvenile justice system more racially aware; it is to eradicate institutionalized racist practices within it.

Likewise, within the social services and probation departments, data analysis might well reveal the ways in which the activities of social workers, probation officers and administrators are worsening the predicament of black young people through recommendation to the court of care or custody or through the neglect of alternatives where they might be appropriate. Gatekeeping mechanisms would then be required to combat these practices. For example, any social worker considering making an institutional or custodial recommendation might need to clear it with the director of social services or another senior administrator. The problem with this approach, which has been tried, is that it is essentially an administrative ruse aimed at putting obstacles in the way of practitioners and, as such, it has tended to antagonize them. An alternative method is to require field workers, who believe that their client is likely to be facing a custodial sentence, to work with the IT section to devise a programme for the young person which will be offered to the court as an alternative to custody. In this model of gatekeeping field workers are supported and helped rather than constrained and confounded. This necessarily puts IT at the centre of a young offenders' policy and requires that the social services court section and IT work as one. They would both have to take seriously the conditions of the 1982 Criminal Justice Act which state that custodial sentences may only be given if the crime committed is a very serious one, if the defendant poses a threat to the community, or if the defendant is unwilling or unable to make use of a community-based alternative to custody. If the courts could be constrained to take these conditions equally seriously, perhaps knowing that appeals would be lodged if they were not, this should ensure, given reasonably well-developed IT provision, that very few young offenders would ever be committed to care or custody. Many juvenile magistrates are effectively ignoring these requirements of the Act. Thus IT must be in a position:

1　To assist defendants with legal aid applications and to approach the Lord Chancellor's department if, as is the case in some courts, legal aid is denied for arbitrary reasons.

2   To assist defendants in gaining adequate legal representation. By adequate we mean identifying solicitors and barristers who are committed to, and understand the relevant legislation which bears upon, young offenders. Adequate representation is a continuing problem in the juvenile court.

3   To assist defendants in making appeals against conviction and sentence. Many appeals under the 1982 Act can be won on technical grounds alone.

4   To support defendants' appeals against the denial of bail under the 1976 Bail Act. This is important because in some juvenile courts it has been the practice for many years to remand defendants in care or custody and to give them a non-custodial sentence at their subsequent court appearance. Thus many young people who are never sentenced to care or custody serve sometimes considerable periods of time in institutions as a form of under-the-counter imprisonment.

Experience teaches that the way in which IT can be most effective as an alternative to care or custody is to assume a permanent presence in the juvenile court, in order that in any case in which the Bench is considering care or custody the court will be asked to adjourn while the possibility of involvement in IT is explored with the defendant.

The political and administrative practices outlined above are the first priority. The next is to train all the workers within the community-based alternative to care and custody, in anti-racist practice. This is the subject of the following chapter. It is not an easy task.

# References

BROWN, C., *Black and White Britain: the Third PSI Survey*, Heinemann, 1984.

COMMISSION FOR RACIAL EQUALITY (CRE) *Report of the Formal Investigation into the Suspension of Black Pupils in Birmingham Schools*, 1985.

DENNINGTON, J., *SUS Does a Phoenix Job in Eureka*, LITA, 1981.

DHSS, *Intermediate Treatment in London*, HMSO, 1977.

HALL, S., et al, *Policing the Crisis*, Macmillan, 1978.

KETTLE, M., 'The Racial Numbers Game in our Prisons', in *New Society*, 1982.

LANDAU, S., 'Juveniles and the Police', in *British Journal of Criminology*, vol. 21, 1981.

MATHIESEN, T., *The Politics of Abolition*, Martin Robertson, 1974.

MILLHAM, S., 'Intermediate Treatment: Symbol or Solution', in *Youth in Society*, no. 26, pp. 22-4, 1977.

OUSLEY, H., *The System*, Runnymede Trust, 1982.

PITTS, J., and ROBINSON, T., *Young Offenders in Lambeth*, LITA, 1981.

PITTS, J., 'Policy and Delinquency and the Practice of Youth Control', in *Youth and Policy*, vol.1, no. 1, 1982.

SMITH, D., *Police and People in London*, Policy Studies Institute, 1983.

TAYLOR, W., *Probation and After Care in a Multi-Racial Society*, CRE and West Midlands Probation and After Care Service, 1981.

TAYLOR, W., 'Black Youth White Man's Justice', in *Youth in Society*, November, 1982.

THORPE, D. H., et al, *Out of Care*, Allen and Unwin, 1980.

# 15 Towards a training for an anti-racist intermediate treatment

*John Pitts, Theo Sowa, Alan Taylor and Lorna Whyte*

What this chapter does not and cannot offer is a blueprint for anti-racist training in IT and the juvenile criminal justice system. It cannot do this because thus far such training does not exist in any clearly discernible way. What it does offer is an approach which identifies issues to be confronted and ways in which this might be done. The present authors' training work has raised many questions and some of these are not yet resolved. We have wrestled with the apparently inevitable tendency of many practitioners to understand the problems they confront as problems of attitudes held by individuals. We have been struck by how little understanding there is of the workings of the juvenile criminal justice system and the legislation which bears upon it. Our problem has been that practitioners have not been equipped in their initial training or their subsequent practice with a paradigm for action into which the material we have presented might be easily slotted. We have, therefore, asked them to act and think in unaccustomed ways which they may have often found confusing. We have offered a threatening, and usually uncomfortable alternative paradigm outlined in the previous chapter. Thus part of the struggle to develop training for an anti-racist practice is that we are simultaneously trying to bring about a new way of seeing and a new way of behaving.

In the past chapter we showed that the treatment received by black offenders was different from that received by white offenders. We indicated that social work practice with young black offenders is influenced by the racism that is inherent within these structures and systems. We went on to argue that the only effective response to racism is an anti-racist one, and that anti-racism seeks to change the structures and systems which perpetuate racism. It does this by strategies which have been developed through a critical analysis of those structures and

187

the power relationships within them. Anti-racism is therefore a political concept which involves and requires political action.

With the exception of the campaigns which took place around the passage of the Police Bill 1983 and which are taking place on the issue of police accountability, there has been very little political analysis or discussion concerning racism within the criminal justice system. There has been even less in the area of the juvenile criminal justice system. The report of the National Association of Probation Officers (NAPO) *Working Party on Racial Issues* (1981) stated:

> It is depressing to record that despite Home Office circulars, a Research Bulletin on Ethnic Minorities and the Annual Seminar held by the Home Office, there is not a single reference to these issues in the recent White Paper on young offenders, despite the substantial evidence from the West Midlands and other areas that youth custody and after-care are particularly important issues as far as working with black clients is concerned.

Within the field of intermediate treatment there has been a reluctance to discuss issues of racism within the juvenile justice system and some groups have actively opposed debate of these issues. Several associations belonging to the National IT Federation effectively absented themselves from the 1984 annual conference because it included workshops on sexism, racism and unemployment in the justice system; these 'political' issues were not seen to be the proper concern of IT workers despite the relationship between government's commitment to policies which limit young people's prospect of employment, reduce their earnings and restrict their opportunities for an independent life, and which have led to large numbers being committed to custody (Taylor, 1981).

To argue that in tackling racism, priority must be given to structural and systems change does not imply that individuals should not confront, or be confronted by, their own racism. Increasing an individual's awareness of his or her own racism may be a part of an anti-racist strategy; but we argue it must only be a subordinate part. To eradicate racism, action must be taken at individual, organizational and structural levels. What we do argue, however, is that power, in the sense of having access to resources or to the decision making process, is not held by individuals but by the State. If we want to change the situation of black people in British society then we must seek to influence and change those systems and structures which support and legitimize inequality. Action must be focused upon systems rather than individuals, upon education rather than teachers, policing rather than police officers, social work rather than social workers.

Because this is a monumental task and because of the difficulties that individuals have in considering their own contribution in such strategies, the less challenging approach of racism-awareness training has become popular. The discomfort that many white liberals experience during such training does at least make them feel that they are doing something. However, racism-awareness training with its primary objective of individual attitude change usually directs both resources and people away from structural and systems change. It is consistent with a powerful ideology within social work and social welfare, including the juvenile justice system, namely that problems are best understood in an individual, usually psychological context. Individual change, reformation or rehabilitation are therefore the goals, and the important issue is an individual's capacity to integrate and function within a firm structure, and not the nature of that structure.

The view that the problem of race is to do with the inability of black people to cope with British social mores is reflected in the report by the Central Council of Probation Committees (1983).

It has been suggested that social work methods generally should be reappraised with the aim of offering 'an appropriate and effective service' which will assist in reducing the number of black offenders in custody. It is difficult to resist this proposal, though it is not entirely clear how it is to be achieved . . . . It has been noted that some black defendants behave impertinently, casually and inappropriately when before the court and this conduct – which is very largely a consequence of cultural discomfort rather than over insubordination – can discourage magistrates from searching for a constructive disposal.

Thus the problem of a disproportionate number of black offenders in custody is argued to be their own fault.

We argued in the previous chapter that the first pre-requisite of effective strategies for intervention within the justice system is a good understanding of how the system works and the power relationships within it. The fact that many workers do not have this understanding has been one of the major problems in our training. This raises questions about the extent to which IT is intervening in the juvenile justice system on behalf of any youngsters. The second component of anti-racist practice is a shift of emphasis away from individual case-work towards a community action approach, which develops constituencies of support, an understanding of political structures, and strategies for joint action.

## Training for an anti-racist IT

Training aimed at helping workers develop an anti-racist IT could be divided into three areas: first, intervention in the operation of the juvenile justice system; secondly, changes in the internal operation of IT projects; and thirdly, the development of alliances with community groups and organizations which will apply pressure on the juvenile justice system from the outside. The training that we have been involved in has concentrated on the first and third areas, partly because the attack on the workings of institutionalized racism within the justice system was a priority for us, for the reasons discussed in the previous chapter, and partly because, in our experience, IT workers are far less willing and able to look at systems intervention than they are to look at a very limited definition of 'practice'. The interventions we discuss mean broadening the definition of practice to include systemic intervention. The definition of 'face-to-face' work needs to be expanded to include work as advocates for young offenders, with social work and probation colleagues, other professionals and magistrates. It also includes work with the local black community, trade unions and local councillors as potential sources of support, action and change. Action may also be needed on a wider front. As indicated in the previous chapter, there is now no alliance at national level which is mounting a concerted assault upon racism in the juvenile criminal justice system. Local alliances also seldom exist. Thus in our training we have asked participants to speculate (a) about those individuals, organizations and community groups which would have an interest in such collaboration, and (b) the ways in which such an alliance might be constructed and serviced.

What has emerged clearly in discussion of alliances is that the victimized group, the black community, is seldom considered as part of such an alliance. Its strengths and contribution have thus been ignored. Discussions have also highlighted massive ignorance and lack of understanding of the black community. Local community relations councils were mentioned occasionally, but black churches, black cultural and political organizations, black friendly societies and the informal, sometimes familiar, networks of the black community were not identified. We have been struck by the irony that once again appropriate pressure is perceived as coming from professional and political groupings within the welfare and justice agencies. This excludes the voice of the black community on an issue which is causing black parents a great deal of concern.

Accurate information about trends in arrests, intervention and sentencing, information about rights, legal services, appeals procedures, and abuses of these procedures should therefore be made readily available to the black community. This provides a basis for action. In addition, access to the juvenile justice system via the local authority IT section for representatives of the black community offers another source of influence. It is in IT's interest that the black community, as part of a broader public, has the information it needs about its justice system and has information which will help it act effectively to fight for racial justice.

Overleaf is a diagram outlining the juvenile justice system as we see it. We have tried to highlight potential intervention points in the system which we see as priorities. Local variations in organization and practice will mean that priorities are likely to vary.

We have used this diagram of the juvenile justice system as the basis of a training exercise aimed at enabling IT practitioners to identify different types of intervention at the points we have already highlighted in the system. Three types of intervention seemed to be common to all points: interventions in terms of the practice of individual workers and projects; in terms of organization, through IT projects, departments and managers; and in terms of politics, through all involved in the justice system, using various means, for example, local council policy changes, campaigning.

We begin the diagram of the juvenile justice system by listing issues such as unemployment, homelessness and education. The effects of institutionalized racism in these areas have been well documented and are outlined in the previous chapter. If IT is aiming to divert youngsters from the justice system, and custody in particular, it cannot ignore other political problems.

The procedures for cautioning are one point of entry for influencing the juvenile justice system. Landau and Nathan (1983) showed that black young people were significantly less likely to be formally cautioned than white young people. It would be likely that this pattern is the same with 'instant cautioning' at the point of arrest. The police exercise a large amount of discretion in their cautioning practices regarding the 'framing' of charges, discretion which is highly likely to be influenced by eurocentric and class prejudices which can lead to less favourable outcomes for black young offenders and a subsequently lesser degree of diversion. The existence of recidivist lists can also create channels in the system along which youngsters can be more hurriedly pushed through to court, as an appearance on this list negates the possibility of being

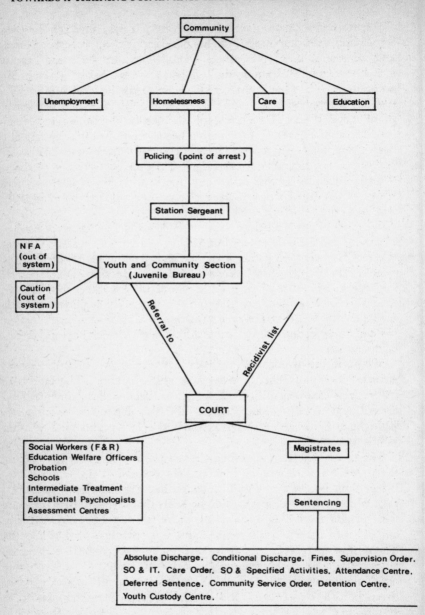

referred to the 'Police, Youth and Community Section'. Here again young black people are more likely to be at risk of swift journeys to the courtroom.

IT workers must identify where within this sub-system they can make inroads. Clearly if IT is to divert greater numbers of black young offenders from the justice system, a lot of work must be done at this early stage in the process. This might include monitoring of police systems, although it is important to bear in mind the 'Hawthorne Effect', in which the presence of outside observers can bring about the modifications that the observers might be wanting to implement. Involvement of IT with both statutory and voluntary police accountability and consultative groups attempting to influence local policing strategies is another possibility. Multi-agency policing panels, where the power does not lie with the police representatives, and campaigning for greater community involvement in policing policies and accountability, both at local authority and national levels, including for example campaigning and lobbying specifically for changes in the recent Police Act 1985, are further strategies. It is fairly easy to become involved with accountability and consultative groups. They are constantly searching for input from community groups and individuals, and IT workers, especially those from community-based projects, should have much useful information to offer.

Work with magistrates has two aspects. The first involves identifying racist processes within specific courts. This could be attempted by careful monitoring of court processes and sentencing and, most important, the establishment of a mechanism through which to feed this information to magistrates; for example, letters or articles in the magistrates' newsletter or in *Justice of the Peace*; structured meetings with local magistrates; study days; meetings with individual magistrates and having them relay the information to their colleagues, and so on.

Some IT projects or departments already have regular meetings with their local magistrates, which could be used to inform magistrates of issues of racism in sentencing. It is essential to provide clear, well-documented evidence of the issues and some suggestions as to ways in which magistrates might be able to respond; for example, the challenging of stereotypes and values reflected in social enquiry reports, requests by magistrates to the Lord Chancellor's Department for training regarding issues of race and the justice system, and so on. This work will not be easy. Many magistrates will be both hostile and disbelieving. However, probably most have never been informed or given quantifiable evidence of their sentencing and the cumulative effect of the juvenile justice process on young black offenders.

The second area of work with magistrates requires political intervention focused partly on their initial selection and training. The current selection process does not produce magistrates from a sufficiently wide variety of class or racial backgrounds. The Bench does not therefore reflect multi-racial Britain, and its composition will affect its perception and treatment of offenders from unfamiliar backgrounds. A great deal of work could be done in improving, indeed initiating, the training magistrates receive, particuarly regarding race and the juvenile justice system.

Clearly IT practitioners could not be expected to do all of this directly, but there is a role for IT departments through local authorities and local IT associations to link their activities with national organizations, such as the National Intermediate Treatment Federation or the Association for Juvenile Justice, to bring pressure to bear on the Lord Chancellor's Office.

The work with other professionals could cover much of the same ground as that with magistrates, that is, monitoring, evaluation and feedback, plus training on race and the juvenile justice system. The need to influence child care policies was discussed in the previous chapter. However, possibly the priority is work on the racism contained in various reports to the court, particularly in social enquiry reports. This racism is manifest in the type of questions social workers ask, the type of information contained in them, the way in which value judgements can be offered as facts and the type of recommendations made. Many of these faults occur in reports by other professionals as well, the problem of values being particularly prominent in reports from psychiatrists and educational psychologists. Examples include reports which start 'X was born in South London; his parents arrived in this country from Jamaica in 1951', both statements offer unnecessary information and implant notions of alienness in the minds of magistrates. Other frequently written phrases include 'owing to the nature of Afro-Caribbean child-rearing methods, X is more likely to understand the clear boundaries of a custodial establishment than those of an IT centre', offering both value judgements and racist stereotypes as fact. These are two very simple examples; the real danger lies in the cumulative effect of such value-laden beliefs and phrases in the final Social Enquiry report.

In their proposed role as advocates for the youngsters they work with, IT workers would have a clear mandate to liaise with other professionals before court appearances to attempt to minimize these manifestations of racism. But first IT practitioners need to improve the quality of their own reports. This would be in addition to the formulation of child care strategies and mechanisms for screening and monitoring SERs by social services departments.

### Anti-racism and IT projects

Anti-racist intervention in the juvenile justice system must be linked to anti-racist practice within IT projects. Their priorities, their staff roles and the basic assumptions, policies and frameworks of the project must be examined and changed where necessary.

When IT has considered black youth within the juvenile justice system it has been from the viewpoint of culture; for example, what do we need to understand about the way that black people think, speak, operate in order to fit them into our projects? Our contention is that IT (and other professions) need to address very different questions such as: how do IT projects adapt themselves so that they begin to operate as alternatives for *all* youngsters? How do IT projects become equally accessible to black and white young people? How, and when, do IT projects stop concentrating on 'understanding' black youth and start concentrating on treating them fairly and equally? How do IT projects begin to tackle institutional as well as individual racism? Anti-racist IT should not be about waiting years while white workers 'sort out' their racism and learn to 'understand' black cultures, but about working towards a *just* IT, a *just* juvenile justice system.

'Understanding' should not be of black cultures, but of racist systems, their operation and their effect on the lives of black youth.

If these were the types of questions IT practitioners were to ask themselves, then the response to issues of race should be radically different from those which are prevalent, if the issue is raised at all. These questions imply action; they emphasize that examination and understanding of racism within the juvenile justice system is not an end in itself; the knowledge is acquired to improve practice and learn to intervene in the system effectively.

Although there is a role for IT projects to ensure that the images they reflect are not racist, all too often workers seem satisfied with having posters or pictures of black people and novels by or about black people in prominent areas of their project, and then feel that their 'anti-racist obligations' have been met. Our contention is that IT practitioners must recognize that anti-racist practice involves *major* changes and that they must accept responsibility for this. Posters of black people on the walls will not change the numbers of black youngsters who are constantly excluded from projects as a result of workers' stereotypes and fears; they do not improve the support given to the usually minimal number of black workers.

Of the issues that projects should consider, questions of staff structure and support, individual staff responses, referrals and curriculum are of particular significance.

The issue of staff structure and support is linked to that of extending the definition of practice. If IT is to intervene actively in the justice system, workers will need time, training and support, and project structures will need to provide this for them. Whether this takes the form of fewer 'curriculum' hours per worker, or increased staffing of projects, or re-prioritization of work tasks must be a matter for individual projects or departments to tackle. It is clear, though, that structures must be adapted.

In order for this to happen effectively, workers, all workers not just management, in IT must see the task of challenging racist systems and institutions as their responsibility and an integral part of their work. All too often workers become enmeshed in internal issues, and the present structure of many IT projects encourages this, so that many project workers feel that their responsibilities and tasks are internal, while workers in management positions are seen as having responsibility for external tasks. It is essential that anti-racist practice be built into the structures of IT projects, from inclusion in their aims and objectives, staff recruitment, policy formulation, referral procedures, right through to curriculum.

Individual staff responses are clearly important in this process. If individual actions or statements contradict policy, major problems are presented. This is another reason why anti-racist practice needs to be a part of the structure of a project. Racist practice by individuals within projects can then be tackled by the project as a whole in the same way as other bad practice, rather than either being ignored or left to particular individuals, usually black workers, to tackle. Part of the training that projects will need to provide should try to ensure that the individual racism of workers does not prevent them changing their working practice. This does not mean racism-awareness training, as it is widely understood. There is not the time to wait for white workers to become 'aware' and go through the process of self-blame or guilt, which seems to be such a large part of racism-awareness training, and is both long and diversionary. What is needed is change in working practices, and this involves identifying where in the project institutional and personal racism is operating, and then working out how to eradicate this.

Referrals to and the use of IT projects are areas where anti-racist practice is particularly necessary. Despite the increasing numbers of black youth in the justice system and the disproportionate numbers of black youth receiving custodial sentences, IT has for years been predominantly white. The emergence of alternative to custody projects which have not made an impact on those figures highlights the need for prompt action, which must include ensuring that black young people are given the opportunity to attend IT when this is appropriate to their needs, their offending history and their wishes. It is equally important to ensure that workers do not over-compensate or allow racist assumptions and stereotypes to push black youth into IT provision too soon. This may prematurely push someone up the tariff of sentences and put them at greater risk, if offending continues, of a custodial sentence.

Other action could be based on internal project issues, that is ensuring that the project structure, staffing and programmes do not alienate or isolate black youth attending projects. For example, if a project has a high proportion of black youngsters appropriately referred to them, but finds that black youngsters are disproportionately excluded or exclude themselves, the project needs to evaluate why this is happening. Part of this process could include evaluating the curriculum of the project. It has already been noted that a project needs to be physically welcoming for *all* its clients, but that this is not enough on its own.

It is important, too, to ensure that activities do not alienate black youngsters and that race issues run throughout a project's curriculum. For race issues to be seen as significant they must be integrated into the curriculum. For example, if as part of an offending programme policing is being examined, then an integral part of that session should be dealing with racism within the police force. If the use of SERs is being examined racist assumptions which arise in them should be examined and challenged.

It is important to monitor and evaluate the project's service to its black clients regularly to ensure that anti-racist practice is being maintained and to evaluate where and when it needs to be strengthened.

Finally it must be emphasized that anti-racist practice must be carried on both inside and outside a project. Internally a project could be a model of anti-racist practice, but if youngsters are not being allowed the option of IT because of the operation of racism in the justice system, or if the black youngsters attending the project are constantly being arrested because of racist policing, then the anti-racism of an IT project amounts to very little. Building constituencies of support amongst co-professionals in the form of social services department race and justice working parties, or support groups at practitioner level made up of social workers, IT workers, probation officers and others would help to keep this 'disappearing' issue on the practitioner's agenda. The external activities of IT are the hardest to keep going, but the most important. We must also consider the need to form an alliance with victimized young people themselves, and IT, social workers and the probation service are in a uniquely advantageous position to do this. What we learn from the National Association of Young People in Care is that despite some difficulty, young people can themselves make an authentic and effective contribution to struggles to improve the structures which bear upon their lives. There are enough black clients and a smaller number of black workers who have experience of the juvenile criminal justice system to make this broad alliance possible.

Beyond this the social workers and welfare trade unions, NALGO, NAPO and NUPE, and professional associations such as BASW could be effective in informing members on issues of racial injustice. Police accountability groups, the Children's Legal Centre, CRCs, councils of voluntary organizations, could all play a part in an alliance, and many are looking for a lead. It is our contention that IT workers, working through their local IT associations, could act as catalysts for such action because their primary professional preoccupation is the operation of the juvenile criminal justice system and the diversion of children and young people from it. Such activity departs fairly radically from the more established modes of intervention encapsulated in case work and group work. Methods of community action, usually directed towards disadvantaged communities and stressing as they do the formation of political alliances to change the functioning of welfare systems, offer a body of experience and a set of techniques which could be used to focus on the juvenile criminal justice system.

This chapter will we hope start a debate about anti-racist training in IT. It by no means begins to exhaust it.

## References

CENTRAL COUNCIL OF PROBATION COMMITTEES, *Probation - A Multi Racial*

*Approach*, 1983

LANDAU, S., and NATHAN, G., 'Selecting Delinquents for Cautioning in the London Metropolitan Area,' in *British Journal of Criminology*, vol. 23, no. 2, 1983.

NATIONAL ASSOCIATION OF PROBATION OFFICERS, *Working Party on Racial Issues*, 1981.

TAYLOR, W., *Probation and After Care in a Multi-Racial Society*, CRE and West Midlands Probation and After Care Service, 1981.

# Index

abandonment of a child, 124
abolitionist alliance, 178, 179, 180
adoption research, long-term follow up to, 32, 33
adoption, transracial, 3, 26, 32, 33, 81–98
African Asians, 11, 12, 18
African descent, people of, 11, 12, 29
Afro-Caribbean,
    children, 7, 15, 18, 19, 22, 29, 30, 40–50, 51, 55, 56, 58, 59, 119, 120, 121, 122, 123
    culture, 64, 122, 123, 126, 127
    families, 6, 11, 12, 13, 14, 17, 18, 21, 22, 119
    foods, 43, 49, 52–53, 59, 72–73, 74, 122, 127
    parents, 29, 30, 40, 41, 42, 43, 44, 45, 46
    voluntary organizations, 122, 127, 128, 129, 130, 131
aggression & realization of one's blackness, 105, 107
agoraphobia & problematic psychological nigresence, 109, 110
American experience, 4, 16, 33, 100, 153
ancillary staff in day nurseries & wellbeing of black children, 60
Anglo-European norms, imposition of, 4, 5, 7, 9, 43, 44, 45, 46, 47, 48, 52, 53, 58, 59, 64, 65, 72, 75, 76, 108, 140, 141, 142, 145, 148, 149, 150, 151, 152, 156, 192
ante-natal services, usage made of, 1, 19, 135
anti-deportation campaigns, 165
arranged marriages, 143, 145, 148, 149, 151

Asian,
    children, 10, 19, 21, 22, 51, 53, 55, 56, 58, 59, 62, 66, 121, 123
    culture, maintaining contact with, 64, 123, 138
    families, 11, 12, 14, 66
    mothers' self-help group, 132–139
    parents, 6, 7, 11, 12, 13, 18, 19, 21, 44, 54, 142–151
    Resource Centre (ARC), Birmingham, 155
    voluntary organizations, 123, 127, 132–139, 155–166
    women, personal & social difficulties facing, 132–139, 140–154, 155–166
    women's refuge, 155–166
assaults on the police, 171
assessment and remand centres, 168, 176
Association for Juvenile Justice, 194
Association of British Adoption and Fostering Agencies, 29, 31
attendance centres, 168, 170

backwardness, prejudiced whites' attribution to blacks of, 45, 46
Bail Act (1976), 185
Bangladeshis, 11, 12, 13
battered & homeless women, 155–166
bereavement & care, 124
beyond control & care, 124, 128, 130
biculturalism, 71, 72, 94, 107, 125, 145, 146, 147
bilingualism, 55, 56, 71
Birmingham and Southall Black Sisters, 166
'black and ethnic minorities', 6
'black British', 6

black,
  children's self-perception &
    placements, 32, 33, 43, 44, 45, 46,
    51, 53, 55, 56, 60, 61, 64, 65, 70,
    81–98, 100, 101, 102, 103, 104, 105,
    107, 118, 119, 122, 123, 125, 126,
    128, 129, 130, 131
  community, age structure of, 11–15,
    19, 20
  community, alienation from, 82, 83,
    84, 85, 86, 87, 88, 89, 90, 91, 92, 93,
    94, 95, 96, 97, 103, 105, 118, 125,
    128, 129, 130
  defined, 5, 6, 66
  families in white skins, 87, 94
  families, strengths of, 3, 5, 7, 70, 83
  identity, establishment of a positive,
    100–114, 121–131
  parents, dilemmas for, 29, 30, 42, 44,
    45, 46, 47, 48, 49, 51, 52, 53,
  usage of social services, 18, 19, 30, 35
  women's advice centres, 49, 50
  Women's Right to Benefit campaign,
    165
borstals, 168, 170, 172, 173
Bradford Social Services Department's
  Review of Care of Black Children,
  31, 117–119, 120–131
British Adoption Project, 32, 33
British Asians, 6
Building Blocks, 56, 57, 64–68

care,
  black vs. white children &, 1, 16, 17,
    29, 30, 31, 35, 57, 58
  disproportionate numbers of black
    children in, 28, 29, 30, 31
  orders & custodial sentences, 167, 168,
    173, 191
  premature reception of black children
    via social worker's fear, 29, 30
  quality of, 1, 2, 3, 5, 51, 117–119
  staff, low proportion of black, 43, 48,
    50, 78
cautioning by the police, 191, 192
Central Council for Education & Training
  in Social Work, 27
Central Council of Probation Committees,
  189

child abuse, 124, 147, 157, 158
Child Care Act (1980), 11
child development unit, gross insensitivity
  & racism in, 133, 134
Child Health and Education Study, 14
child minders, unregistered, 21, 24
child minding, quality of, 21–27
Children and Young Persons Act (1969),
  169, 173, 175
children in care, provision for & positive
  discrimination, 17
City and Handsworth Project, 174, 175
class differences, 29, 32, 51, 61, 62, 86,
  93, 94, 108, 145, 146, 152, 161, 168,
  172, 173, 192
closed family system & transracial
  adopters, 90–91
colonialists as transracial adopters, 87
colourblind approach, ethnic groups &
  social policy, 8, 9, 15, 27, 30, 45, 62,
  118, 163, 164
Commission for Racial Equality (CRE), 7,
  10, 30, 34, 40, 165, 178
communication, absence of, & racism,
  133, 134, 135, 148
community,
  based provision for young offenders,
    34, 35, 167, 169, 174
  health services, 20, 47
  homes with education (CHEs), 170,
    171, 175, 176, 179
  nursery for black children, 69–74
  nurses' prejudice, 47
  service orders, 34, 169
confidence, 32, 69, 86, 87, 110
consensus & ethnic division, 4, 8, 17
cooks in day nurseries & wellbeing of
  black children, 60
coping mechanisms, 55, 81, 85, 108
court's attitude to battered Asian women,
  161, 165
Criminal Attempts Bill, 171
Criminal Justice Act (1982), 174, 184, 185
criminalization, premature & young black
  people, 5, 35, 168, 181
cross-cultural explanations, 148
cultural,
  continuum needed between home &

day nursery, 52, 53, 54, 56, 59, 60, 69, 70, 72–73, 74, 80
deficit model, dangers of acquiring, 53, 64, 65, 150
distortion and caricature, 64
explanations, danger of over-reliance on, 140–153
imperialism, 142–153
needs, insensitivity to, 1, 3, 5, 16, 17, 18, 19, 20, 21, 26, 43, 44, 45, 52, 53, 54, 56, 81–98, 127, 140–153
racism, 140–153
silence & nihilism, 64
tradition, importance of black, 3, 5, 7, 8, 9, 17, 18, 43, 44, 53, 54, 56, 69–74, 81–98, 119, 120, 121, 122, 123, 125, 126, 127, 128, 129, 140–154, 176
custodial sentences, disproportionate & black offenders, 34, 35, 167, 173, 174, 175, 176, 177, 182, 183, 187, 189

day care,
outside the home, 4, 8, 9, 20, 21–27, 39, 40–50
for the most socially & economically disadvantaged, 22, 40, 48, 69, 70
quality of, 1, 9, 10, 17, 21–27, 40–48, 51–63, 69–74
day nurseries, 22, 23, 24, 39, 40–50, 51–63
an alien environment for black children, 52, 53, 56, 57
and grounds for conflict, 42, 43, 44, 45, 53, 54, 55, 56
demography of the black population in the UK, 11–15, 18, 19
de-skilling of young black women, institutional, 47, 144
detention centres, 168, 170, 175, 179
developmental theoretic approaches to self-concept, 106–107
DHSS under-fives initiative, 52, 64
dialect, positive approach needed to, 71, 72, 80, 109, 110, 113, 122, 128
dietary needs of black children, 4, 52–53, 59, 60, 72–73, 74, 122, 127

disabled children, problems faced by the mothers of, 132–137
disipline, differing approaches to, 29, 30, 53, 71
doctors, need for women, 19
domestic violence, 155–166

eating habits, 43, 53, 59, 60
economic recession, consequences of, 143, 144
education,
discrimination in, 10, 14
of ethnic minority children, 10, 69–74, 98, 128
vs. physical care of young children, 23–27, 53, 54, 70
within the Afro-Caribbean community, alternative, 128, 129
educational needs, special provision for & demography, 11, 12, 13, 14, 21, 22, 23
educational priorities in a multi-racial society, 1, 9, 21, 22, 23, 75, 76, 77, 78, 79–80
elderly black people, provision of services for, 5
employment, discrimination in, 10, 14, 21, 46, 165
English, 6, 44
ethnic background, insensitivity towards, 1, 4, 5, 8, 9, 17–18, 42, 43, 49 52, 86, 87, 88, 89, 90, 91, 92, 93, 94, 140–154
ethnic foods, 43, 49, 52–53, 59, 72–73, 74, 122, 127, 160, 163

family, notion of in the black community, 70, 143, 144, 145, 146, 147, 148, 149, 150, 157, 158
'farewell workers', 29, 30
foster-care, 24, 25, 26, 31, 81, 118, 121, 124, 125, 126, 128, 129, 130, 131, 157
foster parents, criteria for choice of, 24, 25, 127
frustration experienced by children, 105, 107, 108, 109, 110, 113, 114, 134

gatekeeping, systems of, 170, 184
gollywog, Robertson's jam, 44, 45
Greater London Council (GLC), 50
    Ethnic Minorities Unit, 178
    Women's Committee, 64

Hackney, 20, 21, 52, 79
hair care, cultural differences in, 42, 44,
    53, 54, 74, 122, 125, 126, 127, 129,
    131
handicap, mental or physical & care, 124
Haringey, 20
health care & social work, 5, 19, 20, 75
health care, centralized, problems of
    dealing with, 19, 133
health service workers' insensitivity &
    prejudice, 47, 132, 133, 134, 135,
    136, 137, 139, 141, 142, 143, 144,
    159, 161
health visitors' prejudice, 47, 142, 143,
    144
home corner in day nurseries, 57, 65
Home Office seminar on ethnic minorities
    in prison, 168, 169, 188
home-on-trial, 121, 124
homelessness & imposition of custodial
    sentences, 173, 174, 182, 191, 192
House of Commons Select Committee
    Report,
    on children in care (1984), 29, 30, 31
    on immigration & race relations, 10
housing, discrimination in, 10
housing poor, 1, 20, 21, 22

identity, damage to black children's sense
    of, 32, 33, 43, 44, 45, 81–98, 100,
    103, 104, 105, 106, 107, 108, 109,
    110, 112, 113, 114, 118, 128, 129,
    130, 145, 146
imitative behaviour in young children,
    104
immigration policy, 10, 14
Immigration Service, 7
imprisonment, abolition of, 178, 179
inadequacy, young black mothers' forced
    sense of, 47, 48
incarceration of young offenders, 167–185
Inner London Education Authority
    (ILEA), 28, 75–78

in-service courses to combat racism, 28,
    46, 49, 57, 58, 59, 60, 64–68, 76–78,
    80, 196, 197
institutional care, 84, 100, 103, 104, 110,
    117, 121
institutionalized racism, 7, 8, 9, 42, 43,
    44, 45, 46, 47, 68, 73, 75, 133, 134,
    135, 140–154, 167, 169, 176, 177,
    190, 192
insulting behaviour, 171
integration, 3, 4, 5, 9, 176
intensive policing, consequences of, 172
intermediate treatment (IT) for young
    offenders, 17, 34, 129, 130, 167–185,
    187–198
internalization of the environment, early
    mental, 104, 105
interpreters, absence of, 135, 136
Iqbal Begum campaign, 165
Irish, 6, 44

joblessness & custodial sentencing, 173,
    174, 182, 191, 192
*Justice of the Peace*, 193
juvenile bureau, referral to, 171, 172,
    181, 191, 193
juvenile criminal justice system, 10, 34,
    167–185, 187–198

Lambeth, 29, 171
    study of antecedents to care, 29
language, racist, 44, 45, 46, 133, 134,
    141, 163
languages, information in minority, 8,
    135, 136–139
law & order, a political issue, 170
laziness, prejudiced whites' attribution of
    to blacks, 45
linguistic ability in English, 14, 17, 18,
    19, 21, 22, 72, 80, 109, 110, 113,
    133, 134, 135, 136, 137, 174
linguistic needs, 55–56, 57, 59, 71–72, 80,
    113
literacy projects, 174
*Little Black Sambo*, 43, 44
local authority resources, scarcity of, 15,
    78, 164, 170

Manjit Kaur, anti-deportation campaign for, 165
Metropolitan Police, 171
mixed parentage, children of, 29, 44, 87, 88, 91–93, 94, 109, 118, 121, 123, 124, 125, 129, 130, 131
multi-cultural, anti-racist training for nursery staff, 75–78
multi-cultural books & play materials, 43, 49, 54, 58, 59, 65, 67, 70, 71, 126, 128, 131
multi-racial society,
 social policies for, 3, 4, 5, 9, 16, 17, 22, 26, 27, 28, 40, 41, 48, 49, 50, 51, 57, 58, 59, 64–68, 73, 79, 80, 118, 167–185, 187–198
 training programmes for, 26, 27, 28, 56, 57, 58–63, 64–68, 73, 74, 75–78, 126, 127, 187–198

Nasreen Akhter, anti-deportation campaign, 165
National Association,
 for the Care & Re-settlement of Offenders, 178
 for Young People in Care, 179, 198
 for Advisers for Under-fives, 67
 of Probation Officers, 178, 188
National Child Development Study, 14
National Childminding Association, 67
National Intermediate Treatment Federation, 178, 194
National Nursery Examination Board, 28, 73, 75–78, 80
 certificate in post-qualifying studies, 76–78
Nationality Act (1981), 170
New Black Families, 83, 84
Newham, 20
nigrescence, psychological, 107–114
non-attendance of school & care, 124, 128
nursery,
 care, need to foster multi-racial, 27, 40–50, 52, 53, 54, 55, 56, 57, 58, 59, 60, 61, 62, 63, 64, 65, 69–74, 75–78, 79–80
 nursing, training for, 27, 28, 48, 49, 57, 58, 59, 73–74, 75–78

staff attitudes to black parents, 42, 44, 45, 46, 48, 52, 53, 54, 56, 57, 59, 60, 69, 70
staff, need of black, 48, 50, 57, 78
staff, racial prejudices of, 42, 43, 44, 45, 69, 70

object relations theory approach to self-concept, 104–105
offences, child in care on account of, 124, 128, 173, 175
Organization of Women from African and Asian Descent, 166
Orthodox Jews, NNEB validated course for, 76

Pakistanis, 6, 11, 12, 13, 14, 18
parent-child relationship problems & care, 124, 130
Parent to Parent Adoption Service, 91
parental contribution to nurseries, maximizing, 44, 49, 50, 52, 53, 54, 70, 71, 72, 80
parental inability to care, 124, 131
penal institutions, disproportionate black offenders in, 34, 35, 167, 168, 176, 177
penal system, reforming the, 178, 179, 180, 181, 187–198
Pentecostal religion, 122
personal social services, demographic implications for, 15–20
play, differing approaches to, 53, 54, 65, 70
play groups, 23
pluralism, 3, 4, 5, 77, 169, 176
police accountability, 188, 193, 198
Police Act (1985), 193
police attitude towards battered women, 158, 159, 160, 161
Police Bill (1983), 188
police harassment, 34, 171
policing, military style of, 171
Policy Studies Institute Reports, 10, 13
politically motivated transracial adopters, 87, 96
'poor blacks', helping, 86, 87, 96
positive action to redress racial disadvantage, 15, 16, 17, 34

poverty, 1, 3, 15, 16, 19, 20, 21, 29, 69
& problems arising from positive
discrimination, 16, 17
pre-school children, day care provision
for, 17, 20–27, 39, 40–50, 51–63,
64–68
Pre-school Playgroup Association, 67
prison, 167, 168, 170, 174
probation orders, 34, 173, 174
probation service, value of interventions
by, 173, 174
psychodynamic theory & self-concept,
102, 104–105
psychological needs, 55, 56, 81–98, 100–
114
public order offences, 171

Race Relations Act (1976), 9, 17, 25, 26,
78
racial,
differences, fear of acknowledging, 8,
9, 17, 18, 82, 83, 84, 85, 86, 87, 88,
discrimination,
& insensitivity, measures to remedy,
2, 3, 15, 17, 18, 20, 21, 22, 48, 49,
50, 51, 56, 57, 58–63, 64–68, 69–74,
79, 82, 84, 128, 132–139, 140–154,
155–166, 187–198
by child minders, 21–22, 24, 25, 26
hostility & positive action, 16, 17
identity confusion, 32, 33, 43, 44, 45,
81–98, 100, 103, 104, 105, 106, 107,
108, 109, 110, 112, 113, 114, 118,
128, 129, 130, 148, 149
pride, development of, 107–114
stereotyping, 6, 7, 18, 34, 42, 43, 44,
45, 46–48, 51, 64, 79, 86, 87, 88,
126, 142, 143, 144, 146, 147, 148–
153, 155, 175, 194, 196
racism, 1, 3, 4, 15, 42, 43, 44, 45, 64, 65,
66, 69, 75, 82, 85, 88, 89, 92, 93, 94,
97, 108, 109, 111, 113, 125, 126,
127, 128, 130, 131, 133, 134, 135,
138, 140, 141–153, 161, 162, 163,
164, 165, 166, 167, 171–185, 187–
198
defined, 6–11
Radical Alternatives to Prison (RAP), 178

Rampton Report (1981), 10, 22
Rastafarian religion, 122, 127, 169
'recidivists' list', 172, 182, 191, 192
religious needs, insensitivity to, 18, 19,
20, 127
residential care, 121, 124, 126, 127, 128,
129, 130, 167, 177
resources, competing for scarce, 15, 18,
19, 20, 22, 78, 164, 170
reviews of children in care, statutory,
117–119, 120–131
routine, differing approaches to, 53
Runnymede Trust, 178

Save the Children Fund, 64
Scarman Report (1981), 10, 15, 17
schools' response to needs of black pupils,
1, 9, 34, 69–74, 98
self-concept, 100–114
self-destructiveness, 105, 107
self-esteem, 32, 33, 42, 43, 44, 45, 46, 47,
51, 53, 55, 58, 59, 60, 61, 65, 70, 85,
86, 88, 89, 100, 104, 105, 107, 108,
110, 111, 112, 113, 114, 143, 144
self-hatred, 110
self-help, 49, 50, 132–139
self-image, 55, 58, 59, 60, 61, 65, 66, 69,
70, 81, 82, 83, 84, 85, 86, 87, 88, 89,
100–114, 127, 128, 129, 149
sentencing policy & young black
offenders, 34, 35, 167–185, 192, 193,
194
sexism, 145, 147, 149, 151, 152, 153, 161,
162, 163, 165, 166
sickle cell anaemia, screening for, 122,
124, 128
significant others in transracial
placements, 84, 85, 86
single-parent families, 9, 10, 21, 22, 45,
70
skin care, cultural differences in, 44, 53,
74, 122, 125, 126, 127, 129, 131
Social Enquiry Reports (SERs), 194, 195,
197
social learning theory approach to self-
concept, 102–104
social services,
& improvement of service for black
people, 117–119, 120–131

racial insensitivity of, 1, 2, 3, 4, 5, 7, 8,
15, 16, 17, 18, 19, 25, 29, 47, 110,
128, 132–139, 157, 158
social work, demographic implications
for, 15–20
social workers,
lack of involvement with black
youngsters, 35
need of black, 83
panic at black familial conflict, 29, 30
support given by white, 132, 136, 137,
138
socialization, white attempts at forcing
white, 43, 44, 45, 46, 47, 48, 51, 81,
82, 83, 84, 85, 88, 90, 104, 105, 107,
119, 125, 126
solvent abuse, 129
South Asian descent, people of, 6, 66,
140–154
Southwark, 67
specialist ethnic minority workers, 117,
118, 119, 120, 121, 124, 126
structural theoretic approaches to self-
concept, 105–107
substitute care, 24, 25, 26, 31, 81, 118,
121, 124, 125, 126, 128, 129, 130,
131, 157
substitute families, 17, 24, 25, 31, 40, 70,
81–98
substitute parents, black, 1, 25, 26, 31,
32, 33, 34, 83, 93, 94, 124
survival skills developed by black
children, 103, 104, 105, 106, 107
SUS law & Vagrancy Act (1824), 171, 172
suspension from school of black pupils, 1
SWAMP 81, 171
Swann Report ( 1985), 10, 15, 22, 34

textbooks for nursery staff training, racist
assumptions of, 68, 73
Thatcher, Margaret, 171
The Bluest Eye, Morrison's, 111
Tower Hamlets, 20
trades unions, 178, 198
training,
for anti-racist intermediate treatment,
187–198

needed for multi-racial caring, 26, 27,
28, 57, 58–63, 64–68, 73, 74, 75–78,
126, 127
needed for transracial placements, 95,
126, 127
programmes, objectives of, 75–78
transracial adopters, characteristics of,
86–88, 89–91
transracial adoption, 3, 26, 32, 33, 81–98
transracial placements in care, 31, 32, 33,
34, 81–98, 118, 126, 131, 157
trial by jury, opting for, 173, 175

underachievement of children,
countering, 51–61, 69–74, 75–78, 79
unemployment, consequences of, 1, 15,
34, 142, 143, 144, 173, 174, 182,
191, 192

voluntary organizations, 122, 123, 127,
128, 129, 130, 131, 132–139, 190

welfare rights, communicating
information about, 132, 136–139,
162, 163, 165
welfare state, white belief of black
exploitation of the, 45, 46
Welsh, 6, 76
white in all but skin colour, 81, 82, 83,
84, 85, 88, 89, 92, 93, 103, 104, 105,
107, 108, 109, 126, 129, 130
Wolverhampton, 20
women's groups, 40, 49, 50, 132–139,
155–166
women's refuge, an Asian, 155–166
working class culture, English, 145–146
working mothers, black, 19, 20, 21, 45,
46, 47, 49, 50
working mothers & provision of day-care,
8, 10, 21, 40–50, 70

young offenders, 1, 5, 17, 34–35, 167–
185, 187–198
youth custody, black youths in, 1, 17, 34,
174, 179
Youth Training Scheme (YTS), 48